Wasserfälle

razos

Little River

ta Anna

Bettina   Castell   Leiningen
Llano
use mount
Bezauberter   Friedrichsbg.   Nashville
Felsen   Tenoxitlan

Flint River, Piedernates

Austin

(Delawar's und Schawnees)
Indianer

Rio
Colorado

Bastrop

Rio   San Marcos

Halbeivilirte

la Grande

Neu-Braunfels

Seguin
Gonzales

troville

San Antonio
de Bexar

Guadeloupe

Comanches and Germans
on the Texas Frontier

Publication of this book was made possible by
a grant from The Summerlee Foundation.

Comanches and Germans on the Texas Frontier

The Ethnology of Heinrich Berghaus

Daniel J. Gelo

AND

Christopher J. Wickham

WITH CONTRIBUTIONS BY

Heide Castañeda

TEXAS A&M UNIVERSITY PRESS
COLLEGE STATION

This paper meets the requirements of ANSI/NISO Z39.48–1992
(Permanence of Paper).
Binding materials have been chosen for durability.
Manufactured in the United States of America

Library of Congress Cataloging-in-Publication Data

Names: Gelo, Daniel J., 1957– author. | Wickham, Christopher J., 1950–
author. | Castañeda, Heide, 1973– author.
Title: Comanches and Germans on the Texas frontier : the ethnology of
Heinrich Berghaus / Daniel J. Gelo and Christopher J. Wickham ; with
contributions by Heide Castañeda.
Description: First edition. | College Station : Texas A&M University Press,
[2018] | Includes bibliographical references and index.
Identifiers: LCCN 2017021367| ISBN 9781623495947 (book/cloth : alk. paper) |
ISBN 9781623495954 (ebook)
Subjects: LCSH: Comanche Indians—Texas. | Germans—Texas—History—19th
century. | Comanche language—Etymology. | Berghaus, Heinrich Karl
Wilhelm, 1797-1884. | Geographers—Germany—Biography. | Ethnology—United
States—History—19th century.
Classification: LCC E99.C85 G45 2017 | DDC 976.4004/974572—dc23
LC record available at https://lccn.loc.gov/2017021367

Cover photo courtesy Forschungsbibliothek Gotha der Universität Erfurt,
Sammlung Perthes

Back cover photo courtesy Katherine Weber

Jacket flap photo by Daniel J. Gelo

CONTENTS

PART I
Berghaus and German Contributions
to American Ethnology

PART II
Berghaus's 1851 Ethnological Article

PART III
The Berghaus Glossary and Map

ILLUSTRATIONS

PREFACE

In 1851 an article appeared in the *Geographisches Jahrbuch* (Geographic Yearbook, Gotha) claiming to establish definitive connections, using language observations, among the Comanches, Shoshones, and Apaches. The author of the article, Heinrich Berghaus, was a well-established cartographer but had no history of original anthropological research. Titled "Über die Verwandtschaft der Schoschonen, Komantschen und Apatschen" ("On the Relationship of the Shoshones, Comanches, and Apaches"), the article was based on lexical data gathered by a young German settler in Texas and included a list of 366 Comanche words and their German translations. To his discussion of this material Berghaus added cultural notes on the Comanches from his informant, discussion of the existing literature on the three tribes, and an original map of Comanche hunting grounds. Probably because it was published only in German, Berghaus's article has been almost completely ignored by US scholarship, even though it offers valuable insights into Native American languages, toponyms, ethnonyms, hydronyms, and cultural anthropology, and at the same time is a significant document in the history of German-Comanche relations in Texas.

It is the goal of this book to make available for the first time a reliable English translation of Berghaus's 1851 article, to provide an account of its historical context, and to present a detailed commentary on its value for the anthropologist, the student of German settlement in Texas, and the general reader. We are especially pleased to think that it will be useful to members of the Comanche Nation who are striving to preserve their native language. In addition, it is hoped that this work will resonate with the burgeoning scholarship in German history and cultural studies on such themes as German contributions to the development of science, the significance of writer Karl May, and the German fascination with American Indian life.[1]

Berghaus's article first came to the attention of Dan Gelo in the 1990s while he was researching his translation of another early Comanche word list, that of the Mexican philologist Manuel García Rejón (García Rejón and Gelo 1995). In 1999 Gelo requested a translation of the Berghaus article from Heide Castañeda, then a graduate research assistant in the University of Texas at San Antonio (UTSA) Department of Anthropology, now a medical anthropologist and associate professor at the University of South Florida. Castañeda, a native German speaker, produced an excellent gloss, and under Gelo's direction also began matching Berghaus's Comanche terms with ones from a contemporary Comanche dictionary. From this effort, it became apparent that the original document held great potential to inform a variety of historical and scientific issues, and Gelo brought the possibility of a more involved Berghaus project to colleague and Germanist Chris Wickham, who had earlier researched and published on Native Americans in the work of German painters (Wickham 1996). The idea simmered for several years while both tended to administrative duties and other publications, until conversations in spring 2013 renewed interest. To properly engage the material, Wickham produced his own independent translation of the article, as published in this volume, and from there we went wherever curiosity led us, and were soon immersed in deep and complex explorations.

These are the days when interdisciplinarity is rightly celebrated, and ours was an eminently enjoyable, model collaboration. Essentially, Wickham, in addition to translating, took the lead in researching and drafting the sections about Berghaus and the German settlers; Gelo handled the Comanche and ethnological discussions and assembled all the parts. All along the way there was vigorous back and forth as each author made discoveries and formed opinions that helped the other. We also made road trips together to view the sites of the German treaty talks and settlements and found leader John Meusebach resting in his grave under some cedars in the forlorn quiet and sunshine of the Texas prairie. In addition, Wickham undertook travel to archives in Potsdam, Berlin, Gotha, and Munich, not to mention the Llano County (Texas) public library and the Llano city cemetery, and these visits were essential in reconstructing the story of Berghaus and his informant Emil Kriewitz.

Organizing our interpretations in relation to the original material was a challenging task, and we have tried to make our decisions plain within the text, but a few preliminary explanations are in order. We have taken

Berghaus's German-Comanche word list and Comanche-Shoshone comparison table out of their positions in the translated article (chapter 9) and presented them in a separate chapter (12). Also, our commentaries on the article and glossary became so extensive that we placed them in chapters by themselves (10 and 11). These steps allowed room for expanded exegesis and enhanced the utility of the different sections, as readers can now study the article uninterrupted by a lengthy word list or long footnotes and can access the word list directly as a working dictionary. In our word list translation, we retained the original unalphabetized order of words but afterward provide an index of all the terms in alphabetical order, in English, to enhance its usefulness as a reference. And whereas Berghaus employed Arabic numerals to mark his article endnotes, we have converted these to small letters, so there is no confusion with our numbered notes throughout. Berghaus's article endnotes are gathered in their original position at the end of his article, that is, at the end of chapter 9. When referring to his endnotes in our preceding chapters we use the letters. Berghaus mistakenly employed the number 14 in his endnotes twice, first in his article text and again in the Comanche word list. His second note 14 includes a statement that the first one has been removed from the text, an apparent attempt to rectify, though in fact it was not removed. By moving the second of these notes to chapter 12 with the word list, we have effectively eliminated this error.

As for editorial conventions, throughout the book our own brief comments, clarifications, and corrections are enclosed in brackets. In our translation of Berghaus's notes we reproduce his variance in the italicization of titles. In addition, our translation preserves Berghaus's use of the word "ethnography" (German *Ethnographie*) to mean cultural anthropology in the broad sense, while in our own writing we observe the modern American distinction between "ethnography," the description of specific individual cultures through fieldwork, and "ethnology," the wider, comparative approach to cultural questions. We refer to the colonists as "emigrants" when the focus is on their leaving Germany and "immigrants" when the focus is on their arrival in Texas.

The authors would like to acknowledge the indirect or direct help of several individuals. Heide Castañeda deserves thanks for her essential preliminary assistance. Venerable rare map dealers Dorothy Sloan and Barry Lawrence Ruderman have each produced exacting scholarly descriptions of the items in their online catalogs, which were a tremendous aid to our research in locating and understanding early Texas maps. The University of Texas at Arlington's Cartographic Connections website and the Texas Beyond History website also provided much useful map information. Jenny Marie Johnson, map librarian at the University of Illinois at Urbana-Champaign, took the extra effort of sending photos of pages and a list of maps when her copy of Johnston's 1848 atlas was too fragile to share. UTSA Special Collections archivist Juli McLoone assisted continually with document retrieval and copying. Tommi Myers of the Llano County library main branch in Llano, Texas, hosted a productive visit from Dr. Wickham. Herr Dr. Wolfgang Stein, North American curator at the Museum für Völkerkunde, Munich; Frau Dr. Petra Weigel and Herr Sven Ballenthin of the Sammlung Perthes archive, Gotha; Frau Anja Lampe of the Stadtarchiv Potsdam; Herr Udo Gentzen of the Bibliothek des Landeshauptarchivs Brandenburg; and Frau Monika Ayers of Die Maus–Gesellschaft für Familienforschung, Bremen, lent gracious assistance in Germany. Over the course of the project, the authors had fruitful exchanges with Nathan Crenwelge of the Fredericksburg (Texas) *Standard and Radio Post*, and regional history authors Glenn Hadeler and Scott Zesch. We are deeply grateful to Amy Fulkerson of the Witte Museum, Cathy Garnica and Jorge Chavez of Barry Lawrence Ruderman Antique Maps Inc., Henrietta Kettner Keener, Frau Dr. Kathrin Paasch of the Forschungsbibliothek Gotha, Connie Seger, and Katherine Weber for furnishing illustrations. Jay Dew of Texas A&M University Press was perfectly wise and positive in stewarding the project, and two anonymous readers provided many helpful comments for which we are appreciative. Patricia A. Clabaugh and Dawn Hall offered excellent editorial guidance. Our research was made possible by the resources of the Stumberg Distinguished University Chair, and we are ever thankful to Mary Pat Stumberg for her generosity and unfailing encouragement. We would also like to express our profound gratitude to the Summerlee Foundation, which supported publication of this book with a generous grant. Finally, we thank our wives Gabrielle Gelo and Sherry Whitmore for traveling with us along the Pinta Trail and contributing to the lively conversations through which this work took shape.

Daniel J. Gelo
Christopher J. Wickham

ORTHOGRAPHIC NOTE

In this book Comanche words are spelled using the alphabet adopted by the tribal language preservation committee (Comanche Language and Cultural Preservation Committee 2010, x–xi). Modern linguists have found it important to discriminate more sounds with additional symbols, but the tribal alphabet is quite precise and serviceable. In this system, single vowels represent vowel sounds like those in Spanish. Dual vowels that are the same (*aa*) represent a lengthening of the usual vowel sound; dual vowels that are different (*oi*) are pronounced as diphthongs. Under-lined vowels (*a̲*) are voiceless or "whispered." In addition to the usual vowel sounds and symbols found in Spanish and English, there is a cen-tral mid vowel, described as similar to the vowel sound in "put," writ-ten by Comanches as *ʉ*. Consonants are generally like those in English, except *b* is soft, like the English *v*, *r* is flapped with the tongue, and the clusters *kw* and *ts* represent single consonantal sounds. One additional consonant is the glottal stop, as in the English expression "uh-oh," shown with the symbol (*ʔ*). When pronouncing Comanche words, usually stress is placed on the first syllable.

Exceptions in using this modern Comanche standard are made for certain personal and group names that have older spellings that have become conventional. Also, when presenting the Berghaus glossary with comparative terms from other word lists (chapter 12), the original spell-ings and diacritical marks used in those lists have been retained.

A few details on German orthography are also provided here to aid pronunciation for readers who do not speak German, and also to suggest the intentions behind Kriewitz's and Berghaus's transcription of Coman-che sounds. The sounds represented by the letters *ch* in German have no direct equivalents in English. These letters are pronounced as a voiceless palatal fricative, somewhat like a soft *sh* in English, after front vowels (*i, e, ü, ö, ai, eu*), and as a voiceless velar fricative, somewhat like a soft *k* or *kh*, as in the Scottish word "loch," after low and back vowels (*a, o, u, au*). When at the beginning of a word, *ch* generally may be sounded as *k* or the soft *sh*, depending on the word. In German, the letters *qu* are pronounced like the English *kv*; *j* like the English *y*; *sch* like the English *sh*; *w* like the English *v*; and *z* like the English *ts*.

In comparing Comanche and German sounds, and noting such correspondences as the Comanche *ts* with the German *z*, it can be seen that German orthography lends itself fairly well in writing Comanche. But even though Berghaus recommends that his Comanche words should be read and pronounced as if they were German, it is not certain that his informant Kriewitz systematically and consistently abided by German spelling conventions when writing Comanche words.

Comanches and Germans
on the Texas Frontier

INTRODUCTION

Comanches and Germans
in Central Texas

When first encountered by German pioneers in February 1847, the Comanche people had a long and colorful history on the southern Great Plains and were coming to grips with new and, ultimately, conclusive challenges to their regional hegemony. Skillful buffalo hunters and superb equestrians, the Comanches epitomized the way of life developed by Native Americans across the Plains. Unlike other celebrated tribes such as the Sioux and Cheyennes, however, the Comanches had western rather than eastern origins. They originated from among eastern Shoshones who occupied the northwestern Plains for a time as pedestrian hunters, but whose earlier homeland was the Great Basin and adjacent Rocky Mountains. Splinter groups gained a separate ethnic identity as they migrated southward along the flanks of the Rockies, into the upper Arkansas, Canadian, and Red River valleys, driving the Apaches, who had preceded them from the north, farther south and west. Along with the Pueblos and Apaches, the Comanches were among the first Indians to adopt the horse, a Spanish introduction; within a few generations they gained mastery of the animal, and with that a greater range of travel and influence.

Much has been made in recent scholarship about the reach and power exerted by this relatively small but highly mobile society (e.g., Kavanagh 1996; DeLay 2008; Hämäläinen 2008; Gwynne 2010). Comanches first appear in a Spanish record in New Mexico in 1706 and had entered Texas by 1743. In addition to displacing the Apaches, they decimated the Tonkawas of Central Texas and thwarted any westward migration by groups such as the Pawnees and Osages. In Texas they inherited ancient Indian trade routes that linked the Native villagers of the southeast with others in the desert Southwest. They functioned as key middlemen in the trade of horses from south to north, supplying other tribes, and between east and west, serving prospective settlers as well as Indians. They also did a brisk commerce in stolen cattle and in human captives, taken for ransom, enslavement, or, occasionally, adoption. Most significantly, they blocked Spanish and Mexican control over the Southern Plains, guaranteeing the eventual failure of those colonial efforts.

These southbound Plains Shoshoneans supplemented their bison diet with smaller game, wild plant foods, and garden vegetables procured through trade with other tribes. They did no farming or gardening themselves. In relying on large horse herds, they also practiced nomadic pastoralism. The best form of social organization for pursuing these survival strategies was a flexible one. In a continuous waxing and waning, small family units gathered into bands of varying size when seasonal resources, trade opportunities, or warfare encouraged congregations, and dispersed across the landscape when resources became scarce or when under pursuit by enemies. Bands maintained wider ties and at times coordinated in yet larger units. The definition of the large units has been debated, for even though they shared a common language, they mostly functioned independently of one another, with their own leaders, ceremonies, treaties, and territories, and thus, in a technical sense, might be considered distinct tribes unto themselves; in modern parlance, they are called divisions. In any case the evolution of bands and divisions was a dynamic process. In the 1700s three divisions were known: Jupes (meaning unclear), Kotsotekas (Buffalo Eaters), and Yamparikas (Root Eaters). In the 1800s there were six divisions, including the Kotsotekas and Yamparikas, plus Kwahadis (Antelopes), Nokonis (Wanderers), Tenewas (Downstream People), and Penatekas (Honey Eaters).

The Penatekas, the southernmost division, were an offshoot of the Kotsotekas, who occupied Central Texas in the early 1800s. Their name Honey Eaters (Pihnaatɨka) follows the Shoshonean custom of designating social groups according to their stereotypic favorite food, which in turn evokes a stereotypic favorite environment. The southern Comanches were said to favor the timbered country where honey was found, and indeed there are many accounts of overflowing hives in the trees and cliff faces of the Cross Timbers and Hill Country, and as the most concentrated source of natural sugar, these were greatly valued by Indians and settlers alike (Gelo 2013, 49–50). In keeping with this theme, an alternate name applied to the southern division in the 1800s was Hois (Huuʔinʉʉ), "timber people." The "honey eater" name was also sometimes glossed as "wasp," "quick stinger," or "quick striking," lending a more martial tone to the characterization. But since honey bees were introduced by Euro-Americans, and feral bees colonized the Plains ahead of the line of white settlement, honey is also potentially evocative of cultural interaction and impending acculturation.

As the leading edge of Comanche migration in the early to mid-1800s, the Penatekas became largely independent of the other Comanche divisions, which at that time remained for the most part on or above the Red River. The Penatekas maintained northward ties initially, and in particular they explored connections with the Tenewas who occupied trading sites along the middle Red River, but in Central Texas the Penatekas had their own distinct economic and political universe. During the period, they generally had more intensive dealings with non-Indians than other Comanches. They were also the first Comanches to face the thrust of Anglo-American settlement and the first to succumb to its pressures, agreeing to occupy a reservation and attempt farming on the Clear Fork of the Brazos River in Throckmorton County, Texas, from 1855 until 1859, when they were driven to Indian Territory, present western Oklahoma.

As a result of these experiences, the Penatekas assumed a special profile both outside and within the Comanche tribe. To Anglo pioneers and early historians, they were "the Comanches." They became an emblem of the supposed duplicity of Indian societies that alternately sought peace and resisted forcefully against an inevitable transformation. It was suspected at the time and has since been confirmed that much of the later violence blamed on the Penatekas was committed by Comanches from the north, other tribes, or outlaw whites. Later non-Indian attitudes toward the Penatekas have been friendlier, in no small part because of the persistent idea that they held true to their peace promise with the German settlers of the Llano country; also, their circa 1875 reservation leaders Esahabbe (Milky Way) and Toshaway (Silver Brooch) were respected pacifists. Other Comanches recognized the Penateka's greater wealth in trade commodities and their more acculturated ways. But once among other Comanches on the Oklahoma reservation, having been impoverished and devastated by disease during their final years in Texas, the Penatekas were easily disparaged. They found themselves subordinated to leaders from the more northerly divisions who had resisted longer, and they were branded as overly conciliatory to whites, not sufficiently proud of traditional Indian life (Hagan 1976, 1993). Another, uncomplimentary name was applied to them: Hanitaibo, "[they eat] corn [like a] white man" (Jones 1972, 13). This image too has been tempered over time, though many present-day Comanche people remain aware of the affiliations and factional tendencies of their ancestors.

Central Texas must have been a very attractive location for the Comanches. The area enjoyed a mild climate compared to the High Plains and more sheltering topography. In a typical year, it received ten more inches of rain than the Panhandle area from which the Comanches most directly migrated (see Stephens and Holmes 1989, 5). It drew huge buffalo herds and offered green winter grass for horse forage. The entire area was generally abundant with deer, bear, antelope, wild horses, and small game. More importantly, living in the region provided easy access to several different ecological zones (Stephens and Holmes 1989, 6), and this variety was an advantage for survival.

The country between the Llano and Colorado Rivers at the heart of Penateka territory lay, technically, in the southern end of the Western Cross Timbers province. This was itself a varied environment with oak and hickory woodlands interlaced with open grasslands. Immediately surrounding this area on the east, south, and west was the inverse vegetation of the eastern Edwards Plateau or Hill Country, with short grass prairies dominant and timber along the breaks and streams. To the southeast, all along where the Hill Country gave way at the Balcones Escarpment to lower ground, was a line of remarkable springs. Other zones ran north to south paralleling the Cross Timbers. To the east and north lay the extensive open grasslands of the Grand Prairie and the long band of Blackland Prairie where deep black soils sustained even more luxuriant grasses, and where Indians sometimes burned off the winter grass to stimulate spring sprouting. These two prairies were partly separated by the narrower, denser eastern branch of the Cross Timbers. To the northwest lay the drier steppes of the Rolling Plains, stretching to the rugged face of the plateau-like Llano Estacado. With this great variety, the Comanches could adjust to periodic or sudden changes in availability of game and grazing. They could do so quickly, since they could travel up to sixty miles per day on their small, scrappy Indian ponies (Roemer 1983, 275). And by moving up and down the Brazos and Colorado valleys they could traverse these different zones without ever leaving major water and pasturage. This strategy is apparent if one reviews the locations of the different Penateka bands as they were recorded in mid-nineteenth-century reports.

Another advantage of Central Texas was its location relative to settled farming populations, both Indian and Euro-American. The Comanches established a symbiotic relationship with the Wichitans (Wichitas, Wacos, Tawakonis, Kitsais), whose villages, surrounded by acres of corn and pumpkin, sat along the Brazos and other streams to the east. They traded buffalo pelts and meat for garden produce, and, as the villages became depots for non-Indian goods, for ironware, guns, and horses also. Over time the Comanches and Wichitans joined in raiding to support their mutual economic interests, and some Comanches became a persistent, haughty presence, living for long periods in the villages of their allies, so much so that it is interesting to wonder how the two ethnicities might have merged, had their partnership not been interrupted by the march of white settlement. Regarding the French, Spanish, Mexicans, and Anglo-Americans, for the Comanches in the early 1800s, Central Texas was close enough, but not too close. They could enjoy trade with these aspiring intruders from what appeared to be a safe distance and play them off each other to forestall advancement. And, they could launch raids on the towns and ranches of Mexico and drive the stolen livestock and human captives back to the protected valleys of the Hill Country. These ventures took the Penatekas all the way to Durango, and they became pervasive and devastating during the 1840s.

The land of Central Texas was also imbued with value in another way, because once the Comanches occupied it they localized their belief system within the landscape (Gelo 1994, 2000). Comanche religion rested on the acquisition of medicine power, *puha*, from spirits that appeared in animal and human ghost form. These spirits were known to inhabit particular environments, such as springs, creeks, cliffs, and mountains. Just as their Shoshonean ancestors identified certain land features as the abodes of powerful spirits in the Great Basin and Rocky Mountains, the Comanches did so on the Southern Plains. Enchanted Rock north of Fredericksburg (figure 1) and Santa Anna Peaks in Coleman County are two sites in the region mentioned in early sources as places of Comanche ritual activity, and doubtless they recognized many other similar sites across the area.

Thus Central Texas, which turned out to be a much harsher than promised destination for Euro-American farmers, truly was, for the Comanches, an ideal landscape—a land of honey, if not milk—and one they were understandably reluctant to give up. How disturbing, then, it must have been to them to hear Republic of Texas president Sam Houston's proposed boundary between the settlements and Comanche land in 1844 (Winfrey and Day 1995, 2:6–9, 103–19). Houston had seen the Colorado River valley up to Austin fill rapidly with Anglo settlers, and he and his agents were looking farther west for similar locations. In a preliminary message dictated in March 1844, Penateka leader Old Owl suggested a boundary line running southwest from Comanche Peak (present Hood County) through the junction of the Llano and Colorado Rivers, and then on to the Rio Grande. This line would have kept settlers out of the Llano and San Saba valleys. When talks resumed in earnest in October, Houston arrived with a draft treaty drawing the line farther toward the southwest than what Old Owl had proposed. He wanted the line to run through the old fort site of San Saba, ostensibly to gain the Llano valley. But since the maps available to him were in error, with distorted stream courses and therefore showing the old fort to the southeast of its actual location (see chapter 13), Houston was asking for even more than he realized: cession of the San Saba valley as well as the Llano, and the area where these rivers, and also Pecan Bayou, join the Colorado—in other words, the Penateka heartland at the time. The Comanches had an accurate sense of where the old fort was located and understood the real implications of Houston's proposal. Another Penateka headman, Buffalo Hump, then countered with a line running somewhat east of what Old Owl had proposed, arguing that the line should follow the Balcones Escarpment, thus preserving the entire Hill Country and its buffalo grounds for the Penatekas. Houston feigned misunderstanding of this requirement and Old Owl's earlier intentions. The parties refused to agree, and the boundary remained unsettled.[1]

In fact, however, much of the same territory had already been taken away from the Comanches on paper in 1842, as a grant of settlers' rights to nearly four million acres from the Republic of Texas to entrepreneurs Henry Francis Fisher and Burchard Miller (Biesele 2010). Their plan was to settle the tract with German, Dutch, Swiss, and Scandinavian immigrants, but after two years of delay they simply sold their rights to a settlers' society recently formed in Germany, the Adelsverein. The following year (1845) Texas joined the Union, and in January 1846, US agents arrived in Penateka country to pursue their own treaty (Richardson 1933, 140–43; Foreman 1935, 1948; Winfrey and Day 1995, 3:43–52). Pierce M. Butler and M. G. Lewis met with Penateka headmen Buffalo Hump and Old Owl at Comanche Peak, then with these leaders and twenty-two more Comanche "chiefs, warriors, and counselors," along with leaders from other tribes, at the old Indian council grounds on Tehuacana Creek near present Waco. By signing the resulting accord the Penateka representatives bound their people exclusively to the United States and promised to surrender all captives and stolen horses, in exchange for trading posts and blacksmith shops to be set up "on the borders," plus $10,000 worth of future presents. Old Owl and another prominent headman, Santa Anna, also accepted an invitation and visited Washington, DC, witnessing the might of the approaching society. Although in one sense a realization of the Houston treaty effort, the Butler-Lewis treaty likewise never specified a boundary line between Indians and whites. Meanwhile, German immigrants had been landing by the hundreds at Matagorda Bay, intent on settling beyond the Llano River in the so-called Fisher-Miller grant.

As the decade of the 1840s drew to a close the Penatekas were active in assessing their situation and responding strategically. They did not simply retreat westward, but rather engaged whites along the line of settlement. On the northeast front of Comanche territory, they traded at the Torrey Trading House No. 2 located at the Tehuacana Creek council grounds from 1843 to 1849, where the proprietors, as good Yankees eager to see a weakened Mexico, were happy to receive the booty from south-of-the-border raids. They visited Fort Gates (1849–52; present Gatesville, Texas) and Fort Croghan (1849–55; present Burnet, Texas), and some befriended the Pidcokes, an English family who settled between the two forts (Gelo 2013). On the southern front, they frequented Fort Martin Scott (1848–53) just east of the new German town of Fredericksburg. From here, in January 1850, a party under agent John H. Rollins negotiated yet another treaty, signed by twelve Comanche headmen and leaders from other area tribes that placed them, again, solely under US jurisdiction and prohibited them from traveling south of the Llano River without permission. Less than six years later the Penatekas were bound to the Clear Fork reserve to the northwest, and their life as free-ranging hunters, traders, and raiders was all but over. But it was probably already quite apparent to them, on the chilly Friday of February 5, 1847, when the Penateka leader Ketumsee first rode up on the Germans just paces northwest of today's Mason, Texas, town square, that the days of Comanche dominance in Central Texas were numbered.

—————oℛℴ—————

The historical forces that brought German settlers into contact with the Comanches during the 1840s included the decisive activity of the Adelsverein. One among many organizations formed to sponsor emigration from Germany to the Americas, the Society for the Protection of German Immigrants in Texas was organized by a group of noblemen on April 20, 1842, at Biebrich am Rhein, a small town near the city of Mainz.[2] The label Adelsverein derives from its German name Verein zum Schutze deutscher Einwanderer in Texas and the German word for nobility, Adel (hence Adels-verein). Its purpose was to purchase lands in the Republic of Texas for Germans wishing to settle there. Two years later, on March 25, 1844, it was reorganized as a stock company, and on May 3, the government of the duchy of Nassau issued a charter permitting the society to operate (Benjamin 1910, 155; Brandenburg 1968, 8; Herff 1978, xv; Shook 1972, 230–31). Known variously as the Texas-Verein, the Mainzer Verein, the German Emigration Company, and the Society, the Adelsverein was responsible for bringing nearly ten thousand immigrants to Texas on ninety-three ships by 1850 (Gish in Solms-Braunfels 2000, 1; cf. Surminski 1992).

The goals of the Adelsverein derived from a mix of social, economic, and political ambitions, some stated programmatically in published documents, some emerging in the light of decisions reached by the leadership. Overpopulation and resulting poverty among the peasantry and lower middle classes in the states, duchies, and principalities that made up Germany in the early and mid-nineteenth century were the aristocrats' immediate incentives to act, with the increasing danger of social unrest and revolution as an additional stimulus. The prospect of trading links with a German community in the New World was certainly also attractive to the organizers, as were personal aggrandizement through naming of settlements and political influence on the world stage. Furthermore, the premise of a New Germany in the Americas with strong patriotic implications and a cultural emphasis on manners, morals, and traditional values and customs was never far from the surface. There is also evidence that British political ambitions in the New World were part of the

Adelsverein's strategic calculus, at least in the mind of its first commissioner general (Shook 1972, 232–33; Solms-Braunfels 2000, 203–25; Morgenthaler 2009, 174–77). The Adelsverein stressed repeatedly that it had no interest in persuading Germans to emigrate (Ehrenkreutz 1846, 187; Bromme 1846, 253; Benjamin 1910, 140). Rather, its role was described as providing a protective organizational structure through which those who had already decided to leave Germany could do so.

The Adelsverein couched its statements and publications in terms of philanthropy, its programmatic goal being framed in 1844 as follows: "Ein Verein hat sich gebildet, dessen Zweck es ist, die deutsche Auswanderung so viel als möglich nach einem einzigen günstig gelegenen Punkte hinzuleiten, die Auswanderer auf der weiten Reise und in der neuen Heimath zu unterstützen und nach Kräften dafür zu wirken, daß ihnen jenseits des Meeres eine neue Heimath gesichert werde" ("A society has formed whose purpose it is as far as possible to guide German emigration to a single, favorably located point, to support the emigrants both on the long journey and on arrival in their new homeland, and to use its strength to work to secure a new home for them on the other side of the ocean" [Bromme 1846, 254; Benjamin 1910, 140]). However, the investment aspect and the intent ultimately to turn a profit are embedded in the society's own budget projections, and the trustee and secretary admit as much in a circa 1848 open letter to the Victoria, Texas, newspaper, the *Texian Advocate*: "The German Emigration Society was originally founded as much for private speculation as philanthropic purposes" (Spiess and Wrede 1848; Bromme 1846, 246; see also Benjamin 1910, 33–37). The constitution of the Adelsverein indicates the profit motive of its members. Citing Biesele (1930, 73, 87), Philip Donald Brandenburg summarizes:

> [The Adelsverein] constitution (Chapter 4) provided for the distribution of profits in the following manner: 80 per cent among the stockholders, 10 percent to the reserve fund, 5 per cent among the employees, 3 per cent among charitable institutions, and 2 per cent for exploration, promotion of the sciences, the founding of institutions, and similar objects. According to the terms of the grant, the empresario was to receive 10 sections of land for every 100 families and 10 half-sections for every single man introduced. After the grant had been settled the land owned by the Society would increase in value and could be sold to new immigrants, thus providing the Society with a profit on its investment. (Brandenburg 1968, 16n18)

In a similar vein, in his report to the members of the Adelsverein in Germany, its first commissioner general in Texas, Prince Carl of Solms-Braunfels, stated that he anticipated working with the Texas congress "to acquire such commercial advantages for the Society as would allow him to take care not merely of the farmers in the German Fatherland, but to give the German industrial activity new markets and to expand German sea trade" (Brandenburg 1968, 19; Constant 1847, 13; see also Biggers 1925, 35, Benjamin 1910, 36). Fifty years later, when outlining the history of the Adelsverein for a court deposition, its second commissioner general, John O. Meusebach, admitted that financial gain had been an early goal but that it was to be omitted later from the Adelsverein's official program. He described the 1844 reorganizing of the society in these words: "it was concluded at a general meeting to drop the idea of financial speculation and to organize as an association with the avowed purpose of aiding and leading the emigration to Texas on a large scale, and to carry the operations on a basis of philanthropical principles, excluding all political or money-making financial projects" (Meusebach 1894, 4). But despite Meusebach's claim of a revised mission, there can be no doubt that financial speculation, investment opportunity, and profit motive were core elements in the self-image of the Adelsverein.

The terms of agreement offered by the Adelsverein were extremely attractive to prospective emigrants. Three hundred and twenty acres were promised to each family and 160 to each single man, also provisions and supplies until the first harvest as well as housing, churches, schools, and medical care. The society also undertook to provide transportation to the society's lands in the interior on arrival at the Texas coast. However, owing to the disastrously inadequate funding the society provided, and its administrative and managerial shortcomings, these ambitious promises were not fulfilled. Apart from the acreage, the contract document provided by the Adelsverein for signature by each emigrant did not even list these commitments, though it did spell out in detail the emigrant's obligations: accept the land as is and as assigned by the society's agent; assume the role of owner of the property, but do not sell any of it within three years; reside on the property for three years; fence and cultivate fifteen acres within that time; erect a dwelling on the land; adhere to the regulations of the society in general; be responsible for the cost of surveying the land; title would transfer to the immigrant after three years, provided all conditions had been met by the immigrant; failure to meet the conditions by the stated time would result in forfeiture of the land and any structures on it to the society.

Observers and students of the Adelsverein have seen in these and other statements a desire to establish a New Germany in Texas (cf. Ehrenkreutz 1846, 176). The emphasis on the German work ethic, manners, morality (Sitten), traditional values and customs (though usually not religion; the final paragraphs in Solms-Braunfels's 1846 *Texas* [Solms-Braunfels 1846a, 133–34; 1936, 140–41] are an exception) recurs with regularity in publications supporting the work of the Adelsverein, and the numerous guidebooks published for German emigrants stressed the desirability of settling where German communities already existed. One reason given is that Anglo-Americans, typically painted as pragmatic realists, have a tendency to seek unfair advantage in transactions and cheat the innocent German immigrant (Berghaus 1844, 368–69; Ehrenkreutz 1846, 142; Behr 1847, 91; Solms-Braunfels 2000, 206). Maintaining ties with the fatherland is a selling point in the Adelsverein's own literature, and the touted cohesiveness of the planned communities as German communities suggests nationalistic aspirations. Some commentators see in the establishing of the slave-holding Nassau Plantation by the Adelsverein's first representatives in Texas an intent to perpetuate a model of feudalism; however, the later trajectory of the society's activity does not support this analysis (cf. Kearney 2010, 4). Nevertheless, there is a clear pattern of the sponsoring aristocrats wishing to make their personal mark. The three Carls among the Adelsverein members gave their name to the destination port Carlshafen (also known as Indianola); the first commissioner general named New Braunfels after his home; Fredericksburg was named for Prince Friedrich of Prussia, an Adelsverein member; the settlements Castell, Leiningen, Schoenburg, and Meerholz also take their names from Adelsverein members (see also Morgenthaler 2007, 58).

Before its reorganization as a stock company, the Adelsverein began its involvement in Texas by dispatching two representatives from Germany to the republic. Count Ludwig Josef von Boos zu Waldeck und Montfort and Count Viktor August zu Leiningen Westerburg-Altleiningen arrived in Galveston in August or September 1842. Boos-Waldeck, the older of the two, recommended taking the time to establish an organizational structure in Texas and beginning with a slow immigration flow; he purchased land near the German settlement at Industry in Fayette County for development as a farm and bridgehead for immigration (Nassau Farm).

Leiningen, on the other hand, favored rapid advancement of the immigration project and persuaded the leadership of the Adelsverein to adopt his approach. As a result, Boos-Waldeck resigned from the Adelsverein in April 1844.

When the French speculator Bourgeois d'Orvanne heard of the plans of the society, he approached its leaders with the offer to sell them a land grant he held for a tract west of San Antonio. The offer was accepted without hesitation (April 1844), even though documents clearly showed that the time allowed for settlement of the grant had expired (King 1967, 35). Evidently, d'Orvanne had persuaded the Adelsverein that it could be extended; however, when he and the newly appointed commissioner general of the Adelsverein arrived in Texas their efforts to effect the extension with the Texas congress were unsuccessful. The commissioner general was Prince Carl of Solms-Braunfels, a member of the Adelsverein, who had taken a yearlong leave of absence from his military duties in the Austro-Hungarian army to make the necessary on-site arrangements for immigration and oversee the first arrivals. According to his successor, John O. Meusebach, when the d'Orvanne plan failed the Adelsverein should have purchased land, then available at five to ten cents per acre, on the open market to avoid the land-grant constraints that required settlement by a certain number of families or individuals within a fixed period of time (Meusebach 1894, 5). However, at just this time Henry Francis Fisher arrived in Germany and offered the Adelsverein the grant he held with Burchard Miller. The Fisher-Miller grant covered 3,878,000 acres and lay between the Llano and Colorado Rivers; Miller knew, but did not explain, that it was situated within the hunting grounds of the Penateka Comanches. It was also 300 miles from the coast and 150 miles from the nearest settlement (Benjamin 1910, 41). On June 26, 1844, Fisher sold an interest in the contract to the Adelsverein, and on December 30, 1845, Fisher and Miller sold to the society their rights in the grant, which now included the stipulation that six thousand families or individual colonists be settled on the land by August 1847.

It is doubtful that the Adelsverein fully understood the realities of the deal; Fisher and Miller did not have land to sell, only the rights to settle it, therefore the society should not have been promising emigrants acreage of what it did not own (cf. Benjamin 1910, 41; Tiling 1913, 109; Meusebach 1894, 7–8). During discussions with President Sam Houston soon after their arrival, Boos-Waldeck and Leiningen had been offered a tract situated between the d'Orvanne grant and the Fisher-Miller grant. Geographically this would comprise a substantial portion of the drainages of the Guadalupe and Pedernales Rivers (see maps in Ehrenkreutz 1846 and Solms-Braunfels 2000, 112). Leiningen declined, as he preferred to seek land closer to the center of settled Texas. William von Rosenberg views Houston's offer as part of a strategy to settle West Texas with European immigrants and to hold the eastern and northern parts of the state for Americans (Brister 1982, 303). While Rosenberg does not say as much, if this was Houston's strategy it would have placed a European buffer between the Comanches and the Americans. Acceptance of Houston's offer by Boos-Waldeck and Leiningen would have radically changed the history of the Adelsverein in Texas.

When the first families arrived at the landing site on Matagorda Bay in December 1844, there was no land for them; purchase of the Fisher-Miller grant rights had not yet been finalized by the Adelsverein administrators. The immigrants remained at Carlshafen (Indianola) until March 1845, when Solms-Braunfels was able to purchase two leagues of land at La Fontana (later renamed New Braunfels), on the Comal and Guadalupe Rivers, to serve as a temporary way station. The project had now become a logistical one of transporting the settlers and their belongings from Carlshafen on the Gulf Coast to New Braunfels, a distance of 152 miles by Solms-Braunfels's own calculation (Solms-Braunfels 1846a, 69–70), and then on to the Fisher-Miller grant land. A second way station also would be necessary, and it fell to the next commissioner general, Meusebach, to establish it at Fredericksburg.

When Baron Otfried von Meusebach arrived in Texas in May 1845, he opted to leave his status of nobility and privilege behind and commit fully to his new, egalitarian home with a new, Americanized name. This was in stark contrast to his predecessor, Solms-Braunfels, who preserved the trappings of aristocracy wherever he could and complained wherever he couldn't. Solms-Braunfels's inability to function effectively as an executive in Texas resulted in part from this attitude, in part from his minimal business sense, and not least from his contempt for Anglo-Americans and their approach to the realities of life. But despite these shortcomings, Solms-Braunfels succeeded in making arrangements with the Republic of Texas and its officials for the immigration, acquired several land tracts for settlement, put in place the basic logistical arrangements for movement of the immigrants, and founded Carlshafen and New Braunfels (Gish in

Solms-Braunfels 2000, 3). Meusebach arrived to find bills due, massive debt, incompetent bookkeeping, and unhappy settlers (King 1967, 52–56). Because Solms-Braunfels, less than eleven months after his arrival in Texas, had already left New Braunfels, Meusebach had to hurry to catch up with him on the way to Galveston, and when Solms-Braunfels was apprehended in Galveston because of his debts, Meusebach was forced to use some of the already inadequate funds he had brought from Germany to free him (King 1967, 56; Gish points to Solms-Braunfels's own differing account of this time in his personal diary [Solms-Braunfels 2000, 7]). Meusebach's frustration at the conditions he confronted can be sensed in his recollection of the events fifty years later:

> I found the affairs of the Society in the greatest confusion and disorder. The prince had already experienced that all the estimates made by the directory in Europe with the aid of Fisher (the vendor of the grant concession) were by far underrated, no matter whether intentionally or unintentionally; that the shipping of frame houses, goods, provisions, and emigrants with unlimited baggage from Galveston to Matagorda Bay; that the camping, moving, transporting, and supplying such a large body with provisions, required more than 10 times the amount of the estimates. (Meusebach 1894, 11)

Meusebach was an experienced administrator, having attended the mining and forestry academy in Clausthal, Harz, in 1828, and the University of Bonn in 1832. During an appointment as mayor of Anklam, Western Pomerania, he had had to resolve difficult tensions between the communities of Anklam and Stettin (King 1967, 30). His new responsibilities included the challenge of looming humanitarian disaster.

The Adelsverein immigrants who had arrived in the first wave between July and December of 1844, having celebrated Christmas on the shores of Matagorda, were moved by Solms-Braunfels to the newly founded New Braunfels in March 1845 (Biesele 1927, 118; 1930, 19–120).[3] A treaty with the Lipan Apaches was made in the interests of security (Benjamin 1910, 44, 127). Because they were not yet at the designated settlement area, instead of the 320 or 160 acres promised them, immigrant families and single men were given half an acre of land in town and ten acres in the surrounding country (Benjamin 1910, 45). This makeshift solution immediately caused tensions, and some declined to accept, as they feared they would not get what they had been promised by contract (Seele 1884,

99). In July 1845, shortly after Meusebach's installation as commissioner general, the second wave of immigrants arrived; however, it was a third wave that arrived in the fall that cost hundreds of lives and proved beyond all doubt that the Adelsverein was not close to being equal to the task it had set itself, indeed was closer to being criminally negligent.

In November 1845, Meusebach received notification that 4,304 emigrants were on their way from Germany. There was no money available to transport and care for them. Meusebach calculated that he would need $140,000; the Adelsverein directors sent a credit note of $24,000 (Benjamin 1910, 48). About 5,250 German immigrants landed in Texas between October 1845 and April 1846.[4] To these already fraught circumstances two more factors were added that the Adelsverein could not have controlled. The Mexican War began, removing promised transportation resources and able-bodied men from the migration project, and the spring of 1846 was unusually wet, causing otherwise difficult trails to become impassable, and undernourished, immobilized immigrants to become sick and frail. Benjamin reports that eventually "[some] 2,500 reached New Braunfels and Fredericksburg. A thousand were left at Indian Point, and on the road towards New Braunfels. Five hundred returned to Germany. Five hundred enlisted in the Mexican war . . . about 250 lost their lives at Indian Point, a hundred on their way to the settlements and a hundred on their arrival in New Braunfels" (Benjamin 1910, 49; cf. Morgenthaler 2007, 45–48; Seele 1883, 44–51). Some were stranded in the unhealthy conditions at the coast for six months. When letters reached Germany concerning this human catastrophe, the already shaky reputation of the Adelsverein was damaged further. As commissioner general, Meusebach was responsible for managing this crisis in addition to moving the settlement project ahead. Now that the Fisher-Miller grant was the designated destination, Meusebach needed to secure the route, establish a second way station between New Braunfels and the southern boundary of the grant on the Llano River, provide for security on the grant land, begin surveying the land, and move settlers onto that land. The Fisher-Miller grant lay well beyond already settled territory and beyond the reach of the US military. As early as mid-December 1845, Meusebach began preparing the site of Fredericksburg, north of the Pedernales River, as the second way station. In May of the following year the first settlers arrived there; by August the population of the town numbered one thousand.

Providing security for Adelsverein settlers on the Fisher-Miller grant called for a different kind of problem solving. Drawing on his diplomatic skills, an Enlightenment education, and a humanistic worldview, Meusebach sought peaceful coexistence with the Comanche residents of the planned new German homeland. In late 1846 his appointed business director in Fredericksburg, Dr. Friedrich Schubert (he also used the name Strubberg), had traveled the 38 miles to the Llano and returned with reports of forty to sixty thousand hostile Kickapoos amassed north of the river (Morgenthaler 2007, 59), but Meusebach (who shortly afterward fired Schubert as an incompetent) gave no credence to this information.[5] Instead, he realized how important it was to counter Schubert's claim and reassure the settler community. Equally as important as confidence building among the immigrants was the safety of the surveyors who would need to enter the Fisher-Miller grant lands in advance of the settlers (Meusebach 1894, 23). Meusebach therefore prepared a party to approach the Comanches with a view to negotiating a nonaggression agreement. The idea that the Adelsverein would seek a peace accommodation with the Comanches had a history that went back at least a year. In his book *Vollständige Beschreibung des Staates Texas in historischer, politischer, geographischer und geselliger Hinsicht* (Complete Description of the State of Texas with Respect to History, Politics, Geography, and Society), in which the preface is dated March 1846, B. von Ehrenkreutz anticipates the treaty: "It is expected that the directors of the Mainzer Verein in Texas will do everything to sign a peace and trading treaty with the Comanche Indians" (Ehrenkreutz 1846, 63).

On February 5, 1847, where the town of Mason now stands, Meusebach encountered the Comanche leader, Ketumsee, and arranged to accompany him to the Comanche camp on the San Saba River, 25 miles from its confluence with the Colorado. They agreed that the Comanche headmen Buffalo Hump, Mupechucope (Old Owl), and Santa Anna would come to that location to meet with Meusebach and his party. Meanwhile, Meusebach's party, which by now included Indian agent Robert Neighbors and geologist Ferdinand Roemer, would continue into the Fisher-Miller grant land to find the old Spanish mission and presidio, which were rumored to be close to lost Spanish silver mines. If the legend proved true and silver was located, the principal impediment to the Adelsverein project, lack of financial resources, might be mitigated. Neighbors had been sent by Texas Governor Pinckney Henderson to dissuade Meusebach from negotiations because the Comanches were supposedly on the warpath

(Meusebach 1894, 24); failing that effort, Neighbors was to stay and assist. Roemer had met Neighbors in Fredericksburg and chose to join him in his pursuit of Meusebach. Roemer's firsthand account of this meeting between the Germans and the Comanches (Roemer 1849a; 1983) is the most detailed and reliable source of information of the encounter (though Meusebach later took issue with some details [Meusebach 1894, 25]). The mines were not found; Roemer pronounced the geology of the immediate vicinity incompatible with silver deposits (Roemer 1849a, 312; 1983, 259; Penniger 1971, 41).

On their return to the Comanche camp, the negotiations with the three headmen proved fruitful, and a ratification ceremony was scheduled for May 1847 in Fredericksburg, after the chiefs had had the opportunity to confer with their tribes (Morgenthaler 2007, 70–72). The specifics of the encounter between the Comanches and the Germans that produced what has become known as the Meusebach Treaty have been laid out in many accounts and will not be rehearsed in detail here (e.g., Roemer 1849a, 285–329; 1983, 237–73; Penniger 1896, 86–108; 1971, 37–45; Tiling 1913, 95–107; Biesele 1927, 122–27; King 1967, 111–23; Morgenthaler 2007, 62–72; Luther 2013, 53–67). Suffice it to summarize the three major points of agreement: that the Germans would be allowed to travel in Comanche territory between the Llano and San Saba rivers without impediment, and conversely the Comanches could visit German communities, provided that they remained peaceful; that the Germans and Comanches would support each other if attacked or robbed by a third party; and that surveyors would be permitted to survey as far as the Concho River. Gifts to the value of $2,000 were promised to the Comanches if they agreed. Not written into the agreement, but concluded orally at some point, was an understanding that a member of the German community would live in the camp of Penateka leader Santa Anna as either an agent, guarantor, intermediary, representative, or voluntary hostage—the terms are unclear. Thus, one of the colonists, Emil Kriewitz, who had not been at the negotiations on the San Saba, though he did meet the Meusebach party as it was returning to Fredericksburg, apparently out of a sense of duty when other candidates demurred, went in May 1847 to live with the Comanches (Penniger 1896, 118; 1971, 49). It was during the following four months that he gathered the data for his German-Comanche word list (see chapters 7, 11, and 12).

Solms-Braunfels had been very aware of the Comanches during his time in Texas, though he had not reached out to them as Meusebach did.

He writes in his 1845 "Memoir on American Affairs" that "[the] Indians are well aware of the difference between Americans and European immigrants" and refers to the Comanche memory of the 1839 Council House massacre in San Antonio as a principal motivator of enmity toward the Americans (Solms-Braunfels 2000, 223). Indeed, he explicitly characterizes them as potential allies against the Americans, praising their courage and bravery and explaining that they keep their word to those they trust. It is likely that he conveyed this confidence in Comanche trustworthiness to Meusebach during their conversation.

Even before he set out into Comanche territory to seek negotiations, Meusebach had already written his letter of resignation to the Adelsverein directorate on January 22. After eighteen months of struggle to bring order to the society's affairs and ongoing conflict resolution with and among settlers, Meusebach was ready to begin his own project as settler and pioneer. In December 1846, settlers in New Braunfels, at the instigation of Henry Fisher, had risen up against Meusebach as the Adelsverein representative, demanding what they considered to be equal treatment and calling for the resignation of Meusebach as soon as a successor could replace him (Morgenthaler 2007, 60–61). In Fredericksburg, too, there had been unrest. The failure of the society's managers in Germany to understand the situation on the ground in Texas and the lack of response to his repeated and urgent pleas for funding had made Meusebach's task impossible. In addition, the Adelsverein directorate had begun a campaign to gather information on Meusebach through Fisher and Philip Cappes that could be used to discredit him. He was succeeded by Hermann Spiess, a member of the Darmstadt Forty, a group of intellectuals that had been organizing itself in Germany to form a utopian colony in North America at the very time the Meusebach Treaty was being concluded.

After discussions with Adelsverein general manager Castell, Spiess and Ferdinand Herff had decided to drop their plan to settle in Wisconsin and instead move with their group of forty idealistic compatriots to Texas. They were promised land in the Adelsverein tract and in September 1847 founded Bettina, the first settlement on the Fisher-Miller grant, at the confluence of Elm Creek and the Llano River. Kriewitz, following his residency with Santa Anna, was their guide. The Adelsverein succeeded in placing only five settlements on its land; all were founded at this time. They were Bettina (named for a leading figure of the German Romantic movement, Bettina von Arnim), Castell, Leiningen, Schoenburg, and

Meerholz. Only Castell exists today and has relocated to the south side of the Llano, which means it is no longer on Fisher-Miller grant land. As 1847 drew to a close, Spiess made it known among the colonists that the Adelsverein was winding down its operations. Offices in Fredericksburg and Carlshafen were closed and bankruptcy was inevitable. In the ensuing years, the society worked to pay off its debts but ceased transporting emigrants and was no longer able to support those settlers already in Texas.

Debate about the Adelsverein and its activities brought out strong opinions during the 1840s. Over a period of at least six years, a discussion unfolded in the German and German American press and in book publications for emigrants, as well as in proclamations and reports issued by the society, on the quality of the achievements of the Adelsverein and the merits of emigration to Texas, especially under its auspices.[6] The following outline of some of the contributions suggests the flavor of this debate (see also Tiling 1913, 114–20).

Texas had probably entered the German popular consciousness as a potential destination for emigration with J. Valentin Hecke's 1820 publication *Reise durch die Vereinigten Staaten von Nord-Amerika in den Jahren 1818 und 1819* (Journey through the United States of North America in the Years 1818 and 1819). Hecke lauds the province (until 1821 still part of New Spain) for its beautiful, fertile, and well-watered land (Hecke 1820, 173). He goes on to recommend that Hamburg, in alliance with what remains of the Hanseatic League, offer to purchase the territory from Spain, because Texas unifies in its boundaries "all the advantages of a rapidly blossoming and blessed colony" (Hecke 1820, 178); he also suggests that Prussia could do the same thing (Hecke 1820, 199; Benjamin 1910, 11–13). In 1834 Detlef Dunt's *Reise nach Texas nebst Nachrichten von diesem Lande* (Journey to Texas with News of this Land) had appeared, and in 1841 G. A. Scherpf's much cited *Entstehungsgeschichte und gegenwärtiger Zustand des neuen, unabhängigen, amerikanischen Staates Texas* (The Origins and Current State of the New, Independent, American State of Texas) (Dunt 2015; Scherpf 1841). At the latest, Texas became a known quantity through the Swiss writer Charles Sealsfield's (nom de plume of Karl Postl) two-volume novel of life in the early years of the republic, *Das Kajütenbuch oder Nationale Charakteristiken* (The Cabin Book or National Characteristics), published in 1841 (Sealsfield 1841). Postl's book was well received in Germany until the censorship that followed the failed 1848 revolution.

The role of the press in the debate about the Adelsverein can be seen in a single issue of the *Allgemeine Zeitung* (no. 351), published in Augsburg on December 16, 1844 (see Walker 1964, 84–85). On page 2802 of the supplement, there begins, under the headline "The Emigration Speculations" ("Die Auswanderungsspeculationen"), an anonymous review of Wilhelm Grisson's book *Beiträge zur Charakteristik der Vereinigten Staaten von Nord-Amerika* (Contributions toward Characterizing the United States of North America) (Berghaus 1844; see also Grisson 1844). The author of the review is Heinrich Berghaus (Engelmann 1977, 298). The reviewer essentially summarizes and concurs with Grisson's warning that prospective emigrants should think very carefully about taking that step, because so many who had would now gladly return to their previous miserable situation in Germany if they could. In a direct slap at the Adelsverein, the reviewer writes that even princes and lords have stooped so low as to give the stream of those sick of their homeland a new direction by elevating Texas to the level of a promised land. From the opposite side, in the same issue of the *Allgemeine Zeitung*, the voice of those princes and lords is also heard. On page 2806, a short article picks up on a criticism in the *Rheinischer Beobachter* (Rhenish Observer) of December 9, of a report from Galveston published in an earlier issue of the *Allgemeine Zeitung* that had chastised the Adelsverein for its work and the considerable obstacles that the society was not dealing with competently. The two newspapers clearly stand on opposite sides of the debate; the *Rheinischer Beobachter* generally supports the work of the Adelsverein, while the *Allgemeine Zeitung* is critical. That said, the December 16 article in the *Allgemeine Zeitung* concludes by printing verbatim an announcement by the Directorate of the Adelsverein, dated December 11, which lays out the termination of attempts to settle the Bourgeois d'Orvanne grant, the acquisition of the "extremely fertile and healthy" Fisher-Miller grant, and the imminent recruitment of the second wave of immigrants as soon as news of the first wave's safe arrival is received.

The writing of Traugott Bromme contributed further to the criticism leveled against the Adelsverein. Bromme was a collaborator of Berghaus and wrote the section on Texas in volume six of Berghaus's *Allgemeine Länder- und Völkerkunde* (General Geography and Ethnography), published in 1846. Already on the second page of his own 1846 book *Rathgeber für Auswanderungslustige* (Advisor for Those Wanting to Emigrate), Bromme launched a withering attack on those in the press who uncritically welcomed the initiative of the Adelsverein, "which the author of this book will never recognize as an authority on emigration and settlement enterprises" (Bromme 1846, 2). The servile tone of those newspapers that sought from the noblemen no accounting of the details of their plans but congratulated them on their good intentions and asserted that they "know what they are doing" was, for Bromme, reprehensible. Later in his book the tone becomes more conciliatory. For twelve pages Bromme is at pains to paint a more complete and balanced picture of the work of the Adelsverein (Bromme 1846, 246–58). The intentions and efforts of the society are described as laudable and its accomplishments so far (July 1846) extraordinary (Bromme 1846, 246). However, its incautious haste to acquire the d'Orvanne and Fisher-Miller grants and its appointment of an unsuitable first leader (Solms-Braunfels) are criticized. Bromme stresses that he is not personally acquainted with any members of the Adelsverein and exonerates all except the founder for these failures. Most members, he claims, were simply speculators seeking profit and therefore beyond suspicion (Bromme 1846, 246). With this statement Bromme comes close to committing the same fault for which he castigated some members of the press: presumption of innocence on the basis of social position. While recognizing the potential of the Adelsverein to accomplish great things, Bromme is dismayed at the apparent contradictions in the society's motives, the lack of openness in the society's operations, and its exclusion of all but the nobility at its top level of management (Bromme 1846, 246). Bromme is clearly well informed about what is happening on the ground in Texas; as early as the middle of 1846 he is aware of the plan to found a town (which he refers to as "Frederickville," but which will be Friedrichsburg/ Fredericksburg) on the "Perdinales" [*sic*]. His spelling reflects the local pronunciation of this river name then and to this day, though the spelling, even at that time, was established as "Pedernales." Fredericksburg had been officially founded in May 1846, just two months before the date of the preface to Bromme's book.

What Bromme did not know as he prepared his manuscript for his publisher, was that at exactly that time the financial crisis of the society in Texas had forced Meusebach, the commissioner general, to take a desperate step. In June 1846 Meusebach asked the society agent in Galveston, D. H. Kläner, to write a letter to the mayor of Bremen for publication in the German newspapers, laying out the dire conditions of the settlers and the absolute need for more funding from the Adelsverein in Germany.

This public shaming produced the desired effect, and a letter of credit for $60,000 was issued immediately (Morgenthaler 2007, 44). The amount was insufficient, but the effect was manifold: yet another damning letter about Adelsverein viability appeared in the German press, Meusebach came under suspicion and was subsequently conspired against by the society leadership in Mainz, and some confidence was restored to Adelsverein creditors in Texas that outstanding bills might be paid.

Among the indefatigable boosters of emigration to Texas and the role of the Adelsverein was the sometime businessman, explorer, and railroad agent from Düsseldorf, Viktor Bracht. His book *Texas im Jahre 1848* (*Texas in 1848*) contains not only a detailed account of the state of the state at that time but also a collection of his own personal letters written between June 19, 1845, and November 1, 1847. Bracht acknowledges the difficulties of the Adelsverein and attributes their cause almost solely to funding problems, specifically, too little and too late (Bracht 1849, 135; 1931, 90). At the time of his writing (the foreword by Bracht's brother is dated November 11, 1848), the settlements on the Fisher-Miller grant had been founded (Bettina, Castell, Leiningen, Schoenburg, and Meerholz) and as of May 1848 were reported to be thriving. Bracht seems to be writing out of immediate personal experience of these settlements, and he writes enthusiastically: "Nowhere else have Germans given more magnificent evidence of what stern diligence and courageous perseverance can accomplish than those have that settled on the banks of the picturesque Llano. . . . In this small German colony lies the germ for real future greatness" (Bracht 1849, 136, 137; 1931, 91).

As if to reinforce his own positive assessment, Bracht quotes at length two pieces from Texas newspapers touting the advantages of the state. The first, from the March 20, 1847, issue of the *Galveston Weekly News* and presumably originally in English, is an open letter from thirty-one citizens of the Adelsverein town of New Braunfels, declaring the health and strength of that settlement. One of the signatories is Emil Kriewitz, who, as we shall see from Berghaus's 1851 article, had written to his mother from Fredericksburg barely six weeks earlier on February 14, 1847, that conditions were extremely bad and that prospective emigrants should on no account come to Texas at this time. This contradiction is perhaps explained by Kriewitz's solidarity with the collective need of the citizens of New Braunfels to make a stronger case than was justified by reality in order to preserve their livelihoods (Kriewitz's noble title is given for good measure); on the other hand, perhaps Kriewitz's name was used without his permission. A shortened version of the same letter also appeared in a different German translation in the Darmstadt paper *Der deutsche Auswanderer* (Wedemeyer et al. 1847).

The second piece cited by Bracht was written by the American editor of the *Texian Advocate* of Victoria (Texas) and appeared in that paper on February 10, 1848. It praises the beauty of the landscape and the intelligence of the inhabitants and paints the picture of an idyllic land awaiting further settlement. It is thus not only Germans, for whom everything is at stake, but also Anglos, who sing the praises of Texas as a destination. At the close of his book, Bracht includes an open letter (to which he is one of thirty-three signatories), intended for all German-language papers and printed in the Galveston *Zeitung* on June 7, 1848, correcting for German readers their misperceptions about Central Texas. The points stressed are: the climate is good and not tropical; the good health of Germans residing there is beyond doubt; fear of Indians is completely unjustified, no settlement or farm has ever been attacked; all German crops and farm animals thrive; safety of persons and property is as good as anywhere in Germany; land prices are lower than anywhere else in the United States; soil yields are better than at the coast; and Germans are concentrated together in the region and anyone with the right means and readiness to work hard can do well (Bracht 1849, 299–303; 1931, 207–9).

Bracht's personal letters to Germany capture the tenor of his individual disposition with respect to Texas and the Adelsverein project (Bracht 1849, 221–94; 1931, 153–202). They also cover the exact time period referred to in Berghaus's 1851 article when Kriewitz was in the Penateka camp compiling the Comanche-German word list. The names of the addressees have, unfortunately, been redacted. Bracht's arrival in Galveston with the Adelsverein is described with enthusiasm in a letter dated June 19, 1845. With the words "Ein Mißlingen unserer Kolonisation wird hier für unwahrscheinlich gehalten" ("We do not feel a failure of our colonization is at all likely"), he seeks to put to rest the negative speculation that prevails in many quarters. He advises his countrymen to emigrate to Texas and affirms that he sees only satisfied and healthy faces; even the blacks are happy and enjoying life, he writes (Bracht 1849, 223; 1931, 154). On December 15, 1845, he became a citizen of Texas, just days before US President Polk signed the bill authorizing the annexation on December 29 (Bracht 1849, 225; 1931, 155). On January 10, 1846, Bracht is in New Braunfels and writes that Meusebach set out on December 28 for the Fisher-Miller grant. He mentions peaceful Lipan Apaches and Delawares, but not Comanches. However, an addition to this letter dated January 11 makes reference to the earlier (October 1845) murder by Indians of settlers Wrede and Claren (Biesele 1927, 120), but here too Bracht tries to downplay the danger by ascribing part of the cause to the carelessness of the victims and anticipates that this will probably be the last instance of Indian violence (Bracht 1849, 233; 1931, 160). On February 9, 1846, Bracht reaffirms his unwavering intention to remain in Texas, though in a second letter of the same date he complains that the Adelsverein is sending over too many vagabonds, idlers, thieves, and criminals (Bracht 1849, 239; 1931, 164).

One letter in particular deserves attention, as it is evidently addressed to somebody who is considering emigration and, because of its detail, appears to be based on journal entries. Bracht strives here to be frank to someone dear to him about the realities of life in Texas, and the picture he paints is rich and nuanced. The (male) recipient is addressed as "Du" and is therefore a very close friend or even family member. The letter contains ten different dates of writing, beginning with July 12 and ending on October 11, 1846, and numerous ellipses. Bracht, like the Adelsverein's own literature, distances himself from any intention to persuade someone to emigrate. Once the decision is made to sail for Texas, he recommends the emigrant not sign on with the Adelsverein, which so far has not met any of its promises, but rather bring 5,000 talers to cover expenses in becoming established (Bracht 1849, 240–41; 1931, 165). At the time of writing (July 12, 1846), the Fisher-Miller grant has not yet been opened up, but the outlook is very promising. Two weeks later the optimistic tone is more muted. On July 26, Bracht writes that financial woes beset the society and that the Fisher-Miller grant no longer seems like a certainty (Bracht 1849, 242; 1931, 166). Disease is a problem in New Braunfels, according to the August 9 entry, though this is the result of people arriving in a weakened state following travel exertions and in very poor health from the catastrophic winter months on the coast at Indian Point (Bracht 1849, 244, 281; 1931, 167, 193). By October 7, Bracht is able to report that earnings are high, merchandise is available, and that residents like to eat and drink well, without the formalities of etiquette (Bracht 1849, 248–49; 1931, 170). In spite of the war with Mexico, Bracht consistently praises life in Texas, provided that the Adelsverein is avoided. On the other hand, Bracht writes favorably about Solms-Braunfels's 1846 published account of his Texas experience and expresses his surprise at the veracity and liveliness of many of the opinions to be found there (Bracht 1849, 255; 1931, 175). He does not, however, agree with Solms-Braunfels's negative assessment of the character of the (Anglo-)Americans: "With the exception of some rabble, including Germans as well as Americans, the people here on the average are just as good if not better, than they are in Europe" (Bracht 1849, 267; 1931, 183).

For present purposes, the letter dated New Braunfels, August 30, 1847, is noteworthy because it makes reference to Emil Kriewitz and his residency with Penateka chief Santa Anna. "Santa Anna, the war chief of the Comanches, spent three days here with a large number of his followers to have a good time. . . . He assured us that friendship for the Germans, which he esteemed very highly, should continue in the future as it had in the past. Mr. von Kriewisz [*sic*], of Potsdam, has for some time past lived with the chief and his tribe in the wilderness—a peculiar idea; however, it seems to serve a useful purpose" (Bracht 1849, 283–84; 1931, 195; Tiling 1913, 85; Biesele 1927, 126). It is notable that Bracht does not say any more about Kriewitz than this. He seems unaware that Kriewitz was with Santa Anna during this visit to New Braunfels and made secret contact with the German settlers. Nor that Kriewitz very soon afterward rejoined the German community under adventurous circumstances (as described in chapter 7).

The fortunes of the Adelsverein are addressed explicitly in the letter of September 17, 1847, where Bracht reports that surveying of the Fisher-Miller grant has been completed, "a small kingdom in itself, . . . provided funds arrive in time to prevent the surveyors from selling the field notes elsewhere" (Bracht 1849, 292; 1931, 201). Meusebach continues to earn the admiration of Bracht: "Through negotiations and the raising of small sums of money Mr. von Meusebach has once more retrieved the Verein, which seemed already lost. But for more than a year the Verein has not sent any money. This indifference, of course, cannot continue without causing great losses to its members" (Bracht 1849, 292; 1931, 201). In fact, by this time Meusebach was no longer commissioner general of the Adelsverein in Texas. On July 20, 1847, Hermann Spiess had taken on that title, though Meusebach evidently continued to work in the interests of the settlers. While not an advocate for the Adelsverein as a competent agency for German immigration to Texas, Bracht nevertheless defended the society, when he felt it appropriate. He warned his correspondents not to believe all the complaints gleaned from letters home from disillusioned immigrants and subsequently published in the newspapers, though he does not deny that many settlers are disappointed and in trouble in their new homeland. He is at his most vehement when he defends the Adelsverein against the criticisms of Louis Constant, whose mistakes, miscalculations, and distortions, he says, do not justify the space devoted to them in the press (Bracht 1849, 309; 1931, 213–14).

Constant's book *Texas: Das Verderben deutscher Auswanderer in Texas unter dem Schutze des Mainzer Vereins* (Constant 1847; translated as *Texas: The Ruin of the German Immigrants in Texas under the Protection of the Mainz Society* [Brandenburg 1968]) was a thirty-two-page tract, published in Berlin in 1847. As its title declares, it is a scathing attack on the record and practices of the Adelsverein, though Constant argues in favor of emigration as a solution to social and economic problems in Germany and also supports organized, managed emigration to a designated destination under appropriate leadership (Constant 1847, 5; Brandenburg 1968, 4). He sees Texas as a suitable location where German culture and morality can thrive, and even praises the intentions of the Adelsverein; however, the society was deceived in its assessment of the means necessary to the desired end and made many unhappy in the process (Constant 1847, 7; Brandenburg 1968, 7). Principal points of criticism are listed as follows:

> 1) that emigrants were carelessly shipped to Texas; 2) that the emigrants found no means of transportation at the landing place in Texas. They remained on the coast for months and as a result many died miserably; 3) that the Society never let experienced men travel through its Texas lands; moreover, it sent emigrants to Texas with promises of gifts of land without owning lands itself, and that as a result of such deceptions demoralization broke out among the colonists. Furthermore, it can be pointed out: 1) that even now [September 1847] the promised lands could not be given to the colonists. In the event land is given, the soil cannot nourish the people. The location of the colonial territory is such, however, that because of the expensive transportation costs the conjectured products could not be shipped out; 2) that the colonial pay-office in Texas cannot satisfy the legitimate claims of the colonists; 3) that the recruiting for the colony has only apparently ceased. (Constant 1847, 16; Brandenburg 1968, 22–23)

Much of this is true; however, Constant hurts his case by allowing his passion to get the better of his judgment. The vitriolic rhetoric escalates to the point where, in conclusion, Constant, claiming to speak for all of humanity, makes explicit demands on the Adelsverein:

> Silence is of no help to the Society. It must speak out and say what it wants and also what a person can expect from it. Errors can occur. Breaches of faith the Society cannot and may not commit. Its character does not permit this. . . . Only one thing remains for you men of the Society: it remains for you to act. If you do not act, then may the hand of God strike you and may humanity hold you to account. . . . You have demoralized the Germans in Texas, and thereby the German nation risks the contempt of the people of Texas. . . . Open prostitutes were un-known in Texas before your arrival. . . . You have ceased your recruiting for Texas only on the surface, because your agents slink among the peo-ple now as before. (Constant 1847, 34–35; Brandenburg 1968, 52–54)

Constant's tract is an extreme expression of a significant current of opinion that dogged the Adelsverein from its early days and illustrates well how controversial the society's efforts were in the sphere of public discourse in Germany. At the same time that Constant was making the case against the Adelsverein, Ottomar von Behr, who like Constant insist-ed on his position as an independent voice with no vested interest, was presenting contrasting arguments. One of the first settlers of Sisterdale, Texas, Behr was a highly educated nobleman who played a leading role in this "Latin settlement" that was visited by, among others, Frederick Law Olmsted, Duke Paul Wilhelm of Württemberg, and Edgar von West-phalen (brother-in-law of Karl Marx) (Olmsted 1978, 191–93; Conzen 2000, 44–47). Behr's *Guther Rath für Auswanderer nach den Vereinigten Staaten von Nordamerika mit besonderer Berücksichtigung von Texas* (Good Advice for Emigrants to the United States of North America with Special Consideration of Texas) was published in Leipzig in 1847. The book compares Texas with Wisconsin and Iowa and concludes with a ringing endorsement for the former and a very strong recommendation in favor of the Adelsverein as a means to settling in Texas:

> The fine, philanthropic plan of the Verein has partially already been fulfilled, and is partially proceeding with rapid steps toward comple-tion. The emigrants have been protected against cheating and harm, ten thousand have already been led to a beautiful and healthy land and have remained united there. Perhaps we shall soon see come into being in the middle of Texas a state populated by Germans that will prove to the Americans that Germans too can be ardently enthusiastic about

the greatness of the American constitution and its liberties. . . . Never
has a society offered emigrants such advantages and guarantees as the
Society for the Protection of German Immigrants to Texas. (Behr 1847,
106–7)

This conclusion is arrived at after a systematically organized discussion of the pros and cons of Texas as a destination and the Adelsverein as
intermediary. Behr is generally quiet about the systemic mismanagement
and delinquency in the financing of the Adelsverein project, but he does
single out Solms-Braunfels for particular criticism on account of his romantic, medieval notions of aristocracy, his contempt for Americans, his
extreme mistrust of any German who had been in the United States long
enough to have been contaminated by democratic, republican ideals, and
his refusal to take advice from those who knew the country better than
he did (Behr 1847, 98). He also chastises the German press for spreading
lies and inciting mistrust, and stresses repeatedly the contentment of the
inhabitants of New Braunfels, including those who have come from other
established settlements and who know firsthand how bad the immigration
experience can be (Behr 1847, 104–5). Of the Fisher-Miller grant land
he writes that it has abundant good soil and lies in a healthy region but
that "a large part of the best land along rivers and creeks is already in
private hands and therefore does not belong to it . . . and the whole tract
lies beyond the boundary line of the currently cultivated areas and is used
by the Comanches and other tribes for their hunting grounds. Of course,
that sounds worse than it is, because in Germany we are used to thinking
of Indians as a sort of devil incarnate, whereas they themselves have an
enormous respect for the White Man and his rifle" (Behr 1847, 99). Behr
is extremely complimentary about Meusebach and his abilities and mentions the founding of Fredericksburg in 1846, though the Comanche treaty of May 1847 is not discussed and we may assume it was not known to
Behr at the time he was preparing his book manuscript. It would certainly
have served his agenda to include an account of it if he had known.

The following year, the counterargument to Behr is presented by Jakob
Thran. Although not explicitly responding to Behr's *Good Advice*, Thran's
cautionary account for those considering emigration to Texas with the
Adelsverein has almost nothing positive to say about his experience with
the organization, beginning with his correspondence requesting information, and continuing with the lack of care and support at Bremen and

Bremerhaven, during the crossing, upon landing, and while seeking to gain a footing in Texas. *Meine Auswanderung nach Texas unter dem Schutze des Mainzer Vereins* (My Emigration to Texas under the Protection of the Adelsverein), which describes experiences between the spring of 1846 and April 1847, was published in early 1848 (the foreword is dated November 1847, which is coincidentally when commissioner Spiess was closing down Adelsverein operations in Texas) and is most clear in its indictment of Adelsverein mendacity and misinformation, though his accusations stop short of ad hominem attacks. Solms-Braunfels and Meusebach are not mentioned by name, nor are the nobles who make up the directorate of the society, though the founders are listed (Thran 1848, 16–17). Thran adheres to tenets of respect and propriety before the aristocratic classes, though he is merciless in his assault of their project. He is not as vitriolic as Constant in his expression but is equally unambiguous in his agenda to deter prospective emigrants from having anything to do with the Adelsverein.

Three final opinions about the Adelsverein's immigration project deserve brief mention. The first of these is found in Heinrich Berghaus's 1848 book on the United States of America, where the author groups the Adelsverein in the category of philanthropic organizations that sponsor emigration:

> Already unfortunate in its selection of land, whose climate is entirely unsuitable for the physical constitution of the German in general and which demands the cultivation of plant life whose names the German farmer has scarcely heard of, the Society and its administrators on site have put in place such inadequate, counter-productive, and incomprehensible measures that the entire enterprise, even after many hundred gullible Germans have been lain in an early grave or been seduced into the most bitter misery because of it, must be viewed as defunct. (Berghaus 1848, 78)

Although couched in gentler terms and informed by sounder argument, the conclusion of Ferdinand Roemer is equally unequivocal. At the close of the eminently readable and informative account of his visit to Texas from December 1845 to May 1847, and in spite of his enchantment with Texas in general, Roemer gives this assessment:

> After careful deliberations I must declare, although with great reluctance, since so many exertions have been put forth, that the land in

question on the right bank of the Colorado and the region of the Llano
[that is, the Fisher-Miller grant] is not the proper place for a settlement
by the Germans, at least not at the present time. I would advance the
following reasons: 1. There are no extensive areas in the whole region
which are of the same fertility as in the lower accessible parts of Texas.
2. The distance from the inhabited sections of Texas is too great. 3. The
Comanche Indians will become (if not dangerous) at least very annoying to any settlement north of the Llano. (Roemer 1983, 286)

At the time of Roemer's departure from Texas the Meusebach Treaty
with the Comanches was on the point of being concluded; however, by
the time of publication of his account (1849) we must assume he knew
that it was in place. Apparently, he had little faith that it would hold.

Finally, an 1850 book by Dr. Ferdinand von Herff, who had been a
member of the Darmstadt Forty, founders of Bettina, the first settlement
on the Fisher-Miller grant, gives a unique perspective (Herff 1978). Although settling the Adelsverein grant land, the Forty were not protégés
of the society in the same way that others under contract were, yet they
did have its support. Herff's account is more an outline for a model of
emigration sponsorship (not unlike that of Constant) than a guidebook
for emigrants. Although the book is critical of the Adelsverein, the society provided funding for its publication. The society must have viewed it
as a last-ditch attempt to promote emigration to its lands in Texas even
though it knew by 1850 that it was no longer viable as an agency. Arthur
L. Finck suggests quite plausibly, it is possible that the Adelsverein liked
Herff's idea for a national, state(s)-sponsored society that would assume
the planning and directing of emigration (Herff 1978, xx). The book's title,
*Die geregelte Auswanderung des deutschen Proletariats mit besonderer
Beziehung auf Texas* (*The Regulated Emigration of the German Proletariat with Special Reference to Texas*) betrays the social agenda of the publication, and about half the text is devoted to explication of the theoretical
concept underlying his colony-building model. The other half provides
context drawn from the experience of the Adelsverein, which Herff refers
to as a thing of the past. The key to the success of organized emigration
is, in Herff's view, adequate funding (Herff 1978, 7, 11). This had been
the primary failing of the Adelsverein, he writes, and in this he is unques-
tionably correct. Texas itself is portrayed as a highly desirable destination, and the high mortality rate of Adelsverein immigrants in 1845–46
cannot, writes Herff, be seen as a result of the climate:

Three thousand persons disembarked without shelter or wood on a marshy coast lacking in drinking water, having utterly unsuitable, often spoilt food for a period of eight long months—this had to result in utter demoralization because of the hopelessness and poverty. The fact that neither dysentery nor scurvy, so prevalent at that time, have ever broken out epidemically in Texas, before or since, alone proves that it was not the country, but a chain of unfavorable conditions and blunders which caused that mortality upon which the opponents of colonization in Texas rely for argument. (Herff 1978, 15)

Herff views the Adelsverein as a pioneer organization that through its mistakes ("blunders") has rendered valuable service (Herff 1978, 29), and his book can be seen as an attempt to translate the positive and negative experience of the Adelsverein into a sort of Hegelian synthesis that looks forward to the progress of history. It would be a mistake to see this as a Marxian project, however. Herff is ostensibly writing on behalf of a proletarian advancement but betrays undisguised elitist tendencies when he stresses how important a strong intellectual leadership (in combination with practical experience) is, and he names as prime examples Solms, Meusebach, and Spiess, along with New Braunfels militia commander Ludwig (Louis) Bene and first German consul in Texas Gustav Dresel. In his words, "perhaps in no other section of North America is there a greater number of educated and talented Germans than in Texas" (Herff 1978, 30), and, like Berghaus and Bracht, he does not shy away from such terms as "the refuse of Europe" to refer to social undesirables (Herff 1978, 5).

After Spiess's announcement of the shuttering of the Adelsverein offices in 1847, wrangling over the remaining assets of the society began. Spiess and Schubert wrestled for control of the Nassau Farm; in an ensuing melee two men were killed, and Schubert was eventually paid to move out (Kearney 2010, 123). Spiess remained commissioner general until 1852, but his role was reduced to representing the society in litigation before various county courts. In 1852, he was succeeded by Ludwig Bene, the last Adelsverein official in Texas. Just short of a decade after its founding, on September 13, 1853, the Adelsverein concluded its presence in Texas by assigning to its creditors all its property in the state and all rights due from the colonization grant (Tiling 1913, 113). Fisher and Miller, who had remained involved in Adelsverein affairs throughout, continued to press the state of Texas for what they argued was their share as agents who had introduced the stipulated number of settlers to Texas, but were ultimately denied in the House of Representatives (Tiling 1913, 113). Even as late as 1893, Meusebach himself was dealing with residual entitlement claims by the families of Adelsverein immigrants (Meusebach 1894). The Adelsverein gave rise to two thriving towns, New Braunfels and Fredericksburg, and brought to Texas thousands who contributed significantly to turning the republic into a state of the Union. However, it did not bring permanent settlement to the Fisher-Miller grant land in any degree (even the sole surviving town of Castell moved off the grant land to the south side of the Llano), and it was directly responsible for the loss of thousands of immigrant lives due to its incompetence and intransigence. For all that, it did bring to Texas Emil Kriewitz, the man who compiled the first substantial Comanche lexicon, and it created, through Meusebach's Comanche Treaty, the circumstances that made possible an important contribution to nineteenth-century Native American ethnology.

Figure 1. *Enchanted Rock near Fredericksburg* by Karl Friedrich Hermann Lungkwitz, 1864. Courtesy Witte Museum, San Antonio, Texas.

PART I

Berghaus and German Contributions
to American Ethnology

1

Who Was Heinrich Berghaus?

Heinrich Berghaus (1797–1884; figure 2) trained as a surveyor and geodetic mathematician. He advanced to prominence as a cartographer of excellence and prolific publisher of maritime charts and atlases for school, home, and professional use. He lived at a time of rapid and far-reaching developments in the field of geography in Germany and Europe, and his professional association with Alexander von Humboldt from 1815 until Humboldt's death in 1859 had a profound impact on his career (Beck 1956, 4). Berghaus had no formal training as an ethnologist but was intellectually invested in the dissemination of new and current knowledge in this area. His interest in Native Americans, and in particular the Comanches, deserves special attention here. The following sketch of his career outlines the context for his work in what we now call anthropology and related fields up to the publication of his essay "On the Relationship of the Shoshones, Comanches, and Apaches" ("Über die Verwandtschaft der Schoschonen, Komantschen und Apatschen") in 1851 (Berghaus 1851; hereafter referred to as "the 1851 article").[1]

Just as German history in the first half of the nineteenth century is inextricably entwined with that of France and later with, on the one hand, increasing nationalist and democratic sentiments, and on the other, waves of emigration to the New World, so Berghaus's personal story plays out across French, German (specifically, Prussian), and global stages. Born in Cleves on the Dutch border, Berghaus was recognized early for his talents as a mathematician and draftsman, with the result that in 1811 he was engaged by the Lippe Department on a project for the Napoleonic administration of the Rhineland mapping the course for a canal to link the German ports of Hamburg and Lübeck with the Maas and, ultimately, Paris. In the new order that followed Napoleon's defeat in 1813 at the Battle of the Nations at Leipzig (Völkerschlacht bei Leipzig), Berghaus quickly found employment with the Prussian military authorities and took advantage of the opportunity to begin university studies in mathematics and geography at Marburg in 1814. The resumption of hostilities with Napoleon brought Berghaus to Paris in 1815, where his commanding officer provided a letter of introduction to Alexander von Humboldt. Berghaus and Humboldt subsequently collaborated closely on numerous innovative projects. Berghaus was engaged in 1821 as an instructor of applied geometry, draftsmanship, and mechanical engineering at the Berlin Academy of Architecture (Bauakademie), where he held his appointment for thirty-four years, being promoted to professor in 1824. Following his move to nearby Potsdam in 1836, he founded the School of Geographic Arts (Geographische Kunstschule) in 1839, which trained some of the leading cartographers of the time (August Petermann, Henry Lange, and Berghaus's nephew Hermann) before closing in 1848. Berghaus was involuntarily retired from his academic appointment in 1855 and moved to Pomerania. He died in poverty in Stettin.

Berghaus's career is characterized by unflagging energy and intellectual curiosity tempered by a difficult personality and personal controversy. He was driven by an indomitable urge to publish what he had learned and to make it available in accessible, often innovative, ways; his biographer, Gerhard Engelmann, lists ninety-four published maps and 281 other publications of various kinds (Engelmann 1977). Many of the projects he began did not find their way to completion. Especially early in his career, he was less than scrupulous about matters of intellectual property. Jürgen Espenhorst and Hanno Beck refer, among other instances, to Berghaus's publication of *Die ersten Elemente der Erdbeschreibung* (1831, The Principal Elements of Geography) without attribution to Carl Ritter, the Berlin geographer on whose notes the work was based (Espenhorst 2003, 368 n560, 387; Beck 1956, 6). Later, Berghaus seems to be more sensitive to the issue of potential accusations of plagiarism. For instance, in 1836 in the introduction to his *Allgemeine Länder- und Völkerkunde* (General Geography and Ethnography) he is careful to note that even though he does not cite complete references for his sources, he does indicate the names of the authors from whom his information comes (Berghaus 1837–46, 1:vi).

One of the curious aspects of Berghaus's 1851 article on the Shoshones, Comanches, and Apaches is that in spite of a precise description of his informant's circumstances, he does not name the individual who provided him with the glossary and notes on Comanche culture; in fact, he seems intent on preserving the man's anonymity. This, in spite of the fact that in 1850 he had already published the section of his informant's account covering customs and traditions of the Comanches, naming the source as Emil Kriewitz. The earlier publication is referred to with complete citation information in endnote *p* (16 in the original) of the 1851 publication.

2

Berghaus and Humboldt

B erghaus's relationship with Alexander von Humboldt (figure 3)
played a central role in both his professional and personal well-
being. Following their initial meeting in Paris in 1815, the collaboration
began to intensify in 1825 with work on *Hertha*. The title page for this
journal reads: *Hertha. Zeitschrift für Erd-, Völker- und Staatenkunde.
Unter Mitwirkung des Freiherrn Alexander von Humboldt, besorgt von
Heinrich Berghaus in Berlin und Karl Friedrich Vollrath Hoffmann in
Stuttgart* (Journal for the Study of Geography, Ethnography, and Nations.
With the Collaboration of Baron Alexander von Humboldt, compiled by
Heinrich Berghaus in Berlin and Karl Friedrich Vollrath Hoffmann in
Stuttgart). It was published by Cotta in Stuttgart and Tübingen. As editor
of *Hertha* (1825–29), Berghaus published his own German translation
of Albert Gallatin's list of North American Indian tribes in the United
States in 1827 (Berghaus 1827a); Humboldt had provided Gallatin's English original to Berghaus in 1826. In 1827 Humboldt moved to Berlin
from Paris, so that the German capital now became home to a formidable
threesome, Carl Ritter (geographer), Alexander von Humboldt (explorer-
scientist), and Heinrich Berghaus (cartographer). Together these men
founded the Berlin Geographical Society (Gesellschaft für Erdkunde zu
Berlin) in 1828.

Beck refers to the period 1820 to 1859 as the classical age of German
geography, led largely by these three scholars. Potsdam, already Berghaus's
working location, became a favorite retreat also for Humboldt when he
needed to avoid the constant attention of visitors at his home in Berlin.

Humboldt was given working space in the palace (Stadtschloss) in Potsdam, and a steady exchange of notes and letters with many formal and informal visits between the two men followed. The reverential tone of Berghaus's commentary in his published correspondence with Humboldt is indicative of the tenor of their relationship. Humboldt, as both a nobleman and prominent man of science, commanded the cartographer's absolute respect, and Berghaus's delight at every gesture of kindness, appreciation, recognition, or outright flattery by Humboldt is cause for the highest satisfaction. In his other writings, wherever an opportunity arose for invoking the name of Humboldt, Berghaus exploited it. For example, in the introduction to his six-volume work *Allgemeine Länder- und Völkerkunde* (General Geography and Ethnography), Berghaus expresses his indebtedness to Humboldt as follows, "Baron Alexander von Humboldt, above all, is due my sincerest gratitude, should this highly esteemed man allow me to give it public expression. It is not merely that he permitted me to utilize his published writings without limitation—and to copy them, but I also am obliged to him for his generous sharing of several of his memoirs and notes in manuscript, not to mention the oral instruction and numerous new insights from all corners of the world that flow together in such profusion in his home" (Berghaus 1837–46, 1:vi).

Yet Berghaus is also protective of his own professional prestige. One page later, when discussing his ongoing plans for his Physical Atlas, Berghaus conspicuously does not mention Humboldt's role in its genesis, but characterizes it as illustrative material not for Humboldt's *Kosmos* but for his own General Geography and Ethnography. When it comes to introducing the topic of plant geography in volume 3 (book 5, chapter 51), however, Berghaus places Humboldt unchallenged as the pioneer of the discipline, in whose wake a list of eighty-nine other named botanists follows (Berghaus 1837–46, 3:7). In 1805, on his return from his voyage to South, Central, and North America (1799–1804) with Aimé Bonpland, Humboldt had published his enormously influential *Essai sur la géographie des plantes*. In the ensuing seven pages Berghaus indicates his admiration for Humboldt by mentioning his name sixteen times.

In spite of their class difference, Berghaus and Humboldt worked together well. They shared a fundamental political outlook that favored the emerging democratic culture of Germany and abhorred slavery. Their academic interests coincided, as did their fascination with graphic representation and their desire to educate through publication. Humboldt petitioned unsuccessfully against Berghaus's dismissal from the Academy of Architecture in 1855 and interceded for him in a misunderstanding with the British botanist William Hooker. The class issue was uncomfortably foregrounded when Berghaus's son Alexander, in response to Humboldt's inquiry, said that he wished to enter the diplomatic service. Humboldt answered that Alexander should put this thought out of his mind because this career was the province of the aristocracy: "If you could show sixteen noble ancestors on your father's side, as you can maternally, à la bonne heure; as it is though, because your father has only middle-class citizens as forebears, even if they can be followed back through the centuries with just as much honorable memory as those of any sir knight, there is no chance" (Berghaus 1863, 77).

His very productive collaboration with Humboldt notwithstanding, Berghaus was notorious for being difficult. Espenhorst writes: "In publishing his work he collaborated with a total of thirty-six different publishing houses, and managed to argue with all of them" (Espenhorst 2003, 370). His falling out with the prestigious and influential publisher Cotta in Stuttgart in 1829 was particularly bitter, and even Humboldt's intervention could not repair the damage. Cotta had been the publisher of the journal *Hertha* that Berghaus edited up to this time (Beck 1956, 6). His temperament may well have been an underlying cause of Berghaus's forced retirement from the Academy of Architecture.

3

Berghaus's *Physikalischer Atlas*

As a cartographer, Berghaus's landmark achievement, among many important publications, was his *Physikalischer Atlas* (Physical Atlas, published in its first edition 1845–48). The complete title of the Physical Atlas is *Berghaus' Physikalischer Atlas oder Sammlung von Karten auf denen die hauptsächlichsten Erscheinungen der anorganischen und organischen Natur nach ihrer geographischen Verbreitung und Vertheilung bildlich dargestellt sind* (Berghaus's Physical Atlas or Collection of Maps on Which Are Pictorially Portrayed the Principal Inorganic and Organic Manifestations of Nature According to Their Distribution and Division) (translation, Espenhorst 2003, 375). The Physical Atlas would be best described nowadays as an atlas of culture and the natural world (Espenhorst 2003, 366). An awareness of the Physical Atlas project is essential for an appreciation of Berghaus's 1851 article on Shoshones, Comanches, and Apaches. By 1827, Berghaus had already established his credentials as a cartographer, having completed assignments for both the French and Prussian military; he had also produced maps of Germany and neighboring countries, the Harz and other German regions, France, a map of Europe for schools, and a map of Africa; in addition he worked on maps for Ritter's 1831 *Hand-Atlas von Afrika* (Engelmann 1977, 272–75). The year 1827 is critical because a letter from Humboldt to Berghaus from December of that year proposes that he provide "a set of explanatory sheets" to accompany Humboldt's planned *Kosmos* project, ambitiously subtitled "A Sketch of a Physical Description of the

Universe." It is likely that this letter provided the impetus for Berghaus's Physical Atlas. Humboldt writes:

> What I would like to convey to you today in a few words is my wish that you would undertake to create a set of explanatory sheets to accompany my book, an atlas of the physical world, something along the lines of the attempt I have made in the atlas of my trip: maps showing the distribution of plants and animals throughout the world, the seas and rivers, the distribution of volcanic activity, the magnetic declination and inclination, the intensity of magnetic strength, ocean currents and tides, wind currents, mountain ranges, deserts and plains, the distribution of the various races of humankind, the portrayal of mountain elevations, the length of streams [major rivers], etc. More than two years ago I indicated that I would like to have you create altitude profiles for a number of countries. Without waiting for your agreement, I have written to Cotta, indicating that such a cartographic work was a necessary part of my project. I would like to see you press forward with your current work on the maps of the world and of Europe, so that the physical maps can be created in the near future. (Translation, Espenhorst 2003, 371)

Humboldt's list of desiderata corresponds closely with the structure of the Physical Atlas as it ultimately appeared, and while there is no mention of Humboldt on the title page of the first edition, the second edition (1852) acknowledges Humboldt's "fördernde Anregung" ("supportive encouragement").

The first fascicle of the first edition of the Physical Atlas appeared in 1838, the last in 1848. Berghaus had begun work on the project in 1829 and resumed it in 1836 after a long pause (Beck 1956, 10). The publisher was Justus Perthes in Gotha, owing to Berghaus's inability to work with Cotta. The work consisted of ninety-two sheets, that is 184 printed sides (Reckziegel 1985, 29). The eight component sections of the Physical Atlas are: I. Meteorological Atlas; II. General Hydrographic Atlas; III. General Geological Atlas; IV. General Geomagnetic Atlas; V. General Botanical-Geographic Atlas; VI. General Zoological Atlas; VII. General Anthropographic Atlas, VIII. General Ethnographic Atlas. Sections I–V, completed in 1845, are generally grouped together as Vol. 1; VI–VIII, completed 1848, as Vol. 2 (Espenhorst 2003, 376). For present purposes, sections VII and VIII are of primary interest.

It is in some ways misleading to think of the Physical Atlas as merely an atlas. Berghaus's gift as a presenter of data lay, as Espenhorst puts it, "in his ability to integrate the latest cartographic techniques with current information in the areas of geography, the natural sciences, and ethnology, and portray them in such a way as to provide a new cartographic overview which one could easily grasp" (Espenhorst 2003, 369). And, alongside innovative mapmaking, we find in Berghaus's "atlas" diagrams, profiles, pictorial illustrations, composite images, tables, and text (Reckziegel 1985, 30). Innovation was an important notion for Berghaus. Not only did he seek new visual ways to represent information for the reader, he was also dedicated to assembling the most current information for dissemination. He did not, therefore, view the Physical Atlas as the last word; rather, he sought ways to augment and update the information it contained in an ongoing fashion. The foreword to the first issue of the Geographic Yearbook states this explicitly: The Physical Atlas must always be a work in progress and "given the present direction of human knowledge the physical sciences cannot stand still but must incessantly and restlessly stride forward in their development" ("bei der heutigen Richtung der Menschen-Bildung die physikalischen Wissenschaften nicht stille stehen können, sondern in ihrer Entwicklung unaufhörlich und rastlos fortschreiten müssen"). He had hoped to do this through the *Zeitschrift für Erdkunde* (Journal of Geography), which he edited; however, the *Zeitschrift für Erdkunde* was forced to cease publication in 1848.[1]

Berghaus succeeded in persuading the reluctant Perthes that a complementary publication to keep users of the Physical Atlas up to date on geographical developments was not only desirable but also necessary, and their solution was the Geographic Yearbook. In fact, the title page of the Yearbook indicates its dependence on the Physical Atlas. It reads: *Physikalischer Atlas. Geographisches Jahrbuch zur Mittheilung aller wichtigern neuen Erforschungen von Dr. Heinrich Berghaus* (Physical Atlas. Geographic Yearbook for Dissemination of All Important New Research Results by Dr. Heinrich Berghaus). The Yearbook was, in Berghaus's judgment, surprisingly successful, and four issues appeared between 1850 and 1852 (Berghaus 1863, 101; Engelmann 1977, 127). It is against this background that the venue in which "On the Relationship of the Shoshones, Comanches, and Apaches" appeared needs to be assessed. Ethnography is clearly an important component of the Physical Atlas project, and this thread is continued with this article in the Yearbook.[2]

4

Berghaus's Interest in Ethnology

Berghaus is remembered primarily for his maps and innovations in cartography, the field for which, as a boy, he had shown unusual aptitude. What brings him then, toward the end of the most active phase of his career, to publish an article on the relationships among Native American tribes? To answer this question, we need to look in three different areas: the age, the discipline, and the man.

In the early nineteenth century, German intellectual life was alive with Romanticism's interest in cultures European and non-European. Johann Gottfried Herder had postulated that the true spirit and voice of any culture was accessible through its folk songs; Achim von Arnim (husband of Bettina von Arnim, for whom the first settlement on the Fisher-Miller grant was named) and Clemens Brentano (Bettina's brother) had sought, through their collection of German folk songs, to capture the essence of Germanness; the Brothers Grimm approached the same goal through their anthology of folk and fairy tales; the Grimms, Johann Andreas Schmeller, and other lexicographers set out to record vernacular and national language in ambitious dictionary projects; German explorers were returning from far-flung destinations with scientific and anecdotal accounts of foreign places and their peoples.[1] In midcentury, Germans, such as Charles Preuss, Frederick W. von Egloffstein, and Balduin Möllhausen, would be reporting back from expeditions to the American West, including encounters with Indians. On the other hand, this epoch was also one of major emigration from Germany to the United States, Texas, and elsewhere, and interest in these potential new homelands and their peoples is reflected in the discourse of newspapers, books, and other publications of the time. Berghaus published a book about the United States for would-be immigrants, and in many publications was free with suggestions about solutions to social and political problems in other parts of the world, not least slavery. By the same token, as Germany was in the throes of an experiment in political reorganization in 1848, alternative models of social and national policy from elsewhere in the world were the subject of energetic debate (cf. Reckziegel 1985, 30).

The discipline of geography as we know it today was only just emerging as Berghaus's career was unfolding. The encyclopedic knowledge and interests of Alexander von Humboldt brought together data from fields as disparate as meteorology, barometry, earth magnetism, hydrology, topography, geology, zoology, botany, ethnography, and astronomy into a unified view of creation, later articulated in Humboldt's *Kosmos*. Carl Ritter is credited, with Humboldt, as a founder of modern geography for the novel conception of the discipline as the study of the earth as an anatomical entity consisting of organs, such as rivers, mountains, glaciers, and such, which together form the physical basis for the subsistence of humankind, determining its life and accomplishments. Berghaus's association with these two pioneering minds places him at the birth of a discipline that includes human diversity as an essential component. The interaction of this thinking with the development of scientific discovery in the United States is discussed in chapter 8.

Berghaus, the man, born on the border between Germany and the Netherlands, growing up with German, Dutch, French, and Low German, was acutely aware of linguistic diversity. All his life he gathered Low German words and phrases, and his final major publication was a three-volume dictionary of Low German dialect. In fact, this project was never completed and only reached the letter "O." This interest in language provided the underpinning for Berghaus's curiosity about tribes, races, and nationalities, and thus for his explorations in ethnography. His publications in this field always stress the primacy of language as a determiner of ethnological relationships, and the 1851 article is no exception. Berghaus's awareness of language, its structures, systems, and the principles of its historical development, was, even for its day, not sophisticated. Nevertheless, he took a more than superficial interest in the topic, and as a result of his labors we have one of the first vocabularies of Comanche ever published.

Berghaus's publications provide a set of reference points for his developing interest in language and its relation to ethnography. In the same issue of *Hertha* in which he had published Gallatin's survey of Indian tribes in the United States, Berghaus also printed a contribution from Humboldt's brother Wilhelm, who was himself a linguist, philosopher, educational reformer, and statesman of stature. This article, titled "Fortschritte in der Kultur unter den Indiern Nordamerika's" ("Advances in Culture among the Indians of North America"; Berghaus 1827b, 320–27), and deriving from handwritten notes provided by Wilhelm von Humboldt, praises the success of Indian schools in bringing Native Americans to a level of civilization and devotes considerable space to the Cherokees and the work of the Moravian Brethren. It also includes a report on the thriving condition of the tribe by the Cherokee George Guess (Sequoia), reprinted in English from the Richmond *Family Visitor*. The Cherokee syllabic alphabet developed by Guess with its eighty-six characters is printed as part of the Gallatin article that follows (Berghaus 1827a, 328–34). The latter, titled "Albert Gallatin's Tabulated Overview of Indian Tribes in the United States of North America East of the Rocky Mountains (Stony Mountains), Arranged by Languages and Dialects," depends solely on etymological (not grammatical) information for its analysis. No linguistic data supporting the taxonomy is provided, only names of tribes and bands, their approximate population in 1826, and their location. Berghaus appears to be more interested in the results of anthropological linguistic investigation than the process or data underlying the analysis. Because Gallatin's inventory is limited to tribes within the territory of the United States, it includes the Shoshones but not the Comanches and Apaches.

By 1837 Berghaus had advanced to the point of publishing a six-volume introduction to geography and ethnography. This work is subtitled, "A Textbook for School and Home for all Classes." His introduction to the first volume of this *Allgemeine Länder- und Völkerkunde nebst einem Abriß der physikalischen Erdbeschreibung* (General Geography and Ethnography Including an Account in Outline of the Physical Characteristics of the Earth; Berghaus 1837–46) explains the origins of the work as a compilation of miscellaneous data and information accumulated during years of study with the intent to "place in the hands of all friends of geography a book in which they may find, in addition to a general survey of essential knowledge concerning the physical properties of the earth, as complete as possible a portrait of the nations and their peoples" (Berghaus 1837–46, 1:v). Berghaus's dual concerns here are for an exhaustive account of human geography and an audience that transcends the world of the professional scholar and reaches the living rooms of citizens at all levels of society. The questions he formulates in his introduction revolve around human diversity in appearance, intellect, customs, traditions, habits, physical abilities, social practices, religion, and morality, and how these might or might not relate to the physical environment (Berghaus 1837–46, 1:1–7). An overarching, Eurocentric (even Germanocentric) notion of civilization pervades much of his text, and the, for Berghaus, self-evident unifying mission of Christianity is articulated *expressis verbis* (Berghaus 1837–46, 1:7). The study of descriptive geography (*Erdbeschreibung*) is presented as the means to reaching an understanding of all these questions.

Surprisingly, human language plays a very small role in Berghaus's formulation of the concept of this work, so that, while we can trace a growing interest in the study of man and his environment at this point in Berghaus's intellectual development, the importance of language recedes for the time being. Volume 6 of this work contains a thirty-six-page chapter on the Free State of Texas. These pages discuss Texas solely as a destination for immigration and give an account of the population almost exclusively with reference to immigrant groups. The opening sentence dismisses Native populations laconically with the reference: "The inhabitants of Texas are a mix of Mexicans, immigrants from the United States, English, German and French, and different Indian tribes, of whom the Cumanches are the most numerous" (Berghaus 1837–46, 6:367). Statistics concerning percentages of these different groups ignore Native populations. It may be that these deficiencies were not of Berghaus's making directly, for authorship of this chapter on Texas was claimed by Traugott Bromme (Bromme 1846, 266).

Die Völker des Erdballs (Peoples of the Globe) reasserts the key position of language as the basis for defining a people. "Language is the primary, the first feature of national distinctiveness, and when we study the cultural condition [of a distinct nation] along many paths, the state of its customs, habits, and traditions, its legal system, its civic constitution are all to be seen as subordinate" (Berghaus 1860–62, 11). However, while language yields the primary data for establishing the relatedness of peoples and tribes, it is not Berghaus's primary interest for this project. The single overriding object worthy of study is the creative power of the human mind in its diversity, that is, cultural phenomena. This is perceived as both individual and community achievement and represents the "elevation and expansion of mankind's inner existence" ("Erhöhung und Erweiterung des inneren Daseins") visible in the distinctive "indestructible property" of nations, out of which great individuals inevitably emerge. According to Berghaus's methodological model in the mid-1840s, having determined ethnographic groupings by means of languages and dialects, attention is turned to cultural achievement to characterize and evaluate peoples, tribes, and nations. This approach is reflected in his brief account of the Comanches in the first volume of this work:

> The Comanches [Kamantschen, Camanches, Cumanches, Comanches (according to Spanish spelling)] also occur under the name Hietans, Jetans and that of the Paducas, by which they are supposedly known to the Pawnee [Pahnie] nation. The northern arm of the Platte River is still called the Paducas Fork. As particular divisions or bands of the Comanche we identify: the Kayguas or Kayguen, also called Kiawas or Kioways, who along with the Utahs [Jutas] live on the western steppes between the sources of the Wichita [Wischita], the Colorado and Brazos Rivers, the Red River and the Texas border; the Wetepatahos, the Nanahas, Kanenawish, Katteka, Dotame, the Kaskayas or Bad Hearts, the Castahana, the Stubborn Heads [Trotzköpfe] (Bald Heads). The Comanches are at present perhaps the most powerful people among the Indians of the North American continent; their unrivalled horsemanship, their fearsome attack and their unequaled speed in loading and firing their weapons, as well as their inextinguishable hatred for the whites, make the animosity of these Indians more terrifying than any other indigenous tribe. They never stay more than a few days in one and the same place, but wander north with the buffalo in the summer and return with them when winter comes to the plains west of Texas. They transport with them their conical tents made from hides and where they stop they set up their camp that forms a regular town with streets and open squares. The lands in which the Comanches and the tribes allied with them roam seem to extend from the Arkansas in the north to near the Chihuahua in the south, or across ten degrees of latitude. They trace their origin to one of the most distinguished tribes that resided in Mexico at the time of the Spanish conquest but that, instead of becoming subject to the conquerors, opted to migrate and are said to have settled in the mountains of Texas. Their ferocious hatred of the white inhabitants of Mexico may be a result of this. This hatred is mutual, hence the epithet used all over Mexico to refer to a degenerate individual: "He is a Comanche!" The Comanches have a shared principal chief and many

sub-chiefs who hold quarterly councils, while a great deliberative gathering of the whole tribe takes place once a year.

The Arropahos or Arrapahays, whose language is essentially the same as that of the Shoshones and Comanches, live south of the Snake Indians.[2] In winter they move across the land around the great gorge of the western Colorado and for a significant distance downstream along this river; in summer they hunt buffalo along the Rio Grande etc. They too possess horses, and in addition mules, sheep, and dogs in large number. They feed and consume the latter, hence their name, which is said to mean dog-eaters. They are skilled in weaving the wool from their sheep into artistic blankets which are impermeable to rain.

The [Apatschen] Apaches (according to Spanish spelling) are spread on the eastern side of the Californian peoples not far from the Pacific Ocean, through New Mexico eastwards as far as Cohahuila [*sic*], up to the grazing and hunting grounds of the Comanches. They are known as the enemy of the Comanches and at the same time are terrifying for the Spanish because of their ferocious attacks, which also cause constant unrest among the settled Tarahumaras. Among the Apaches we distinguish the Tontos, Gilenos, Chiricagues, Llaneros, Lipanes and Nabajoas or Navahos, names that are always linked to the primary name Apache. (Berghaus 1860–62, 289–90)

A similar set of methodological principles underlies Berghaus's 1850 publication *Grundlinien der Ethnographie* (Principles of Ethnography). Here too the Comanches receive explicit attention. The title already reveals the preoccupations of the volume: "Principles of Ethnography. Containing in two sections a general tabulation or documentation of all peoples of the earth's surface, by language groups and language families, organized ethnographically and geographically, and a comparative, summary description of their traditions, customs and habits." Berghaus indicates his role as that of editor (*Herausgeber*); however, though he uses materials from other sources, it is clear that as compiler/author he does not doubt their validity. In the introductory chapter, we find a clear expression of part of the ideological disposition that underpins Berghaus's work on ethnography. Mid-nineteenth-century Christian zeal combines with Enlightenment faith in reason, as a distinguishing feature of mankind as well as the means to understanding his environment. The first paragraph opens with a declaration that mankind is at the pinnacle of creation among animals; it closes with the assertion that reason embraces, by means of intellect, the entire world, and this exploration is "the natural history of the mind"

(Berghaus 1850b, 1). As his title suggests, language is indispensable as a determiner of peoples: "Language is the primary characteristic for identifying and differentiating nations" (Berghaus 1850b, 5).

In a—from our perspective—clumsy attempt to align his methodological statement with fashionable thinking of his time, Berghaus adapts the natural philosophy of Lorenz Oken (1779–1851). Oken had established a five-level order of animals based on the senses (Oken 1833–42); Berghaus takes this and modifies it to apply it to racial groups and skin color. At the lowest level, corresponding to Oken's *dermatozoa* (skin users), are the black-skinned inhabitants of Africa, the Indian-Australian islands, and the Australian continent; at the second level, where Oken has his *glossozoa* (tongue users), are found the brown-skinned peoples of the Indian archipelagos and Malaysia; the red-skinned peoples of the Americas inhabit the third level, corresponding to Oken's *rhinozoa* (nose users); the yellow-skinned races of East Asia to Japan are at the fourth level, where Oken has his *otozoa* (ear users); and where all coloring disappears from the skin, the Caucasian white races appear, corresponding to Oken's fifth category of *ophthalmozoa*, in which all the organs of sense are present and complete. Berghaus leaves no ambiguity about his conviction that this fifth group is where the pinnacle of the pinnacle is reached. He states, "They have now settled in all parts of the world and seem destined to subject all peoples of the earth's surface and lead them to culture" (Berghaus 1850b, 4). References to Oken do not appear to inform Berghaus's other writings, so it is difficult from our vantage point to understand why he would invoke this philosopher. If Berghaus was seeking a principle by which to organize his material concerning ethnic groups, surely, he could have used linguistic groupings; he had, after all, already declared this classification criterion to be the primary one. The most that can be said is that in subscribing to Oken's typology, Berghaus anticipates the preoccupation with social and cultural evolution that would dominate the new discipline of anthropology for the remainder of the nineteenth century.

Principles of Ethnography contains a systematized summary of the account of the Comanches already given in Peoples of the Globe five years earlier. Over twenty-seven pages he discusses the tribes of North America, of which two pages are devoted to the "Komantschen," who include the Shoshone, the "true" Comanche, the Arrapahos, and the Apache. Berghaus's thinking concerning the Comanches has not advanced significantly since 1845:

XLVI. Comanches. Under this name we group together several tribes that, although they go by separate names and here and there differ from each other in their traditions, nevertheless seem to be so closely related to each other by their idioms that we cannot speak of a group or family of related languages but rather of a single nation whose branches differ only by dialect variations. This nation, which from the point of view of the present is the most populous and mightiest among the Indians of North America, is distributed over a very broad range; for it reaches from the area of Oregon, from the southern branches of the Columbia River as far as the Gulf of California on one side, across the Cordillera on the other side to the Gulf of Mexico, where in most recent times, however, it is being pushed back by Anglo-Americans and German settlers in Texas. The individual groupings of this nation are the following:

1. the Shoshones or Snake Indians. They form the most north-westerly division of the nature [misprint for "nation"?] and stretch almost from the coast of the Pacific Ocean to the Rocky Mountains, and from the southern tributaries of the Columbia to the unknown extremities of the far Californian deserts.

2. The true Comanches, Camanches, Cumanches, also known under the names Hietans, Jetans, Tetans, and Paducas, are distributed primarily on the east side of the Cordillera, where they are the greatest and most feared Indian nation in Texas. As bands of the Comanches we may list:

   1) The Kayguas, Cajugas, Kiawas, Kioways who, along with

   2) the Jutas [Utahs] are most widespread in the western lands and are scattered on both sides of the Cordillera from the North of New Mexico to the Snake River and the Rio Colorado. A division of the Jutas spends winter in the mountain valleys north of Taos.

   3) The Watepatahos.

   4) The Nanhos.

   5) The Kanenawish.

   6) The Katteka.

   7) The Dotame.

   8) The Kaskajas or Hard Hearts (Baldhearts [*sic*, misprint for Badhearts]).

   9) The Caslahana.

   10) The Stubborn Heads (Baldkeads [Baldheads]).

11) The Tonquewa or Tonqueys and

12) The Waccons or Wäbuh.

3. The Arrapahos, i.e. Dog Eaters, because they enjoy the meat of the prairie dog, dwell south of the Shoshones.

4. The Apaches are spread on the east side of the Californian peoples throughout New Mexico as far as the grazing and hunting grounds of the Comanches. Those who stay east of the Rio del Norte are usually called Mezcaleros by the Spanish in Mexico after the *mezcal*, the baked root of the maguey plant, that is so popular with them as food; however, the far greater number of this name live in the western regions and are known by the nick-name Coyoteros, supposedly because these Indians eat the meat of the Coyota, the prairie wolf. We distinguish six bands:

1) Tonto-Apaches	4) Llanero-Apaches	
2) Gileno-Apaches	5) Lipan-Apaches, and	
3) Chiricague-Apaches	6) Navajo-Apaches;	

among whom the last-named Navajos or Nabajoas speak a dialect that corresponds very closely to the vernacular of the Jutas [Utahs], though the latter is spoken more from the throat and in a deep tone, like ventriloquists.

In general, however, the four main dialects of the Comanche nation do not seem to differ significantly from each other; and all bands, with the exception of the Shoshone, have learned Spanish. (Berghaus 1850b, 132–34)

What is striking about this account is the lack of reference, except in the most superficial way, to language. Having set up language as the essential characteristic by which ethnic groups are to be identified, Berghaus fails to provide any detailed analysis or even incidental example material supporting his classification. The inventory of tribes and their range are his main concern; cultural notes appear sporadically; but linguistic descriptors from systematic phonological, morphological, syntactic, semantic, lexical, or etymological analysis are entirely missing. Berghaus also omits any indication of his sources. Nevertheless, it is clear that, as in 1845, he does associate the Comanches with Texas, and at this time (1850) with explicit reference to the increasing German settlements. However, he is evidently not yet in possession of the firsthand information from the settlements that would distinguish his 1851 Comanche sketch.

In 1846, prior to his 1850 publication of Principles of Ethnography, Berghaus had published his translation of George Catlin's *Letters and Notes on the Manners, Customs, and Conditions of the North American Indians Written during Eight Years' Travel amongst the Wildest Tribes of Indians in North America in 1832, 33, 34, 35, 36, 37, 38 and 39* (Catlin 1851).[3] This work contains a narrative of Catlin's experiences while visiting the Comanches with a regiment of US Army dragoons, anecdotes heard on the way, and cultural notes concerning the Comanches, along with word lists of various Indian languages. Catlin's work, however, does not appear to have influenced significantly Berghaus's 1851 writing about the Comanches. In quoting his informant's account of aspects of Comanche culture in the 1851 article, Berghaus includes Kriewitz's passing reference to Catlin's description of Comanche horsemanship but does not expand on it or footnote it, though he certainly could have done so.

We have thus traced Berghaus's publications concerning the Comanches up to the time of the key work that underlies the 1851 article in the Geographic Yearbook. This key work is Section VIII of Berghaus's Physical Atlas, titled "Ethnography." It appeared in January 1847 as the fourteenth fascicle of the Atlas.[4] It contains Berghaus's Ethnographic Map of North America, compiled in 1845, and is referred to in Berghaus's second footnote in the 1851 article as the point of departure for that article. The fascicle contains thirty-three two-column pages of introductory text, followed by two maps showing the global distribution of Indo-Germanic and Semitic races, and of Germans respectively, and ethnographic maps of the Austrian monarchy, Africa (including inserts showing Australasian and Polynesian peoples), and North America (including an insert indicating the distribution of Europeans and Africans in North America). The introductory text (which is dated October 31, 1846) begins with two pages that comment briefly on the content of the maps and reinforce the ideological position of the author and his identity as European, German, and Christian and as such a member of the group of "transporters of humane values and Christian, i.e. therefore of genuine and true, civilized behavior" (Berghaus 1845–48, 1:193). The remainder of the introductory text (thirty-one pages) comprises a German overview of North American Indian tribes, excerpted by Friedrich Rehbock from Gallatin's 1836 *Synopsis of the Indian Tribes within the United States East of the Rocky Mountains, and in the British and Russian Possessions of North America* and augmented with additional information on the Koloschen

(Koluschan, i.e., Tlingit) group. Berghaus justifies reproducing Gallatin's material by stating its unavailability in Germany. He further expresses his indebtedness to Johann Carl Eduard Buschmann, Custodian of the Royal Library, for making accessible the only copy to be found in Berlin. And it is Gallatin's *Map of the Indian Tribes of North America* (1836) that provides the basis for Berghaus's "Ethnographic Map of North America" in the Physical Atlas.

The 1846 Berghaus/Rehbock narrative says the following about Comanches:

Indians between the Mississippi and the Great Ocean.
The Indians belonging to this region are separated by the Rocky Mountains into two large divisions.

The Indians living to the east of this mountain range are the Sioux, the Pawnees, the Fall-, Rapid- or Paunch-Indians; the Blackfeet and several other, less well-known tribes may be subsumed under the general, if outdated name Padoucas. Some bands of the Snake-Indians or Shoshones, who live on the Columbia River, and the Hietans or Camanches, whose main homeland is south of the Red River and the United States border, sometimes find their way to the headwaters of tributaries of the Missouri or north of the Red River (Berghaus 1845–48, 1:222).

It remains only to mention the Indians within the territory of the United States east of the Rocky Mountains who roam between the upper part of the Platte and Red Rivers, west of the Pawnees, Kansas, and Osages. In 1724 Bourgmont calls them Padoucas, a name that now seems to have disappeared. The Pawnees [Panis] or Towiaches on the Red River have well established villages and have already been mentioned. The Hiantes or Camanches live in Mexican territory and only occasionally do individuals appear in the United States. In the territory of the latter in that area or along the Mexican border between latitudes 34° and 41° N three tribes seem to roam and hunt, namely the Kaskaias or Bad-Hearts, the Kiawas or Kioways, and the Bald-Heads, who were discovered by Major Long during his first trip to the Arkansas, along with several scattered bands of Arrapahoes, Cheyennes [Shyennes], and even Shoshones [Shoshonis]. The word lists that Dr. Say had compiled of the languages of the Kaskaias and Kiawas have unfortunately been lost. We know only that both these languages were rough, with many guttural sounds, and were extremely difficult to learn. It is notable that none of these tribes understood the others and that they used partly the Crow language, which was native to neither of them, and partly sign language to communicate with each other. Their number is estimated by the Department of Indian Affairs to be only 1400 and probably cannot be more than 3000 even counting a few other small bands that Lewis and Clarke, following uncertain sources, mention (Berghaus 1845–48, 1:225).

Clearly, this information adds little to what Berghaus had published about the Comanches earlier. At the same time, it makes completely understandable Berghaus's desire to publish the firsthand material he received from Kriewitz and his interpretation of it in the Geographic Yearbook, which served as the vehicle for updates to the Physical Atlas. By the time the second edition of the Physical Atlas appeared in 1852, Berghaus was able to refer to the 1851 Yearbook article in his introductory narrative to the ethnographic map of North America. Here the overview of North American Indian tribes is reduced to five pages, however, the listing of the sources of his data is far more complete:

> *Shoshones* and *Camanches* and *Apaches*. This triad is considered to be one single linguistic group, which in its three branches divides into the three named tribes and languages. The relationship between the Shoshones and Camanches may be viewed as conclusively proven, though this cannot be said of the third group, for whom we have no language sample. The first branch occupies the northwestern, the second the southeastern, and the third the southern area of the range of distribution, which is among the largest of all North American Indian families. (Berghaus 1852 [7. Abtheilung, Anthropologie], 57)

Berghaus continues to describe the range of subtribes in more detail, assigning the languages of the Utes, Paiutes, and Timbabachi to dialects of Shoshone; with even more certainty, he ascribes the languages of the Kij Indians and Natelas of California to the Shoshone family. He then concludes: "I believe I have demonstrated conclusively that this is also the case with the Camanches or Comanches," and in endnote 15 repeats: "I believe I have proven the relationship of the Shoshones, Comanches, and Apaches,—at least as far as the first two tribes are concerned—based on linguistic evidence. Geogr. Jahrbuch, 1851, III, p. 48–62" (Berghaus 1852 [7. Abtheilung, Anthropologie], 66).

5

Berghaus's Ideology

No sketch of Berghaus's development as a scholar publishing in the field of North American Indian ethnography in the mid-nineteenth century would be complete without reference to his broader worldview. His writings contain multiple indicators of his opinions on social obligation, religion, humanity, civilization, colonization, emigration, the role of government, the place of science, and related topics. An overview of these general positions helps to provide a personalized ideological context for a reading of Berghaus's specific assessments of the Comanches.

Reference has already been made to Berghaus's fundamental desire to share knowledge as widely as possible (as a teacher, through scientific and popular publication, and through school materials) and his development and embracing of new cartographic and typographic techniques for presenting information in engaging ways. This democratization of science and awareness of target audience in his professional activity is a correlate of his sense of social responsibility in his private life. As a prominent citizen in Potsdam, Berghaus played a role in city government as a *Stadtverordneter* (city councilor), taking a particular interest in schools, and directing from November 1848 to November 1850 the distribution of alms in the Department of the Poor (*Armen-Direction*). For this work he was recognized informally by Queen Elisabeth of Prussia, who personally asked Alexander von Humboldt to express to his friend Berghaus her appreciation of his dedication to the well-being of the impoverished in the city (Berghaus 1863, 133–34, letter of January 16, 1850). Social responsibility underlay Berghaus's political impulses that in 1848 had drawn the disfavor of King Friedrich Wilhelm IV of Prussia. As a supporter of the reform movement that eventually led to the March Revolution of 1848, Berghaus had published a short-lived monthly titled *Der preußische Staatsbürger* (The Prussian Citizen) (Häntzsch 1902, 379; Beck 1956, 7; Reckziegel 1985, 34). Retribution for this activity was probably also a reason for Berghaus's dismissal from the Academy of Architecture in 1855 and for the government's repeated denial of his petitioning for a pension as his own economic situation deteriorated in the early 1850s.[1]

Berghaus's attitudes are informed in no small measure by religious convictions. A member of the German Reformed Church, Berghaus repeatedly affirms his belief in certain Christian tenets in introductory statements to his published work. In addition to those already mentioned, we find in the foreword to the first issue of the Geographic Yearbook (1850; written November 7, 1849): "this progress toward knowledge of the laws of nature is seen everywhere on the globe where mankind lives and thinks under the shining star of Christian intellectual freedom and enlightenment." He continues: "The increase of knowledge does not merely serve to satisfy a harmless and trifling sense of curiosity; it is dedicated to a higher and more noble purpose, to life itself, which will enrich it with new ideas." The advance of science is viewed as a project of Christianity, though in this formulation the religious zeal is tempered.

Earlier language had been less moderate. The introductory paragraphs to the first edition of the Physical Atlas referred to earlier encapsulate central threads of Berghaus's ideological fabric. In referring to his map of the global spread of Indo-Germanic and Semitic peoples, he states that the civilized behavior of Europeans is what it is because it is built on faith in the savior of the world. Where human pride has allowed this faith to diminish, it must always in turn yield to "the spirit of truth that emanates from the Father" (Berghaus 1845–48, 1:193). Berghaus then quotes eight lines of selectively chosen, paraphrased New Testament scripture and follows with: "The consequences of two thousand years of these words of the Lord can be seen in the geographic distribution shown in this map. Of course, one must ignore here the Asiatic division of the Indo-Germanic peoples" (Berghaus 1845–48, 1:193).

Berghaus's religiously determined view of mankind as the pinnacle of creation includes the notion that the created universe exists for the benefit of mankind. Thus, in the third volume (Book 5) of the General Geography and Ethnography issued in 1838 we find such formulations as: "the number of different species of plants, with which the face of the earth has been adorned by the all-powerful love of God, in order to serve as nourishment, clothing, heating, protection and the general sustenance and well-being of the human race" (Berghaus 1837–46, vol. 3, book 5, 13). The structure chosen by Berghaus for this sentence unambiguously expresses purpose (*um . . . zu . . .* ; "in order to"). One year after the publication of the 1851 article on Shoshones, Comanches, and Apaches, Berghaus opens his introduction to the ethnographic section of the second edition of the Physical Atlas with the words: "Asia, that part of the earth that we are used to calling the cradle of humanity, following the Mosaic story of creation, has to stand at the beginning of a collection of ethnographic maps" (Berghaus 1852 [8. Abtheilung: Ethnographie], 1). He continues uncritically, "If we proceed from the genealogy of peoples in Genesis (Chap. 5 and 10), then Noah's three sons Sem, Ham, and Jafeth are the ancestral fathers of postdiluvian humanity, whose antediluvian unity, represented by a mythical primal couple, has accordingly divided itself into the trifurcation of Semites, Hamites, and Jafethites, or into the peoples of the middle, the south, and the north" (Berghaus 1852 [8. Abtheilung: Ethnographie], 1). This terminology is maintained through Berghaus's ensuing discussion of Asian and European peoples.

Undisguised national pride is articulated in the Physical Atlas, where Berghaus introduces the map of the distribution of Germans in both hemispheres. It is no exaggeration to say his words are infused with a sense of pique, even inferiority complex, as he laments the minimal recognition of German influence on the world stage. "[The German is sometimes] even subject to a foreign nation that exploits his skill, his industriousness, his learning for its own advantage, but only sees him as a tool to be cast aside when worn out! National feeling is a divine right! . . . The German people [has] lived through a thousand-year-long childhood of Christian civilization and is just now beginning the start of its adolescence. Let us not forget that!" (Berghaus 1845–48, 1:194). In interpreting these comments in a historical context, we must guard against the distraction of seeing only a linear trajectory of sentiment that leads to German expansionist politics of the late nineteenth and early twentieth centuries, culminating in National Socialist ideology. While this link is certainly there to be made, the more appropriate focus for understanding Berghaus's accomplishment is the development of his thinking in the context of German

Romanticism, with its strong religious, democratic, and national impulses, in the context of scientific advances, especially in geography and anthropology, and in the political context of post-Napoleonic Europe.

Indicators of Berghaus's ideological predilections can also be gleaned from his statements about emigration (specifically German emigration) and the policies of destination countries (Mexico and the United States) concerning future social and economic development. A precursor of Kriewitz's remark incorporated in the 1851 article about the unhappiness of German immigrants in Texas and their desire to return home is found in Berghaus's review of Grisson's *Beiträge zur Charakteristik der Vereinigten Staaten von Nord-Amerika* (Contributions toward Characterizing the United States of North America). Berghaus refers to the desire of his contemporaries to emigrate as a social addiction and epidemic. Modern pied pipers are luring stupefied masses to the ports to transport them to other climes "to place them in a wilderness full of ravishing beasts and venomous serpents, among people who have scarcely or not even emerged from a state of savagery; even princes and lords have lowered themselves giving a new direction to the torrents of those sick of home, and praise Texas, the Eldorado of vagabonds and criminals, as a land of promise" (Berghaus 1844, 2802).

Berghaus concurs with Grisson's admonitions to prospective emigrants to be extremely cautious about leaving their homeland and cites with approval Grisson's claim that most would return to Germany if they could. Author and reviewer criticize the hollow hospitality of Americans that conceals the desire and intent to rob new arrivals.

> America is the land of contrasts; it is a land of the most majestic natural beauty, but is also full of swamps and quagmires; it is the land of poisonous snakes, of birds sporting the richest, most colorful plumage but without song, most brightly hued flowers without fragrance, the land of the most magnanimous institutions and most narrow-minded people, the country where next to unlimited freedom there exists the institution of slavery, where adjacent to the crassest bigotry dwells the greatest indifference; it is the land that at one and the same time brought forth a Washington and an Arnold. (Berghaus 1844, 2803)

Berghaus picks up and repeats Grisson's observation that in religious matters the American swings from profoundest indifference to most heated enthusiasm for some sect or other, in which he becomes the fieriest of zealots. Alongside high-principled rule of law the practice of lynching is widespread. Do the emigrants, Berghaus asks, know that the dominant Anglo-Americans continue to look to England as their model and disparage all other immigrant nationalities, so that any thought of a German state in the New World is out of the question? Grisson and Berghaus laud the lofty ideals of law and order on which the United States is founded; however, the Americans do not possess the moral wherewithal and education to put them into practice. Such is the tenor of Berghaus's review, or rather channeling, of Grisson's disaffected take on North America. Some of the judgments (and prejudices) found here recur in Berghaus's own book on North America for emigrants, the Physical Atlas, and contributions to the Geographic Yearbook, including the 1851 article.

German publishers in the 1840s and early 1850s did a booming business with books and other publications about North America, especially with respect to prospective emigration.[2] Berghaus himself contributed to this wave when he published *Die Vereinigten Staaten von Nordamerika, geographisch-statistisch vorzugsweise nach Van der Straten-Ponthoz geschildert mit besonderer Rücksicht auf die Deutsche Auswanderung* in 1848 (The United States of North America, geographically and statistically described primarily according to Van der Straten-Ponthoz with special consideration of German emigration). The volume contains much factual and statistical information about the United States and its makeup, from political structure to the sailing schedules of Atlantic shipping companies. Berghaus recognizes a historic shift in the motivation of emigrants from Germany from religious to material or economic causes (*sittlich* to *sinnlich*). Migration in the nineteenth century is driven by overpopulation and hunger in Germany and Europe generally, especially among laboring classes and the agrarian population (Berghaus 1848, 1–2). His recommendation is that the midwestern states make the most promising destinations for Germans who feel they must emigrate (Berghaus 1848, 11); however, he cautions that farmers with means are most likely to succeed, restless intellectuals should stay at home in Germany, and the outlook for manual workers is precarious. He distinguishes between the opportunities offered by the Eastern Seaboard and the inland states, between agricultural and urban destinations, and between Anglo and German communities. He advises finding an established German community to move into.

Berghaus does not spare his reader horror stories of what emigrants have experienced. Certain passages are bold-faced, such as these: "One must not hesitate to speak the bitter truth with direct words, that the European who settles among Americans, inexperienced as he is, is facing misery in all its various shades" (Berghaus 1848, 81); "Europeans who wish to settle in uncultivated areas—one cannot repeat this often enough—must work with their hands, a rule that knows absolutely no exceptions" (Berghaus 1848, 81); and most emphatically, "It is a duty to warn every German who is contemplating emigration against this Mainz Protection Society and against Texas in general" (Berghaus 1848, 78). This last admonition follows a paragraph highlighting the Adelsverein as one of the worst examples in the category of philanthropic settlement organizations and declaring their Texan enterprise as good as dead! In summary, Berghaus states: "Texas, with its almost tropical climate, with its annually recurring yellow fever, with its wild Comanches, from whom the ground for settlements has to be won by fire and the sword, is no country for the German" (Berghaus 1848, 78).

Berghaus's perception of the superiority of German and, by extension, Anglo emigrant populations, emerges in remarks about how the US government should address certain political and social problems. Implicit in these is a favoring of Protestant Christian morality over other religious views. The 1851 article contains explicit dismissive references to the Mormon "sect," which is in the process of setting up political administration in Utah "based on religious fanaticism." In the same (final) paragraph Berghaus calls on the US government to curtail the unregulated and destructive practices of '49ers in the California gold rush, referring to them as the "rejects and refuse of Indo-European peoples," who threaten what remains of the native tribes (Berghaus 1851, 60).

A year later this thread is developed further in the second edition of the Physical Atlas, where Berghaus inveighs against the greed and depravity of gold seekers:

> It is high time that the Californian [native] peoples and languages be thoroughly studied, for it is reasonable to fear that soon many of them will have vanished from the earth. They are unable to resist the eradicating and annihilating onrush of the countless adventurers, vagabonds, and good-for-nothings, who, as the dregs of all the Indo-Germanic nations of Europe and America, have been crammed together into the gold rich valley of the San Sacramento and its tributaries by their laziness and fear of hard work, their greed and acquisitiveness, and who have for several years been leading an existence here that is unworthy of a civilized human being, and of which any neutral observer must be ashamed

in the depths of his soul. May the enlightened government of the United States soon put an end to this state of affairs; and generally enact measures for the health of the American common good that are able to discourage or even prevent the flood of so many depraved sons of the Old World, with which the Union has been overrun, especially since 1849. May the government also consider acquiring more precise knowledge of the Californian Indians and at least try to save for historical study what still might be saved, before these unfortunate peoples also meet the inevitable fate of the redskins: The linguistic emissary Horatio Hale is the ideal person for the execution of this task that is of the utmost importance for the history of humankind in America. (Berghaus 1852 [8. Abtheilung, Ethnographie], 66n14)

Berghaus's recommendations do not stop at the situation in California and the West. He, like Humboldt before him, speaks out unequivocally against slavery. Already in his review of Grisson (Berghaus 1844) he had referred to the untenable defense and justification of slavery and how it is irreconcilable with principles of natural law. His criticism is most pointed when he attacks Methodist clergy in the South, mentioned by Grisson, who preach the teachings of Christ and yet hold slaves themselves (Berghaus 1844, 2803). A more guarded presentation of the slavery question is found in Berghaus's book on the United States, where he presents in a sober, dispassionate way the distribution of slave states and nonslave states and the history behind the North-South divide with reference also to the peculiar position of Missouri (Berghaus 1848, 3–4). Here geographical description prevails over social commentary.

In the same work, a very different tone dominates when the United States is compared with Mexico. Here racial and religious prejudice (masked as ethics) infect the rhetoric. Referring to the 1848 treaty between the United States and Mexico, he writes: "it is, in our view, merely a cease-fire between the Germanic peoples of the United States and the romano-hispanic race, which, since the days of the conquest, has subjugated the Aztecs and the other peoples of the Anahuac Plateau; but which now, divided, torn, weakened as it is, must yield to the courageous and vigorous Anglo-Americans. It is a political necessity for the Anglo-Americans that they put an end to the Spanish regime in Mexico; they must unite the entirety of Mexico with their empire if the Oregon Territory and the new acquisitions in New Mexico and California are to be as useful to them as they promise to be" (Berghaus 1848, iii). This tone is sustained as the author turns to continental economic politics. A coast-to-coast railway across North America is a far-off dream in Berghaus's view; however, a canal linking the Atlantic with the Pacific is a different matter: "For the United States it is a matter of survival to create a sea passage to the West Coast of the continent. And what other way is there than the way across the Isthmus of Tehuantepec!" (Berghaus 1848, iv). The technical feasibility of the project has already been demonstrated, he says. "The execution is only possible by a people that, like the Anglo-Americans, is young and strong, ethical and intellectually highly educated." To make this possible the United States must have full control, he continues, either by conquest of the land or by unification of the states; the first solution is preferable (Berghaus 1848, v). In this way the Mexican character could be remade—"neuer, besser"—according to the model of the Germanic race. "Spanish nationality and language would of course, in time, go to their grave; that is, however, in our estimation not a disaster if it means the spreading of true and genuine humanity!" (Berghaus 1848, v).

One of the sources Berghaus indicates for the data concerning Apache band names in the 1851 article is Friedrich Adolph Wislizenus. In 1850, in the first issue of the Geographic Yearbook, Berghaus had published a twenty-five-page article on Wislizenus's travels to northern Mexico and New Mexico.[3] At the conclusion of that article, based on Wislizenus's journal that had been published for the US Senate in a limited edition (Wislizenus 1848), Berghaus formulates his view of the future of Mexico.

> Since their declaration of independence [from Spain], the Mexicans have gone through a continuous chain of local and general turmoil, which is evidence that republican institutions have not taken root among them and they are not in a position to govern themselves. Additionally, it is scarcely to be expected that a people consisting of two distinct races that may have mixed but have never assimilated, could suddenly, having lived for three centuries under oppression, be mature enough for a republican constitution. Fanaticism can overthrow an old regime, but there is a lack of calm, clear-thinking heads who are equipped to give the people a new and adequate constitution, just as the people as a whole lacks a certain intelligence necessary to sustain the republican system of government.
>
> Where is the enlightenment of the masses to come from? I cannot but believe, says Dr. W., that Mexico, weakened by the present war, if it is left once again to its own devices, will restart its internal struggles and that these will lead to its complete collapse, and [Mexico] will in coming years be delivered to the United States as a voluntary gift, which now the U.S. scornfully declines to acquire as the spoils

of war. Mexico's fate is sealed! Unable to govern itself, it will fall to the domination of some other power, and it will need all the luck it can get if it falls into worse hands than those of the United States, because this country at least respects its nationality and will guarantee it what it has lacked hitherto, namely the republican constitution. There can be no doubt that Mexico would gain great advantage from such a change, and likewise the whole civilized world, if this wonderful land is opened up to the industriousness and enterprise of a stronger race of humans. However, there is doubt about policy on the United States' side, whether it would maintain possession of the whole of Mexico, even if it could, considering the heterogeneous mass of seven or eight million Mexicans, who would need to be transformed from enemies into friends and elevated from a condition of ignorance and repression to the level of citizens in a republic. Their assimilation with the republic would not be as easy as it would be with the same number of European immigrants arriving on the shore of the Anglo-American federation at extended intervals bringing with them a greater intelligence and the firm desire to live and die as Americans . . . Yet politics, as well as humanity, demands this kind of expansion of the 'Area of Freedom' in the interests of humankind! (Berghaus 1850a, 52)[4]

A curious contradiction in Berghaus's thinking emerges when we consider this strong affirmation of the republican underpinnings of the United States alongside comments found in the second edition of the Physical Atlas of 1852. Here Berghaus is more concerned with general anthropological trends in the organization of human societies and argues himself into a position where he is forced to predict an inevitable return to the conditions of a monarchy: "one cannot say that the 'tree of American freedom' will withstand all the storms of human passions for eternity! Democracy will have to yield to aristocracy, for which there are already indications enough in the old or Atlantic states. From among the aristocrats a monarch will ultimately come forward!" (Berghaus 1852 [7. Abtheilung, Anthropographie], 4). This inconsistency in Berghaus's statements suggests that at least some of his strongly worded conclusions are the result of momentary enthusiasm rather than sustained, systematic thinking and should be treated with some caution. That said, the range of interests and opinions selected and summarized here provides an impressionistic sketch of the ideological underpinnings that inform Berghaus's ethnographic scholarship as it relates to the Comanches and German immigration to Texas.

6

Evaluating Berghaus's Achievement

How have succeeding generations of scholars assessed Berghaus's accomplishments as a man of science? Before addressing this question, we can ask first how Berghaus saw the value of his own work. Two documents help us answer this.

The first is a curriculum vitae, written in the third person and in traditional German discursive style, dating from 1852 when Berghaus was seeking (unsuccessfully) a secure, paid appointment with the Prussian department of education. While this CV does not give a summation of Berghaus's entire career, it does provide a view of how Berghaus saw his professional life up to about the time of the article on the Comanches (1851). While most of the sixteen finely penned pages enumerate his early life, military experiences, education, and further studies as a geographer, surveyor, and cartographer, the final two paragraphs attempt to clinch the sought-after appointment by declaring his position during the republican movement preceding the 1848 revolution as politically beyond reproach, even though the Prussian authorities knew he was not without ideological blemish:

> Keeping clear of all societies and clubs, not belonging to any party, and standing solely on the solid ground of law and order, he was always at pains, in his official capacity as Captain in the civil defense during the months March to May 1848 and particularly as inspector of the largest of the municipal elementary schools, to uphold the authority of the official bureaucracy.

Perhaps protesting too much, he continues:

> Because he spurned all club meetings and party memberships he
> was, as he is fully aware, considered by one side to be an arch-reaction-
> ary and by the other to be a dyed-in-the-wool demagogue; however he
> accepted all of these insinuations with a smile and in the full knowledge
> that, within his circle of responsibilities, he had only ever wanted and
> done the right thing in the struggle against the anarchic efforts of the
> educated and uneducated mob.[1]

To reinforce his standing as an educator of national and international
reputation, Berghaus closes the CV by pointing to his ongoing project,
in collaboration with other European educators, to produce textbooks
for Hindustani schools in India (possibly also to be published in Tamil)
in order to bring to them European traditions of learning and to wean
them gradually away from Brahmadom and Islam. Berghaus takes the
opportunity to mention that Humboldt was the one who put his name
forward for this project as a collaborator in the field of geography. While
the instrumental nature of this CV narrative as a means to a desired end
is obvious, it also allows us to glimpse those facets of his professional
and civic person that Berghaus himself saw as relevant to a positive self-
representation before the Prussian administration.

The second document is the title page of his final major publication
(Berghaus 1880; 1883), which marks a return from the global optic of
his atlases and sweeping geographic treatises to the local focus of a provincial dictionary. It is a Low German lexicon published (though never
completed) in three volumes under the title *Der Sprachschatz der Sassen.*
Ein Wörterbuch der Plattdeutschen Sprache in den hauptsächlichsten
ihrer Mundarten (Language Treasury of the Saxons. A Dictionary of the
Low German Language according to its Principal Dialects). Volume 2,
J–N, published in 1883, provides the following list of titles and learned
societies associated with Berghaus's name:

> Professor at the Royal Academy of Architecture in Berlin, retired.
> Member of the Royal Academies of Science at Amsterdam, Milan, and
> Venice, as well as of the Asiatic Society at Paris; Initiator and Founding
> Member of the Berlin Geographical Society, April 18, 1828; Member
> of the Geographic Societies of Bombay, London, Paris, St. Petersburg,
> Stettin, and Vienna; of the Silesian and Westphalian Societies for Na-
> tional Culture at Breslau and Minden, of the Society for Pomeranian
> History and Antiquities, also of the Arts Council for Pomerania and

Stettin, of the Brandenburg Economic Society at Potsdam; of the Society for Nature and Medicine at Dresden, of the Society for Natural Sciences of the Harz, of the Rhenish and East Frisian Societies for Natural Research at Mainz and Emden, of the Association of Pharmacists in Northern Germany, of the Germanic Museum at Nuremberg, Honorary Member and Master of the Freies Deutsches Hochstift [Free German Foundation] for the Sciences, Arts and General Education at Frankfurt a.M.; also Member of the German Colonial Association at Frankfurt a.M. Senior Member of the Congregation Elders of the German Reformed Church at Stettin.

Berghaus is following tradition in laying out his credentials below his name as author of the dictionary, and we can sense a level of pride in the ten lines of small print that convey this information. He has indeed made his mark on European intellectual life of the mid-nineteenth century and been recognized for this by leading international scholarly institutions of his day.

This status is borne out by enthusiastic early responses to the Physical Atlas found in the review material used by the publisher Justus Perthes to market the second edition of the atlas. In the English press, the *Athenaeum* gushes over the stippling and hatching that characterize the cartographic representations and summarizes hyperbolically: "The book before us is, in short, a graphic encyclopaedia of the sciences—an atlas of human knowledge done into maps. . . . In short, we have a summary of all the cross-questions of Nature for twenty centuries—and all the answers of Nature herself set down and speaking to us voluminous systems *dans un mot*." *The Scotsman* is similarly impressed: "one of these maps combines a mass of information, which if expressed in words, would fill a volume; and the volume, when written, would not tell its tale half so distinctly, or impress it half so vividly on the memory, as the map, which pictures the whole details to the eye, with their relations and dependencies" (advertising front matter to Berghaus 1852).

As early as 1842 the ripple effect from Berghaus's *Physikalischer Atlas* was being felt across the world of cartography. In this year, Alexander Keith Johnston visited Berghaus and arranged to publish some of the maps in an English version in Edinburgh. Additionally, with the help of Berghaus's students Henry Lange and August Petermann, Johnston published an abridged edition of the complete Physical Atlas in 1845–48 (Johnston 1848; Espenhorst 2003, 384; Reckziegel 1985, 35; Engelmann 1964).

Beck (1956), Engelmann (1977), and Espenhorst (2003) offer appraisals of Berghaus from the latter half of the twentieth century. For Beck,

Berghaus's primary achievement lies in his influence on others, which resulted largely from his indefatigable industriousness and his gift for processing and presenting with precision the results of others who had traveled to the corners of the earth and sent back data. For these reasons he is, according to Beck, historically the most significant of the crop of classical German geographers (Beck 1956, 7). Engelmann recognizes that Berghaus features consistently in the biographical dictionaries of Germany and other European countries up to the beginning of the twentieth century, but thereafter diminishes in prominence in such publications. Engelmann chooses in his final comments to return to Berghaus's misfortunes in life: his melancholy; his restless energy that, while it drove him to some astonishing achievements, also was detrimental to his health (and his sociability); his inability to finish ambitious projects; his financial troubles after 1848; and his premature intellectual decline. Nevertheless, Engelmann concludes, "the brighter sides of his personality, his persistence in turning the accumulated knowledge of geographical science critically into cartographic images, come to the fore and allow Heinrich Berghaus to appear as a man who 'soared like a lark that aspires to climb to heights that only the eagle is capable of reaching'" (Engelmann 1977, 187). Espenhorst, in his richly detailed account of Berghaus's Physical Atlas and its importance, summarizes the cartographer's achievement as a step in a process rather than a culminating final product—much as Berghaus himself saw his work. Espenhorst writes: "the physical atlas had opened entirely new perspectives and made clear that the profession of geography included far more than just the topographical depiction of the earth's surface" (Espenhorst 2003, 374; see also Camerini 1993, 511–12).

As the development of geographical science as a discipline, or set of disciplines, advanced in the latter half of the nineteenth century, the state of the art swiftly surpassed what Berghaus had produced, and others, among them his students (particularly Petermann but also Lange and Hermann Berghaus), took on the task of further pushing back the frontiers. At the time of writing, Berghaus is not prominently acknowledged in either popular or academic circles, in Germany or elsewhere.[2] The English-language Wikipedia entry grants him a biographical sketch of 250 words and a listing of major publications; the German-language entry is slightly more generous at 300 words and provides a more complete reference apparatus (accessed July 21, 2014). The importance of Berghaus's 1851 article on the Shoshones, Comanches, and Apaches for the study of Native Americans and anthropology in general is assessed in chapter 8.

7

Who Was Emil Kriewitz?

The decisive circumstance that places Berghaus in a position to write his 1851 article on Shoshones, Comanches, and Apaches is his acquisition of information from his source in Texas. This individual is not named in the article, but endnote p points to an earlier publication where he is named as Emil Kriwitz (more usually spelled "Kriewitz"; figure 5).[1]

The relationship between Berghaus and Kriewitz is unclear, but it is possible, given a reference in endnote k of the 1851 article, that Kriewitz's mother, who may have been a resident of Potsdam at the time Berghaus lived and worked there, played a role as intermediary. The substance of Berghaus's article rests on three blocks of original information: (1) Kriewitz's Comanche-German glossary and (2) his account of Comanche traditions, knowledge, and cultural practices; (3) to a lesser extent, Kriewitz's comments on his own life in Texas and the condition of German immigrants. The following paragraphs outline what is known about Kriewitz and speculate about how Berghaus came into possession of Kriewitz's data. For his article, Berghaus also draws on his wide reading of ethnographic literature on Native American tribes and languages to contextualize Kriewitz's material and to provide a basis for his argument concerning the relationship between the Shoshones, Comanches, and Apaches. In his annotations Berghaus names the following as his sources: Umfreville, Adelung and Vater, A. v. Humboldt, Violet, Ruxton, Hale, Gallatin, Holley, Gregg, Pike, Wislizenus, and Emory.

Little is known of Kriewitz's life prior to his travel to Texas. Chester and Ethel Geue indicate that he was born on January 18, 1822, into the nobility at Kloster Zinna, near Jüterbog in the present-day state of Brandenburg

(Geue and Geue 1972, 113). However, the authorities in Zinna are unable to confirm this information with local records. A document held at the US National Archives, supposedly completed by Kriewitz himself, shows Potsdam as the place of birth (Claim of a Survivor of the Mexican War for a Pension 1887). Yet no verification of a Potsdam birthplace can be found in the Catholic and Protestant baptismal records of that city or Brandenburg. His full name is recorded as Baron Emil von Kriewitz de Czepry (Anonymous 1860, 369; Morgenthaler 2007, 79). The 1860 and 1870 US census forms list his place of origin only as Prussia. Nothing is known of his education, except that transcripts of his predeparture correspondence with the Adelsverein indicate "Forst Candidat" below the signature, suggesting training in forestry (cf. Wurster et al. 2008, 34). We may conclude, however, from the information that appears in Berghaus's article, that he was a man of acute curiosity, perceptive and systematic in his observations, experienced in writing, and with an aptitude for language study.

Kriewitz came to Texas through the Adelsverein, though the facts of his arrival are obscured by inconsistencies. Transcripts of Adelsverein records held in the Sophienburg Museum in New Braunfels show that Kriewitz had contacted the Adelsverein in August 1845 with his request to join a group of emigrants heading for Texas (cf. Hadeler n.d.; Luther 2013, 50). In this letter Kriewitz inquires about legalities concerning the emigration of service personnel (Solms Archive, New Braunfels, 14:85–86). Hadeler notes that he planned to take a ship from Bremen in November and dates his arrival at Galveston as February 5, 1846, as also stated in *Pioneers in God's Hills* (Gillespie County Historical Society 1960, 1:251). Geue and Geue indicate that the shipping record shows him on the *Franziska* (Geue and Geue 1972, 113), but that the departure date from Bremen was October 28 (Geue and Geue 1972, 159). The Staatsarchiv Bremen has a record of a ship *Franzisca* [*sic*] departing Bremen for Galveston on November 8, 1845. Knopp says Kriewitz sailed from Bremen for Galveston on December 18, 1845, arriving on January 11, 1846 (Knopp 1999, 2). The Victoria Regional History Center gives his arrival date as April 1846.

The fog of uncertainty surrounding Kriewitz's arrival in Texas lifts when we consider a fortuitous contemporaneous source. A fellow traveler on the *Franziska* was Alwin H. Sörgel, who had contracted in advance of his departure to write, in a series of letters, an account of his crossing and stay in Texas under the auspices of the Adelsverein. His agreement was with Professor Karl Biedermann, editor of *Der Herold. Eine*

Wochenschrift für Politik, Litteratur und Gerichtsverfahren, a weekly newspaper published in Leipzig. The letters were published first in the *Herold* and then, in 1848, as a book. Sörgel's first letter begins: "On my passage to Texas, our ship, the *Franziska,* was battered by stormy seas in the [English] Channel for five days before we took refuge here [Ryde, Isle of Wight] on November 20" (Sörgel 1992, 5). This would place the departure date on November 15. It is likely that Sörgel is referring to departure from Bremerhaven; typically, emigrants were transported in small boats from Bremen to the embarkation point at Bremerhaven, a journey that could take three days (Thran 1848, 21). Allowing for delays waiting for favorable winds, it is likely that the *Franziska*'s passengers left Bremen before November 12, and quite possibly on November 8, as indicated by the Staatsarchiv Bremen information. The Adelsverein agent in Galveston, D. H. Kläner, records the arrival of the *Franziska* on February 5, 1846, but his passenger list does not include a "Kriewitz" (Sörgel 1992, 171–74). Passenger 33 on the list is "E. Kiersitz," age twenty-four (Kriewitz's correct age), while number 137 is "Emil Riewitz," (no age given), but this man is indicated as traveling with his wife; we are sure that Kriewitz was not married at this time. One of these two entries seems to represent Kriewitz.

Once he was on land in Texas, the accounts of Kriewitz's activities show more agreement. The following summary is based principally on the narratives of Hadeler (Hadeler n.d., 2010). In December 1845, during Kriewitz's crossing, Texas, in accordance with a July 1845 agreement, joined the United States and ceased to be an independent republic; war with Mexico ensued. Kriewitz joined a US military company being formed at Carlshafen (Indianola, Texas) under Captain Augustus Buchel in May 1846. He served as first sergeant in Company H, First Texas Rifle Volunteers, under Colonel Albert Sidney Johnston, together with other young Germans recruited at the landing point in Carlshafen (Hadeler n.d.). The unit was stationed in Mexico at Matamoros and later Camargo. After his discharge and return to Carlshafen about three months later, Kriewitz was hired by the Adelsverein to provide protection for the party of John O. Meusebach (now commissioner general of Adelsverein affairs in Texas) that was preparing to leave for the Fisher-Miller grant north of the Llano River to negotiate peace with the Comanches. Kriewitz arrived in New Braunfels after Meusebach had left and caught up with Meusebach's party only after the March 2, 1847, negotiations on the San Saba River with the Penateka Comanche chiefs Santa Anna, Buffalo Hump, and Old Owl had been completed. Kriewitz was then assigned to protect Richard Austin Howard, who was to survey the grant lands (Luther 2013, 51). In his own brief account of the events of this time, Kriewitz says that without this order he would have likely returned to the "lower country" (probably referring to New Braunfels), instead of remaining in the Fredericksburg area (Penniger 1971, 48). The assignment is therefore key to Kriewitz being in the right place at the right time to compile his Comanche-German glossary.

Meusebach's negotiations were the other critical element that led to Kriewitz's word list. The initial agreements made between the Comanche chiefs and Meusebach in March were to be confirmed and ratified at a second meeting to be held two months later. The nonaggression pact was thus sealed in Fredericksburg with celebrations and gifts from the Germans to the Comanches on May 9, 1847. Terms included protection by the Comanches for German settlers on grant land between the Llano and San Saba Rivers, and German protection for Comanches visiting German colonies, towns, and settlements "as long as they walk in the white path"; a promise from the Comanches not to disturb or molest German colonists in settlements on the Llano River, indeed to help them and report any misconduct by individual Indians, and similarly the Germans promised to aid the Comanches against their enemies when there was a threat of injury or horse theft; permission for the Germans to survey the grant as far as the Concho River and even up to the Colorado without fear of being disturbed or molested, in exchange for which Meusebach would ensure the Comanches received additional gifts and provisions amounting to at least $2,000; fourthly, an agreement by both parties to "use every exertion to keep up and even enforce peace and friendship" between them and to include other colonists "always and forever." Not written into the agreement but requested, perhaps insisted on, by the Comanches was the placing of a representative of the German settlers to live among the Indians to serve as an intermediary.[2] Kriewitz took on this role, and it was during his residency at Santa Anna's camp that he gathered the data that became his word list.

Interpretations differ as to appropriate characterization of Kriewitz's time with the Indians. Was he a hostage, an agent, a (paying?) guest, a goodwill ambassador? Because of the lack of a written agreement about the terms of his stay, it is hard to be sure. It is also difficult to be certain whether or not the nature of Kriewitz's relationship with his hosts, or theirs with him, changed over time. The published translation of Kriewitz's own recollections fifty years later (1896) states: "In addition a German was to be designated as an Indian agent. He was to serve as a mediator in the exchange of trade relationship, and, in order to better understand the Indian, he was to live among them" (Penniger 1896, 118; 1971, 48).

More light can be shed on Kriewitz's curious status by considering Comanche customs of alliance. Among Plains Indian societies it was not unusual to either explore or cement political agreements by swapping members who would go to live with the alternate group and possibly assimilate through marriage or fictive kinship. Persons assuming such a role were at once hostages and diplomats, but could easily become friends or family members, and their continuing presence with the alternate group mitigated against failure of the overture or the eruption of hostilities.[3] This Native custom was at times invoked in some fashion in relations with Euro-Americans. Thus in spring 1786, following an accord between the Comanches and Spanish of New Mexico, Francisco Xavier Ortiz spent three weeks living in eight different northern Comanche camps. Later in the year it was stipulated that four Spanish interpreters would reside among the Comanches, plus two with the Navajos (John 1975, 681–83, 710–11). Such interpreters were "somewhat akin to modern diplomatic representatives," with defined duties—spending most of their time in the Indians camps, even during war expeditions, supervising when New Mexican traders called on the camps, and above all communicating between the camps and the Spanish governors (Kenner 1994, 55–56). In turn Comanche headmen were invited to send their sons, with guardian relatives if need be, to Santa Fe or Mexico City for schooling. The Comanches who took in the Mexican political refugee José Francisco Ruiz during the 1810s (e.g., Ruiz 1972) or who hosted Anglo visitor David Burnet in 1818–19 (see chapter 8) may have expected that these outsiders would serve some similar purpose as representatives of advancing societies.

When Meusebach and company sought an interpreter to help them open negotiations with the Comanches, they hired someone whose experience was comparable to these earlier intercultural emissaries, one "Lorenzo de Rosas, a Mexican who had been kidnapped by the Comanches as a child and was familiar with their ways" (Zesch 2004, 27; Penniger 1971, 38). And when the German party was first greeted by Comanches, two among the Indians caught Roemer's attention, an eighteen-year-old fully assimilated white captive named Lyons, and a twelve-year-old chief's son who had been held prisoner by the Anglos in San Antonio after the Council House Fight and who spoke fluent English (Roemer 1983, 243, 279–80).

Kriewitz's function seems most like that of Noah Smithwick. In late 1837 this young ranger from Coleman's Fort near Austin spent three months at the invitation of some Penatekas in the camp of headman Muguara on Brushy Creek in present southern Williamson or Milam County, Texas, to talk about the possibility of a treaty (Smithwick 1900, 172–97).[4] Smithwick related in later years that the Indians had requested a "commissioner," and that he functioned as a "mediator" (Smithwick 1900, 172, 195), but also noted that he was given an Indian name (Smithwick 1900, 175), the first step in assimilation, and that "the old chief and his head wife always called me son" (Smithwick 1900, 192). While Emil Kriewitz went with the Indians only after the German treaty was executed, his role and Smithwick's were much the same in satisfying the Comanche desire for a resident member of the alternate group. Alliance exchanges were ideally reciprocal, but not always perfectly so. When accepting a German representative, the Comanches in turn reserved the right to visit the houses of the Germans, though all concerned probably understood that proud nomads were not very likely to spend much time in town.

When other candidates for the Comanche assignment withdrew, Kriewitz says he "decided to risk his 'scalp,'" because the safety of the proposed colonies along the Llano and of Fredericksburg itself depended on the friendliest possible relations with the Indians" (Penniger 1971, 48–49). As Smithwick put it, "the Indians were so treacherous that the office of commissioner was not one to be coveted" (Smithwick 1900, 173). The risk to Kriewitz's scalp was likely real because the Comanches reportedly had been subjected to an anti-German propaganda campaign by a white trader whom they had visited on the Brazos River, who feared losing commerce if the Indians came to favor the Germans in the Fredericksburg area. The Germans would take all their land and their horses, this man told the Indians, and he urged them to exterminate the community that threatened his business.[5] No doubt these worries compounded other ones. Hadeler (e-mail to Gelo, March 21, 2015) has suggested that the Comanches, having been swindled in the past, wanted a hostage to ensure payment of the promised treaty goods. This explanation is entirely plausible; at the very least, they associated "agents" with goods, as one was stationed at the Torrey Brother's trading post near Waco (Roemer 1983,

195). Also, the Penatekas were still smarting from the treachery of the Council House Fight in San Antonio eight years earlier, when a trade visit turned into a bloody melee; Old Owl said as much in his speech at Meusebach's treaty council (Penniger 1971, 44–45; Brice 1987; Kavanagh 1996, 261–64). Kriewitz's first challenge therefore was to allay fears among the Comanches that something like the white trader's allegations might be true. He evidently succeeded, and by and large the relationship between Kriewitz and Chief Santa Anna was one of trust and good faith (cf. Luther 2013, 51; Hadeler n.d.; Hadeler 2010). Berghaus states that the information for the map of locations of Comanche divisions and bands included with his article originated from Santa Anna. It is likely that much (perhaps all) of the lexical information also came from Santa Anna, who according to Kriewitz spoke Spanish and a little English. Santa Anna died during a cholera outbreak in December 1849.

A colorful and much repeated episode marks the end of Kriewitz's residency with Santa Anna. In August 1847, three and a half months after the conclusion of the Meusebach Treaty, the great chief and a group of Penateka Comanches visited New Braunfels. Meusebach was no longer Adelsverein commissioner general, so the German reception was led by Hermann Spiess, Meusebach's successor. Kriewitz was a member of Santa Anna's party, but was not recognized at first by the Germans, as he was in Indian attire and apparently thoroughly acculturated. Santa Anna had forbidden him to speak with the settlers during the visit. According to reports, one of the settlers became suspicious of Kriewitz during the meeting and in order to preserve his anonymity Kriewitz obtained pencil and paper and passed a note under the table identifying himself and stating his intent to separate himself from the Comanche group.

Louis Reinhardt, reporting the incident over fifty years later, tells how at age thirteen he accompanied the Darmstadt Forty to Texas in 1847 to create the Bettina colony on the Adelsverein land grant (Reinhardt 1899). Reinhardt describes the importance of the Meusebach Treaty and events surrounding the founding of the early German settlements. Despite this firsthand viewpoint, many details of Reinhardt's account of the New Braunfels episode are inaccurate (Biesele 1930, 156), but the account was reproduced not only in the July 1899 issue of the *Quarterly of the Texas State Historical Association* but also in the August 13, 1899, edition of the *Houston Daily Post*, giving Reinhardt's version of the events some credibility and currency. The relevant passage reads:

Kriewitz had been among the Comanches several months as commercial agent of the colonists at New Braunfels [here Reinhardt is mistaken] and Fredericksburg according to the wish of the savages themselves. But the Indians did not trust him, looking upon him as a spy; and it is said that his life was thrice saved by Santana's daughter. Kriewitz at the making of the treaty was dressed like an Indian; but at last one of our party recognized him and gazed intently at him. Hereupon Kriewitz then touched him under the table with his foot. Kriewitz was then handed a piece of paper and pencil, and he wrote back that he was Kriewitz, but that he could not hold open communication with them now; that on the journey back to the Indian camp he would try to get away. He went back with the savages as far as Comanche Spring [a location now inside Camp Bullis, a US Army installation north of San Antonio] and camped, and lay hid in New Braunfels three days while the Indians came to look for him. (Reinhardt 1899, 36–37)

Although unreliable in its detail, Reinhardt's account serves a valuable purpose in adding to our knowledge of Kriewitz, because Kriewitz himself formulated a response to it in which he corrects the record from his own recollection. In a nine-hundred-word letter drafted to the *Houston Daily Post* in reply to the August 13 article, Kriewitz refers to his role as "Indian Agent" and "hostage" but states that he never regretted volunteering and considers his "past among the Indians as the only white man at that time among a powerful warlike tribe as his best reminisces [*sic*] of his adventorus [*sic*] life" (Kriewitz 1899). Then, in contrast to his earlier statement that the reason for the Comanches' visit to New Braunfels was "the desire among the Indians for more presents" (Penniger 1971, 49), Kriewitz writes that their purpose was to introduce Santa Anna to the Darmstadt Forty, who had just arrived and planned to settle on the Fisher-Miller grant, north of the Llano River, and to make a second treaty for their protection. "[For] this purpose after a good deal of diplomace [*sic*] Santana and other chiefs consented to go to New Braunfels under my guidance. . . . As the Indians never had been so far South they were always afraid of treachery and I was virtually a prisoner during this time." The delicacy of Kriewitz's situation is illustrated by his attempt to talk with the German settlers while Santa Anna was taking a buggy ride around New Braunfels with Meusebach. The Comanches became uneasy when they noticed him missing, and he returned to find "mules packed, bow and arrows out of their quivers, the whole affair looked serious.—The Indians got quieter by my being again in their midst and the misery was cleared up. Santana could not stand the Buggy ride, got quite seasick, the Indians believed him poisoned, and me absent and feared an attack was plotted against them."

Kriewitz rejects as "very romantic" Reinhardt's claim that he left the Indians at Comanche Springs, hid several days in New Braunfels, and that his life was saved three times by Santa Anna's daughter. However, Kriewitz narrates how his life was in danger on the return trip when a Mexican member of their party, who, thinking that Kriewitz had eyes for his young "squaw," tried to shoot him. When the party arrived at Fredericksburg, Kriewitz was given permission to visit Captain Jean von Coll and Dr. Wilhelm V. Keidel until the evening, when he would reunite with the Comanches at Seven Mile Creek. "Our meeting with some good wine was prolonged till midnight. I started, hoping to find the Indians in camp, but arriving at the place there was nothing to be found, other than the coal and boughs where they had barbecued the beef.—By the trail I saw the Indians were in full flight. I followed them as rapidly as I could, hoping to catch them on the San Saba, and not there I went about 10 miles further on, and no Indians—my horse gave out, and luckily a branch with water was near, so I stopped for the night and next morning I went back and in two days came back to Fredericksburg, to the great surprise of my friends."

According to his account, Kriewitz made a good faith effort to reunite with Santa Anna's party; indeed, he could have risen to prominence in the tribe. "I often think my life might have been entirely changed, if I had kept my promise to join them in the Seven Miles Creek, as Santana insisted to make me his Son-of-Law, and offered me the Sub Chieftain-ship of Kotemoczy's band. In conclusion I have to state that 53 years ago the Comanches, warlike and powerful were faithful to their promise and could have driven every settler, Fredericksburg included, back to New Braunfels, and as this has not happened I claim the credit for."

Kriewitz's letter was apparently never printed; perhaps it was not even sent to the editors of the *Houston Daily Post*. Nevertheless, it is the more vivid and revealing of only two autobiographical perspectives from Kriewitz on his experience with the Comanches, during which his Comanche dictionary was compiled (see Penniger 1971, 48–49). It also raises the question: if Kriewitz left the Comanches more or less on a whim, did he have his word list with him in some written form? Or could he have created the dictionary from memory later?

Thus Kriewitz returned to Fredericksburg and ended his role as resident intermediary with the Indians (cf. Hadeler n.d.; 2010; Todd 2009). Shortly after this, in early September 1847, Kriewitz led groups of German immigrants (including the Darmstadt Forty) to the Llano to begin settlements; in this way Bettina, Leiningen, and Castell (in March 1848), which appear (albeit inaccurately located) on Berghaus's map, were founded.

The consensus is that Kriewitz's stay with Santa Anna was beneficial to the peaceful coexistence of the German settlers and the Comanches, whose hunting grounds they were appropriating. Biesele (1930) cites two affirmative sources: Viktor Bracht wrote to Germany from New Braunfels on August 30, 1847, "Santa Anna, the war chief of the Comanches, was here three days. . . . He assured us that the friendship for the Germans, whom he respected, would continue to be observed honestly, as had been the case thus far. Mr. Kriewicz [*sic*] of Potsdam has been living for some time with Santa Anna and his tribe,—a remarkable taste, but the affair seems useful" (Biesele 1930, 187). Bracht seems under the impression that Kriewitz's stay with the Comanches was entirely voluntary. Tiling (1913) summarizes, "the German Indian Agent Emil Krieswitz [*sic*] was very prudent and circumspect in his dealings with the different Indian tribes and secured the friendship of their chiefs for the German pioneers" (Biesele 1930, 187). It is unclear what Tiling means by "different Indian tribes," but clearly the community consciousness and the historical record retain an image of Kriewitz's accomplishment in the role of intermediary as valuable and positive. Kriewitz, too, felt that he had performed an important task (Penniger 1971, 49).

Nothing in what is known about Kriewitz tells us clearly why he compiled his Comanche-German word list in the first place. Was it out of his own curiosity and for his own satisfaction? Did he need something to occupy his mind during the months of his stay with the Penateka at Santa Anna's camp? Was it to help him communicate better with the Comanches? Or to assist other German settlers on the Texas frontier in their dealings with the Native inhabitants? Any evidence there may have been of dissemination of the list in Texas has not survived. Was it done as an assignment from Berghaus, the leaders of the German settlement project, or some other agency? We have no clues.

For four decades Kriewitz continued to lead a productive life in Texas, moving to Castell in 1852 and opening a general store with Franz Kettner in 1853. He had been signatory to the December 1847 petition to found Gillespie County, of which Fredericksburg is now the county seat. In 1857 he married Amalia Markwordt, eighteen years his junior, and they had eight children. The expectation Kriewitz expressed in the letter to his mother of February 14, 1847, that he would soon take a Mexican "squaw," apparently never came to fruition. In 1860 he is on record as signing a petition letter to Governor Sam Houston urging increased military security in the area of Mason, Llano, San Saba, Gillespie, Kerr, and Medina Counties, following the murder of settler Tom Milligan in his home near Mason (Bierschwale 1998, 550–51; Wurster 2008, 92–93). He was elected justice of the peace in June 1870, and served as postmaster in Castell from 1876 to 1883. Economic difficulties following removal of tariffs on imported wool, and a real-estate crisis around 1890 brought Kriewitz close to bankruptcy. He was ultimately forced to sell his ranch and home and died living in a small boarding house in Castell on May 21, 1902.

The question then remains: How did Berghaus come into possession of Kriewitz's information? No definitive answers are possible, though we may speculate based on the content of Kriewitz's contribution to the Berghaus article, the specifics (insofar as we know them) of his personal story, and the chronology of the historical context. Kriewitz himself makes reference to a visit he made to Germany after his stay with the Comanches: "If the Indians had decided to destroy those isolated settlements [on the Fisher-Miller grant], even Fredericksburg, they could have done so. But they remained true friends, and profitable trade relations were maintained. The writer claims credit for this relationship because even long after his return to Europe his Indian friends made inquiry concerning him" (Penniger 1971, 49). When was this return to Europe, after which Kriewitz clearly came back to Texas? Could it have been between late 1847, when we know he was conducting Adelsverein settlers to the Llano and when he signed the Gillespie County petition, and April 1851, when Berghaus was corresponding with Wilhelm Perthes, the publisher of the Yearbook, about Kriewitz's contribution to his article? The Sammlung Perthes archive in the Universitäts- und Forschungsbibliothek Erfurt/ Gotha holds a letter dated April 20, 1851, in which Berghaus writes: "Most Honored Friend! Pursuant to your stipulation I have made another map for the Yearbook, 1851 (III in the series as a whole). It is a very simple one of the hunting grounds of the Comanches in Texas, and I am enclosing it in addition to the article it belongs with and three other essays that will bring variety to the contents of the Yearbook" (Sammlung Perthes MFV 19A/4).

It appears from comments Berghaus makes in his article that he discussed some of the contents with Kriewitz in person. In describing his informant's contribution, for example, Berghaus refers to Kriewitz's explanation of the exact pronunciation of the word "Comanche," while in endnote *m* he remarks, "I must note that my informant was not sufficiently familiar with the ethnography of the rest of North America to know anything about the existence of the Shoshones." This suggests that Berghaus had attempted to follow up with questions to his informant about the Shoshones; while it is possible that this was done through correspondence, the more likely answer is that at least one conversation took place between them. Two other references in Berghaus's footnotes provide information about their communication. The clearest is the indication in endnote *p* that Berghaus had already published Kriewitz's notes on Comanche culture in 1850. It is possible, perhaps likely, that these notes were received first; that could explain why they were published separately. No mention is made of any Comanche glossary or word list in the 1850 publication of the cultural notes, and given Berghaus's evident excitement at having possession of it and his life-long tendency to publish every new discovery quickly, we might suppose that he had the cultural notes in his possession first and that the glossary followed.

The second footnote reference that reflects on the Kriewitz-Berghaus communication is the long quotation in endnote *k* from Kriewitz's February 14, 1847, letter to his mother. Written in Fredericksburg, the letter states that in two days Kriewitz will be heading into Indian territory; though he doesn't say it, we know that this refers to his journey to catch up with Meusebach, who is laying the groundwork for the treaty with the Comanches that will later necessitate Kriewitz's stay in Chief Santa Anna's village. This document therefore predates the glossary by seven months or so. (Berghaus refers in the 1851 article to Kriewitz's "long acquaintance" with the Comanches.) Did Kriewitz's mother live in or have connections in Potsdam and pass the letter along to Berghaus? The name Kriewitz is well known in that city, and the directory for 1849 lists five people by the name Kriewitz/Kriwitz (see Schulz 2012). There is even a Kriewitz Strasse. Did Berghaus become aware of Emil Kriewitz in this way? A comment by Eduard Buschmann, who was well acquainted with Berghaus and later built on Berghaus's 1851 article in his treatise on traces of the Aztec language in northern Mexico, ties Kriewitz unambiguously to residency in Potsdam when he notes the diverse spelling of Kriewitz's name: "Berghaus spells the name this way [Kriwitz] and this is the way it is spelled in the address calendar for Potsdam from 1847 to 1849; from that time forward (1850–4) *Kriewitz*" (Buschmann 1859, 365).

From the Texas end, there is little information. Hadeler (n.d.) reports that Kriewitz received title to town lot no. 235 in Fredericksburg from the Adelsverein on March 29, 1848. So he was probably still in Fredericksburg at that time. This is also the time that the Castell settlement was founded. Hadeler also tells us that Kriewitz sold the Fredericksburg lot on October 21, 1850, and again we may assume he was on location for that sale. We may speculate then, that sometime during the period April 1848 and October 1850, Kriewitz made the visit to Europe that he mentions in his "Recollections" (Penniger 1971, 49), and we may further suppose that during that time he met with Berghaus, perhaps discussing the glossary and his sketched map with him. If that is the case it would have given Berghaus time to prepare his article manuscript for Perthes by late April 1851.

It is also worth noting that Kriewitz makes reference in his cultural notes to Catlin's description of Comanche horsemanship and Cooper's representation of Indians. As an educated offspring of the nobility, Kriewitz could be expected to be familiar with James Fenimore Cooper's works (*The Last of the Mohicans* was published in 1826). He probably knew Catlin's *Letters and Notes on the Manners, Customs, and Condition of the North American Indians* in its original English version, first published in 1841, as Berghaus's German translation of this work appeared only in 1846, the year after Kriewitz departed for Texas. If he heard about the translation later, that might have been sufficient for Kriewitz to seek contact with Berghaus. Firm answers to these questions are elusive at the present time, nevertheless the substantive value of the Kriewitz/Berghaus glossary and article as contributions to and documents of Comanche ethnology is beyond doubt, and for this reason they merit closer evaluation in the context of the development of anthropological science in the United States and elsewhere.

8

Berghaus and the Development of American Anthropology

Berghaus produced his article on the Shoshones, Comanches, and Apaches at a time when geography, ethnology, and linguistics were forming and differentiating as modern disciplines. It is appropriate then to consider, for the first time, his influence on the course of ethnology and linguistics in North America.

Berghaus's personal relationship with Alexander von Humboldt and their shared approach to a broader geographical project and its dissemination have been outlined above. According to Humboldt, the human world in all its permutations, along with landforms, climate, and other geophysical features, had to be accounted for in a theory of a unified and orderly cosmos (Bowen 1981, 240–55; Bunzl 1996, 36–40). Humboldt affirmed to Berghaus in an 1848 letter the reassurance he took from the notion of a cosmic order during those politically troubled times (Bowen 1981, 255). Berghaus's principle of mixing cartographic, cultural, and linguistic information meshed well with Humboldt's holistic approach.

Berghaus also aligns with Humboldt's vision when he ends his Comanche sketch with warnings about the ill effects of "Indo-European" expansion on Native peoples and Kriewitz's critique of the German Texas immigration program. These comments, and similar remarks in the Physical Atlas and elsewhere (see above), resemble Humboldt's indictment of social inequality in Mexico, published in his 1811 essay on the politics of New Spain (Humboldt 2014), which Berghaus cites. Neither author is uncomfortable advocating political and social solutions even while remaining generally committed to dispassionate scientific inquiry. The underlying goal of amassing knowledge for the betterment of humankind had its roots in the philosophies of Immanuel Kant, Johann Gottfried Herder, and Antoine-Nicolas de Condorcet (Bowen 1981, 227–31) and can be traced also in the writings of Humboldt's early collaborator, Georg Forster, and to the accounts of Adelbert von Chamisso and other German naturalists and travelers.

Alexander von Humboldt's interest in human geography and his "sympathetic consideration of native civilizations" (Bowen 1981, 227) has a correlate in the scholarship of his brother Wilhelm, a founder figure of German anthropology. Wilhelm was particularly concerned with language and its value in reconstructing specific ethnic histories and mentalities (Bunzl 1996, 19–36). As early as 1827, Berghaus had used Wilhelm von Humboldt's notes on cultural progress among North American Indians for a publication in his journal *Hertha* (Berghaus 1827b). In his later years, Wilhelm von Humboldt was engrossed in North American Indian languages, which he learned about mostly through the grammars prepared by Jesuit missionaries, as well as those of Europe and southeast Asia. Berghaus's documentation of the Comanche language and his comparison with Shoshone are very much in keeping with this aspect of the all-Humboldtian agenda.

Meanwhile, other German scholars and adventurers were involved in home-grown proto-ethnology (Penny 2008) akin to similar developments in America (Bieder 1986). These movements articulated with each other and the geographic impetus in various interesting ways. It is clear from Berghaus's 1851 article that Germans were conversant with the work of American pioneers such as George Catlin, Albert Gallatin, and Horatio Hale, but there were also complementary German efforts. Prince Maximilian of Wied-Neuwied and Swiss artist Karl Bodmer recorded Native cultures during their exploration of the Missouri River in 1832–34 (Wied 1995, 2008–12). Wied was a protégé of Alexander von Humboldt and both were students of Johann Friedrich Blumenbach. The sources of the Missouri River had been located in 1829 by another German naturalist, Duke Paul Wilhelm of Württemberg, whose explorations beginning in 1822 included visits to Indian tribes (Paul Wilhelm 1973; figure 4).

In the same year that Berghaus's Comanche Yearbook article was published, Paul Wilhelm was headed for the western frontier once more, ending up this time in the vicinity of Fort Laramie, Wyoming. Württemberg's companion on the 1851 trip was artist and topographer Heinrich Balduin Möllhausen. Upon returning to Germany after this trip, Möllhausen became fast friends with Alexander von Humboldt. Then, with Humboldt's solicitation to Secretary of War Jefferson Davis, Möllhausen joined the 1853 transcontinental railroad route survey expedition through Comanche country under Lieutenant Amiel Weeks Whipple (Foreman 1941; Whipple, Ewbank, and Turner 1855; Wright and Shirk 1950, 1953). Following this trip and Möllhausen's reportage in Europe, Whipple and Humboldt launched a vigorous correspondence.

After his 1851 journey Paul Wilhelm visited Baron Ottomar von Behr in Sisterdale, Texas (Lich 2010; Ragsdale 2010). Behr, a founder of Sisterdale, was a prominent advocate of emigration to Texas and promoter of Adelsverein efforts (Behr 1847, 97–107), and an able naturalist who maintained ties with Germany and who counted Alexander von Humboldt among his associates. Behr was also friends with Bettina von Arnim, the German progressive writer for whom the freethinker commune of Bettina, Texas (a location included in Berghaus's map), was named. Another resident of Sisterdale was the geographer Ernst Kapp, described as a follower of Carl Ritter; Ritter has been characterized as a protégé of Alexander von Humboldt, though his science may best be seen as a reflex to Humboldt's (Crone 1970, 19–22; Bunzl 1996, 40–41; Jordan 2010). As mentioned above, Ritter, Humboldt, and Berghaus together founded the Berlin Geographical Society. In 1855 Paul Wilhelm was in the Texas German settlements again, visiting artist Carl G. von Iwonski in New Braunfels. Iwonski was famed both for his pencil sketches of Texas pioneers and his sculpted bust of Alexander von Humboldt (McGuire 2010). And the circle closes tidily in the person of Ferdinand Roemer, whom Kriewitz must have met in Fredericksburg in March 1847. Roemer had arrived in Texas to compile a geological report with a letter of introduction in his pocket from Alexander von Humboldt (Roemer 1983, i).[1]

This is one way in which the reach of the Humboldtian project extended to North America. It formed a bridge linking the academies and museums of Germany with the explorations and settlement of western North America, not least Texas. Berghaus and Kriewitz were participants in this phenomenon, at either end of the span. But what direct influence did the Humboldtian tradition, and Berghaus in particular, exert in the development of American anthropology?

"One of the founders of modern cultural anthropology, Franz Boas, was immersed in the geographic tradition initiated by Humboldt" (Tang 2008, 253n12); "Boas' anthropology may be viewed as uniting the intellectual currents emanating from both Wilhelm and Alexander von Humboldt" (Bunzl 1996, 19); "[Boas] often claimed that much of his intellectual inspiration derived from his fellow Prussian, Alexander von Humboldt" (Sachs 2006, 328). Franz Boas (1858–1942) was born in Minden, West-phalia, and trained at Heidelberg, Bonn, and Kiel universities. His doctoral advisor at Kiel, Theobald Fischer, was a student of Carl Ritter. Boas also worked with other heirs and respondents to the Humboldtian tradition, notably Rudolf Virchow and Adolf Bastien at the Royal Ethnological Museum in Berlin.

In 1887 Boas relocated to the United States, taking positions succes-sively at Clark University, the Field Museum in Chicago, the American Museum of Natural History in New York, and Columbia University. At Columbia he mentored two early generations of prominent American an-thropologists, among them German-born Edward Sapir, Austrian-born Robert Lowie, and children of German immigrants Alfred Kroeber, Ruth Bunzel, and Esther Schiff Goldfrank. Along the way, Boas and his students functioned as interlocutors with the various German schools that were transitional between Humboldtian geography and modern anthropology, such as Bastien's nascent professional ethnology, the "anthropogeogra-phy" of Friedrich Ratzel, and the *Kulturkreis* movement. A legacy of these engagements was Boas's suspicion of ready nomothetic explanations in favor of the patient collection of ethnographic detail. This approach, called historical particularism, was the hallmark of American ethnology in the early twentieth century (Harris 1968, 250–89; Penny 2008, 85–86). Fur-thermore, Boas's own personal career epitomized the evolution of (Ameri-can) anthropology out of (German) geography and physical science, as his research interests morphed from physics (the perceived color of seawater) to polar geography, then to Inuit ethnography, ethnography and folklore on a wider scale, and on to other branches of the American four-field ap-proach, including biological anthropology and linguistics.[2]

As far as Heinrich Berghaus in particular is concerned, his influence was much more concentrated, and confined to the field of linguistics. A

sense of urgency hung over the world of Native American language study
at the time Berghaus was writing his 1851 article. Knowledge of the Shoshonean and neighboring language groups was recent and only formative
(Schoolcraft 1851–57, 1:197). In 1824, as the first details of Comanche
and Navajo culture were making their way into print in English, the naturalist C. S. Rafinesque lamented that "the writers have totally neglected to notice the languages of those nations . . . often the only clue to
trace their origin and history" (quoted in Wallace 1954, 116). By 1826
the American statesman and ethnologist Albert Gallatin had set out on a
mission to amass Native American vocabularies by sending circulars to
traders and missionaries, but by 1846 his effort was no longer funded and
had stalled. That year, with his record of Texas languages remaining de-
ficient and his health in irreversible decline, Gallatin wrote to the Commissioner of Indian Affairs imploring that vocabularies be collected from
the Comanche and Pawnee delegations then visiting Washington, DC, but
his request went unanswered; those in the federal government who earlier supported him evidently had become preoccupied with the outbreak
of the Mexican War (Schoolcraft 1851–57, 3:397–400, 403). Shoshone
country had proven a special obstacle: "The attempts to penetrate this
region have been attended with sufferings and death" (Schoolcraft 1851–
57, 4:551). Another American linguist, Horatio Hale, collected success-
fully in the far West and discerned relationships among the Shoshonean
tongues, but Berghaus was poised to step into the breach with his own
important contributions.

Kriewitz and Berghaus's Comanche word list is indeed the earliest glossary of the language in print—almost. It immediately precedes the published lists collected by Texas Indian agent Robert Simpson Neighbors
(Schoolcraft 1851–57, 2:129–30, 494–505; it is interesting to note that
Neighbors and Kriewitz must have met at least briefly, as both were members of Meusebach's treaty expedition when it ended) and US Army explorers Randolph B. Marcy (Marcy 1853, 307–10; the vocabulary is not
reproduced in the later edition of Marcy's journal [Marcy and McClellan
1968]) and A. W. Whipple (Whipple, Ewbank, and Turner 1855, 54–55,
71–77). (Whipple's list was solicited using a blank schedule with English
and Spanish words obtained from the American Ethnological Society, and
thus appears to be a continuation of the Gallatin agenda, since Gallatin
was a founder of that organization.) The German list is also the longest of
these early ones, with 366 entries, compared to Neighbors's 213, Marcy's

146, and Whipple's 192. The only work to deny Berghaus's absolute claim to first rights is that of David Burnet, who published a "brief desultory and imperfect vocabulary of the Comanche language" in the July 3, 1824, *Cincinnati Literary Gazette* (Wallace 1954, 139–40). Burnet, the future first president of the Republic of Texas, had spent 1818–19 camped along the Colorado River headwaters, in close contact with Comanches. Burnet's list was submitted in direct response to Rafinesque, and consists of eighty-nine entries. Also, in 1841 William Kennedy had given Comanche words for the numerals 1–20 with some brief comments on the structure of the language (Kennedy 1841, 1:348). Berghaus did not acknowledge Kennedy's contribution to Comanche linguistics, modest though it is, though Kennedy's book had been translated into German (Kennedy 1845). Berghaus also neglected to make note of Wied's small Shoshone vocabulary published in 1841 (Wied 1995, 2:340), though he was aware of Wied's account of his trip up the Missouri and had mentioned it in annotations to his 1846 translation of Catlin (Catlin 1851, 354, 376, 380, 382).

The only other known Comanche vocabulary predating Berghaus's is found in the manuscript notes of the Mexican Comisión de Límites scientific expedition through Texas in 1828–29 compiled by French botanist Jean Louis Berlandier, yet another Humboldt admirer (Berlandier and Chowell 1828–29). While Berghaus might be faulted for missing Burnet's list, it is understandable that he remained unaware of the unpublished Mexican source. Apart from these two word lists, the record of Comanche before Berghaus's work consisted of a smattering of translated terms and personal names here and there in the then-unpublished official records of Spanish New Mexico (Espinosa 1907, 13–16; Thomas 1929, 296–98; 1932, 294–342), six names in artist George Catlin's account of the 1834 First Dragoon Expedition (Catlin 1841, 2:67–68), names of several signers of the 1846 Butler-Lewis Treaty (Winfrey and Day 1995, 3:49–50), and some names and terms, some spurious, noted in a paper by the English scientist William Bollaert (Bollaert 1850, 273–74).

Later manuscript Comanche vocabularies would include those compiled by Albert S. Gatschet of the Bureau of American Ethnology (BAE) (Gatschet 1884; 1893) and Charles H. Detrich, post trader at Fort Sill, Indian Territory (now Oklahoma) where the Comanches were settled in the 1870s (Detrich 1894; 1895). The earlier dated of Detrich's lists employs the linguistic schedule devised by John Wesley Powell and therefore appears to have been solicited by the BAE. Subsequent published lists, dictionaries, and texts include those by García-Rejón (1865; García-Rejón and Gelo 1995); Gatschet (1876b, 52, 62, 68 75, 84–85, 117–38); ten Kate (1885); St. Clair (1902a; 1902b, 271–340); Curtis (1930, 230–38); Becker (1931; 1936); Casagrande (1954a, b; 1955); Canonge (1958); Harston (1963, 187–94); Wistrand-Robinson and Armagost (1990); Kavanagh (2008, 515–22); and Comanche Language and Cultural Preservation Committee (2010). This corpus in turn has enabled a vigorous scholarship on Comanche phonology and grammar (e.g., Osborn and Smalley 1949; Canonge 1957; McLaughlin 1983; Armagost 1986; Charney 1993).

Berghaus's impact on linguistic research was practically instant. In pursuing connections between Comanche and other languages he stimulated the delineation of the Uto-Aztecan language family by his acquaintance at the Royal Library, German linguist Johann Carl Eduard Buschmann. In an 1854 scientific report, Buschmann reproduced the Kriewitz/Berghaus word list, using it, along with those of Neighbors and Marcy, to support his theory of linguistic affiliation (Buschmann 1859, 371–75). The classification was then refined by the Mexican philologist Francisco Pimentel, Swiss-American ethnologist Albert Gatschet, and the American anthropologists and linguists Daniel Brinton, Alfred Kroeber, Edward Sapir, and Benjamin Whorf during the later nineteenth and early twentieth century. Thus Berghaus was in the forefront of the impulse to record and classify Comanche and related languages. His linguistic contributions are all the more admirable because he was a polymath rather than a specialist.

Despite this pivotal role, many aspects of Berghaus's Comanche study have until now remained unappreciated. The first citation of Berghaus in the United States appears in Whipple's 1855 report on Indian languages, where brief mention is made of prior vocabularies (Whipple, Ewbank, and Turner 1855, 77). It seems likely that Whipple came to know of Berghaus through Humboldt. In his notebook on the Comanche language, Albert Gatschet wrote down Berghaus's Comanche river names, though without further comment, as well as items from Buschmann's version of the Kriewitz/Berghaus list (Gatschet 1884, 58, 107). Pimentel (1875, 2:19) credits "E. Kriwitz," whose work he obtained via Buschmann 1859. In addition to these authors, only Gatschet (1876b, 5) (a German publication) and García-Rejón and Gelo (1995) among all the subsequent Comanche language publications acknowledge Berghaus. He is not mentioned along with Buschmann and Whipple in the standard summary of North American language research before Boas (Goddard 1996b). The ethnographic detail that Berghaus published has likewise been neglected. The earliest standard twentieth-century history (Richardson 1933) and cultural description (Wallace and Hoebel 1952) of the Comanches do not cite him, nor do any of the numerous more recent Comanche histories and cultural studies. The ethnonyms that Berghaus recorded are generally absent from the foundational synonymies produced by American ethnologists, such as those appearing in Hodge (1907) and Sturtevant (2001).

Figure 2. Heinrich Berghaus. Courtesy Forschungsbibliothek Gotha der Universität Erfurt, Sammlung Perthes.

90

Figure 3. Alexander von Humboldt. Courtesy Everett Collection.

Figure 4. Duke Friedrich Paul Wilhelm of Württemberg. Chalk drawing by an unknown artist. Photo: Foto Besserer, Lauda-Königshofen. With permission Department of City History of the Museum of the Teutonic Order, Bad Mergentheim.

Figure 5. Emil Kriewitz. Courtesy Henrietta Kettner Keener.

PART II

Berghaus's 1851 Ethnological Article

9

The 1851 Article in Translation

PHYSICAL ATLAS

GEOGRAPHIC YEARBOOK

OF

COMMUNICATIONS ON ALL NEW DISCOVERIES OF IMPORTANCE

BY

DR. HEINRICH BERGHAUS

1851

III

GOTHA: JUSTUS PERTHES

On the Relationship of the Shoshones, Comanches, and Apaches

By the Editor

Accompanied by a map of the Comanche hunting grounds in Texas, Plate X

In my ethnographic picture book[a] and in the ethnographic section of the Physical Atlas[b] I grouped together under the heading "Shoshones or (and) Comanches" the long list of Indian tribes that stretch from the southern tributaries of the Oregon River on the one hand to the Gila River and beyond on the other hand across the Rocky Mountains to the plains of Texas, as belonging to a single linguistic family.

We probably received the first report about the Shoshones, under the name Snake or Serpentine-Snake Indians, from Umfreville, then a more complete account from Lewis and Clarke [sic], but without any information about their language.[c] However, we know of the Comanches and the other peoples of the northern regions beyond the Gila and in the surrounding area of New Mexico—among whom the Apache appear as the principal nation—through the excellent work of Alexander von Humboldt and the compilations that Vater has provided about their linguistic relationship, even though these are based on sources that leave a lot, if not everything, to be desired.[d]

The traveler Violet seems to have been the first to explain the Shoshones, Apaches, and Comanches as a single nation, connected by a common language.[e] According to him, the Shoshones, or Snake Indians, live in a wide area that reaches from the great ocean almost to the Rocky Mountains, or is from west to east 540 miles long and from north to south 300 miles wide. This area lies between the latitudes 38° and 43°N and stretches from 116°W to the Pacific Ocean or to longitude 125°W. It is luxuriant and fertile land, lies on the banks of numerous rivers that dissect it, and belongs to the so-called "undulating prairie," which is, however, frequently interspersed by wooded areas. The number of Shoshones is estimated to be 60,000, excluding the tribes living in the mountains, which could be another 10,000 strong; the Apaches are calculated at 40,000, the Arapahos[h] at 20,000 and the Comanches, with their subsidiary tribes, at 60,000 individuals. They all speak the same language, all have the same form of religion, the same customs and traditions.

Ruxton[f] too says explicitly that the Comanches who live in the flatlands of Texas are descended from the Shoshones or Snake Indians. Even though now, as he observes, 100 miles and more separate the hunting grounds of the two peoples, they were at one time, if not one people, certainly tribes of one single great nation; for even now they both speak the same language and have in addition many similar religious customs and folk tales in common with each other. The two are still even today the most numerous of all Indian peoples of the West; and the Comanches dominate uncontested in the eastern plains, as the Shoshones do in the Rocky Mountains and in the land stretching to the west. One branch of the latter is the Tlamath Indians,[g] the most warlike among the western tribes, and also the Utes, who, as it were, connect the Shoshones to the powerful Comanche people.

Ruxton goes on to observe that among the Shoshones, who are considered to be the most numerous of all Indian peoples, many tales have survived that purport to explain all those natural occurrences that go beyond their comprehension. Thus they tell of springs of fresh and undrinkable water that occur next to each other in their hunting grounds, and tie this phenomenon to a tale that sheds light on how Shoshones and Comanches have considered themselves to be one people from the beginning. In this tale, Wakananga is the father of the Comanches and the Shoshones, and the former have Wakomish and the latter Asaqua as their chief; but the Comanches claimed that their chief Wakomish also ruled over the Shoshones, who even owed them tribute, which the Shoshones did not agree with. The tale tells of the murder of Asaqua by Wakomish, as a result of which the great Wakananga turned the spring where the murder took place into bitter water and created another spring next to it with fresh water.

Since that day the powerful tribes of the Shoshones and the Comanches have been torn apart from each other and separated because out of the treacherous murder of the Shoshone chief there arose a protracted and bloody war, and in order to avenge that death scalps have been torn from Comanche heads in large quantities.

In the Rocky Mountains, between the headwaters of the Platte and the Arkansas, lies a small valley with a forest creek rushing through it and closed in by high, vertical limestone cliffs. *Les fontaines qui bouillent* [the springs that boil] is the name used by the Canadian beaver trappers for many mineral springs of various kinds impregnated with gas that emerge in close proximity to each other from the rock in this valley; the American hunters though, have found a special name for each of these springs and know exactly where to locate the "Soda Spring," the "Beer Spring," or the "Steam Spring."

For the Indians all these springs are objects of veneration; for them they are the dwelling place of a powerful spirit whose breathing produces the bubbles on the surface of the crystal clear water. The Arapahoes[h] in particular attribute to the water spirit the power to determine the success or failure of their war ventures, and when their warriors pass by the mysterious spring to search for their traditional enemy, the Utes, in the "Salt Valley," they never fail to offer a sacrifice to gain the favor of the "Manitu of the Waters" and be successful on their "war path."

There, a spring of crystalline water hisses and bubbles from a round hole in the white cliff wall, but it has such a bitter and revolting taste that the white man and the Indian spurn it; for the spring is cursed by a powerful spirit. But not two steps away, bubbling out from the same rock, there is a foaming, effervescent spring whose pleasant and refreshing tasting water, quite similar to seltzer water, is swallowed with equal gusto and satisfaction by reds and whites and even mules and horses. This is the "Soda Spring" of the hunters.

It is these two springs that the preceding tale of the Shoshones refers to. At the same time it locates for us the original homeland of the Shoshone and Comanche people, which we must look for at 39°N on the southmost of the three plateaus of the Rocky Mountains that Frémont introduced to geography under the name "Parks" (South, Middle, North Park; this north plateau at latitude 40⅔°N).

Bounded to the north by the Sahaptins, to the west by the Waiilatpu, Lutuami and Palaiks, the Shoshones (Shoshonees) or Snake Indians extend eastward to the east side of the Rocky Mountains ("extend eastwardly east of the Rocky Mountains"). The land of the Shoshones proper lies on the east side of the Snake or Lewis River. The western Shoshones, or Wihinasht, live on the west side. Between them and the Shoshones proper another branch of the same family, called Panasht or Bonnaks, has occupied both banks of the Snake River and the valley of the Owyhee (Hawaii?) tributary. The eastern Shoshones are always on a war footing with the Blackfeet and the Upsarokos. Hale says that the Utes (Utahs, Eutaws) and the Comanches (Cumanches) speak dialects of the Shoshone language. He adds, "The fact that the Comanches of Texas speak an idiom that is intimately related to the language of the Shoshones, if not identical to it, is supported by documentation from so many sources that it can scarcely be doubted."[i]

Contrary to these three testimonies by Violet, Ruxton, and Hale—among which that of the last named traveler, the philological researcher of the languages of the Oregon peoples, is of special importance—A. Gallatin asserts, "The claim by Hale that the Utes and Comanches along with the Shoshones speak one and the same language, seems doubtful to me and deserves closer investigation. If it proves to be founded in truth, this would be a very valuable addition to our knowledge of Indian languages."[j]

I am in a position to share a glossary of the Comanche language that I believe makes a small contribution to shedding light on the doubts raised by Gallatin. I received this word list from a young man who joined the Mainz Emigration Society in 1846 in order to build his own home in Texas.[k] I am including it in its entirety below because it is, as far as I know, the first that we possess in the language of the Comanches and ought to be suitable for investigating not only the relationship to the Shoshones but the position held by the Comanches in the entire long chain of North American peoples, especially also with respect to the Mexican nations.

With reference to the main word list that the remarks below relate to, I have added a comparative vocabulary of the Shoshone and Comanche languages,[1] from which it is evident that both tongues use exactly the same word for some concepts, and for others have very similar words, while for a third category of concepts no similarity at all obtains.

As the final conclusion from this comparative table I believe we can accept that Violet's, Ruxton's and Hale's conclusions are correct and that Gallatin's doubts are unjustified; that in fact the Shoshones and Comanches do belong to one common language family, and that this relationship is to be taken not only in the extended philological sense, such as arises when we speak of an Indo-European, Indo-Germanic, Aryan or Iranian family of peoples, but in the narrow sense of sister-languages, e.g. Italian, Romanian, Spanish; German, Danish, Swedish, English, etc.

As far as the pronunciation of the name "Comanche" is concerned, my informant, the young Texan settler, observes that in his long acquaintance with this people he has always heard the first syllable pronounced "Ko" and never Ka or even Ku; he is even inclined to pronounce the final syllable of the Spanish spelled name, i.e. "ches" not with "tsch" [tš], but with the pure sound of the German "ch" [ç]; therefore to say not "Komantschen" but "Komanchen." But here he is not quite in agreement with himself, because, according to his statement, the syllable "ches," "chen" is supposed to be an intermediate sound between a sibilant and a guttural sound, which is scarcely reproduceable by a European mouth.

Besides the word list, I am also indebted to my informant for an improvised hand-drawn sketch, elucidated by a table, of the dwelling locations of the Comanches in Texas, and also a description of their customs and traditions.

"The map," he says, "cannot and does not claim to be absolutely precise as to the course of the rivers. However, I am reasonably confident about the location of the grazing places within the separate tributaries of the upper Rio Colorado and of the Rio Brazos, together with the names of the individual tribes and of the tributaries. I have them from the mouth of Chief Santa Anna (named after the ex-president of Mexico), who is the leader of the principal (judging by the settlements) tribe of his people and is a very intelligent man, who speaks Spanish and also mangles some English."

Dwelling Locations of the Comanches in Texas

The Comanches, the most numerous Indian people in Texas, range across
the endless stretches between the Hog River (*Rio de Puercos*), the Colored River (*Rio Colorado*) as far as the source of the Red River (*Rio Roxo
de Nachitoches*); and frequently extend their raids to the other (i.e. right)
bank of the Great North River (*Rio grande del Norte*), leaving devastation and murder behind them. Because of these continual invasions whole
stretches have been deserted by their former inhabitants and are desolate.
In particular, the area of the northern Mexican provinces that lies between
St. Bernardino, Dolores, Jaguana, Revilla, and Monclova is afflicted by
the frequent incursions of the Comanches.

I. Tribes having their grazing places in the area of the Rio Colorado.

a) *Rio de San Saba* and *Conjo*.

1. *Santa Anna*; this chief with his tribe covers the grazing
    places between the Llano and St. Saba as far as the
    Conjo or Enehokue.

2. *Pahajoko* (i.e. in English: "*fuck in the water*"), first
    chief of all Comanche tribes known in the settlements,
    covers with—

3. *Kateumzi* (i.e. Old Owl) and with—

4. *Buffalo Humb* [*sic*] (i.e. Buffalo Hump) the hunting
    grounds between the Rio San Saba and the Rio Conjo,
    but extending more to the east.

b) Between the *Enehokue* and *Uranazwene*

5. *Nokoni.* 6. *Essekuita*; and 7. *Puheua*

c) Between the *Uranazwene* and *Narohono*

8. *Tanemoe.* 9. *Pero*

d) Between the *Narohono* and *Woquequahono*.

10. *Teua.* 11. *Nonenoe.* 12. *Taeuaraoe.* 13. *Quitarae.*

e) Between the *Woquequahono* and *Tagkanohi*
or *Pissapejunowa*

14. *Japarishka.* 15. *Quassare* (and the tribe of the Wichitas, which is a branch of the formerly great nation of the Chikasaws, and thus doesn't belong to the Comanches).

f) Between the *Pissapejunowa* and the *Passiwono*

16. *Kaesua.* 17. *Manakiko.* 18. *Nabachho* (and the Kitscha tribe, which is a small tribe consisting of the remains of the Keacheyes, Jonies; but especially feared as talented [?] [Berghaus's question mark] horse thieves).

II. Tribes having their grazing places on the watershed between the Upper Colorado and Brazos.

The area between the *Passiwono*, *Peoan* and *Pato Pinto* or *Ekaoque* (the latter drains into the Rio Brazos).

19. *Sariteka.* 20. *Aracho.* 21. *Togaroe.*

III. Tribes in the river area of the Rio de los Brazos.

Between the *Ekaoque* (*Pato Pinto*) and the *Tascoque* (*Rio Bosque*).

22. *Juchta*, and 23. *Waqoes* (*Wakoes*, i.e.: the Expelled)

The latter tribe has no more than 40–50 warriors.

IV. Between the Brazos, upper reach, and the Trinidad.

25. [*sic*]. *Tuachhare*, and 25. *Sozonis.*[m]

Between the Hog River (*Rio de Puercos*) and the mountains of Gua-delupe [*sic*] live the Li-Pans or Mezcaleros, who call themselves Haiz, i.e.: cousins of the Comanches, in other words, are related to them.[n]

The Spanish had a mission and a Presidio (*fort*) on the Rio San Saba both for the purpose of converting the Indians and especially for the exploitation of the very rich silver mines that were said to be nearby, and in the manner of all of these fortifications were manned by a strong garrison of 600 soldiers, not counting the large number of workers and their families.

The garrison is said to have, in its arrogance, killed the horses and even some of the warriors of a group of Comanches camping peacefully near the Presidio; as a result, all the Comanche tribes, including the Li-Pans and Apaches, who were related and friendly with them, formed an alliance against their oppressors, and with a force of many thousands surrounded the mission and took it after a siege of two and a half months. The legend says: because of hunger; and only one monk is said to have escaped, before whom the waters of the Colorado parted as he fled and swallowed the pursuing Indians in the waves as they crashed together again behind him. Hence the earlier name *El Brazos de Dios*. The destruction is said to have taken place in 1780.

The two word lists follow, whereby it is to be noted that the Comanche words must be read and pronounced as if they were German and the words of the Shoshone language as English.

Word List of the Comanche Language [The list is reproduced in translation and expanded form in chapter 12]

It will not escape the attentive reader that some words in the preceding vocabulary are borrowed from Spanish, e.g. the word *casa* = buffalo tent. In this case the borrowing is conspicuous because it concerns the naming of an object that the Comanches knew before the arrival of the Spanish. On the other hand, it is notable that they have invented names for objects that they came to know only after the arrival of the Spanish that seem to be derived more or less from their own vocabulary; this is particularly true for all words that refer to firearms.—Furthermore, I must note that the responsibility for the accuracy of the Comanche glossary is to be accorded to my informant and his not entirely clear handwriting.

Comparative Word List of the Shoshone and the Comanche Language [The list is reproduced in chapter 12]

We have recently received so many descriptions concerning the customs and traditions° that it might seem superfluous to add yet one more to their number. Nevertheless, it may be all the more worthwhile to read the remarks of my informant in so far as they betray a talent for keen observation and impartial judgment.ᴾ

Customs and Traditions of the Comanches in Texas

General View. Crudeness and wildness, disloyalty, cunning, cowardice and brutality are their most telling characteristics; whether all these flaws are more attributable to the negative influence of the white man himself seems to me beyond doubt, because in spite of all these flaws and vices several cases are known that would do honor to the most cultivated nations.

I was never able to elicit a poetic side from the Indians, any more than, during my long dealings with them, I saw one of those extraordinary riding displays that Catlin and several writers have provided such fabulous accounts of; nevertheless, the Comanche is a very good rider and unsurpassed in the use of the lasso and in the art of taming horses and mules.— He is serious and taciturn, even dignified in his council meetings, but jovial and fun-loving, not averse even to crude jokes in normal social behavior; and often I could not suppress a smile when contemplating an Indian in reality and those of Cooper and his like.

The Comanches are the tribe that has best resisted the corrupting poison of brandy, and I have only seen very few of them who really drank it, and then only in moderation, so that a corrupting effect never occurred.

Religion. As far as I have been able to find out, they worship a good and an evil being, the first in the sun and the second in the effect of diseases, misfortune, etc. The servants of their idols are the medicine men or Oakatas, unpopular and feared by the whole tribe, because superstition believes them to have direct dealings with both gods; they are supported by the tribe, never take a wife, and in old age take on an Indian boy to whom they teach their secrets and knowledge, and who then, following the death of his master, practices in his own right. When carrying out their art they act in a mystical and mysterious way; usually, the sick person is laid on a buffalo hide after he has ingested the medicine and a small fire is lit near him next to which the Oakata sits, wrapped in his blanket. Now the charms, spells, and the stroking of the body begin. From time to time, he uses a buffalo bladder to catch smoke as it pours from the fire which he then presses into his mouth with a strange clicking sound and then blows out again onto the afflicted parts of the body and rubs them with his hand. A strange instrument, in the form of a turkey wing where the feathers and connected bones with the flesh gone are still attached, complete this ceremony. At the upper end of the bone there is a pipe from which the magician produces shrill notes between spells, while he fans air or the smoke from the fire towards the sick person with the wing itself. The magicians have an important voice when it comes to deliberations about war and peace, and for this reason ambitious and hawkish chiefs always try to gain their favor. The belief in invulnerability is very widespread among the Comanches, and every warrior wears on his braid a small pouch filled with a certain powder; a main ingredient of it seems to be a small, resinous, aromatic-smelling nut.

Hunting and war are the warrior's sole occupations outside of his tent, and it is here that he develops all the acuity or instinct that the red race is gifted with; the former provides the livelihood for him and his family, the latter serves to increase his number of horses and to enrich him with blankets and other things. The numerous buffalo herds located between the Colorado and Brazos provide the tribes with their livelihood; either the whole tribe moves here or just individual families as required by the need for meat, to obtain dried meat to last for months; and when all the pack animals are loaded they move back to their old grazing places, where their herds, women, and children have remained. Hunting in the grazing places is very poor, which is why these hunting expeditions have to be extended over great distances. The Comanches have been living in a state of bitter warfare with the Mexicans since time immemorial, and each year the warriors of any tribe may make several raids into Mexico, where they attack individual villages, drive off the herds of horses and mules, slaughter every living thing in the separate ranchos with horrible brutality, and spare only small boys and pretty girls to take them back as slaves and prisoners. This is why with every tribe you find Mexicans, who, when they are grown up, have been trained to be brave warriors and, as Comanches within the tribe, have even turned into worthy tribe members. The captured Mexican girls are either taken as wives or, as also frequently happens, are bought back by the government.—One and a half years ago, Americans bought several Mexican girls and paid on average 60 dollars for each one.

Body adornment and clothing. When in camp, the Indian spends most of his time with jewelry and adornment; he spends hours with his painting, and he will quite calmly erase painting that has taken hours to do just because of a single bad line and will start over again. His painting follows no pattern and only the tribal mark, the red line around the eyes, is common to all.

The hair is parted and is worn half long, on both sides, forward and at the back of the head, woven in braids; in addition, a long, artificial braid plaited from buffalo hair is attached to these and adorned with broad silver disks. Feathers or bones are frequently used for decorating the hair. The ears are pierced by many brass rings, on the lowest one on each side hangs one of the larger mother-of-pearl shells, which they trade for from tribes whose range extends to the Pacific Ocean.

For decorating their necks, they take only beads of 4 to 6 inches in length, that are made out of one shell; 3 or 4 good mules usually have to be given to acquire one of these. Frequently this jewelry is decorated with a sun beaten out of silver.

The arm adornments are brass rings that are worn only on the upper arm and are usually artfully filed by their owners.

Their footwear is moccasins with buffalo soles, more or less decorated with beads and fringes, according to the taste of the owner. The leggings are of leather, and red and blue cloth, the latter worn more on ceremonial occasions and then usually having a long piece of embroidery in the front; they are fastened to a belt around the hips, which also holds the long red or blue loincloth, where the two ends hang down in the front and back. They wear shirts only rarely, and then only chiefs who have received them as gifts.

The main article of clothing is the blanket, in which they wrap themselves and which is either a tanned buffalo hide or one of the large woolen varieties that are woven in Europe. For ceremonial processions or peace treaties they wrap themselves in blankets of red and blue cloth sewn together and decorated on the back side with a long tasteful piece of embroidery. This costume gives especially a troop of mounted Indians a picturesque and fantastic appearance. Every facial hair, even eyebrows and lashes, is carefully plucked out with a small tweezers, which results in a gruesome expression for the eyes.

Weapons. The majority of them are equipped with firearms, more specifically the long American rifle, in the use of which they have attained as high a level of skill as their white neighbors. Besides this gun, the Comanche also is equipped with a bow and arrow and is unsurpassed in the art of using these, especially when hunting buffalo. The lance is very widespread; the tip is usually a dagger blade, and it is decorated at the upper end with a horse tail or the scalps of slain enemies. The use of the shield, made from the circular piece of a buffalo hide and covered hollow with a tanned buckskin, seems to have been fairly well eliminated by the use of firearms, for I have seen them used by only a few and then it seemed as if the purpose was to display the scalps that hung from them.

Tomahawks, although known and having their own name, are not in use, unlike the long knives in a home-made sheath; these are worn in the belt.

Saddles and tack. The Comanches are very skilled at making saddles from wood or bone, and though they have some similarity with the Hungarian buck-saddles [stock saddles] they are much lighter and delicate in the way they are worked. The women ride like the men, but with shorter stirrups; these are very wide and made of wood. The bits are Mexican, and they get them by stealing them from Mexican territory and by bartering; the tack is often covered with silver discs and crescents, a luxury that they seem to have adopted from the Mexicans.

Huts. The huts or tents of the Comanches are conical, consisting of tanned buffalo hides sewn together that are stretched over a mass of poles, which provide the support for the tent, and at the same time form a flap for an opening to the tent toward the top that can be opened or closed, as desired. The opening or entrance is covered by a hanging blanket. The interior of the tent is covered with pelts, on one side the weapons and trophies are arranged, close to which are the dried meat supplies wrapped in skins, while across from this the beds of the parents and children can be found. When it is cold, there is always a small fire lit in the middle, and the smoke exits through the upper opening.

Mourning the dead. When an Indian dies, the closest relatives cut their hair very short, go to the residence of the deceased, and intone here with the surviving wives and children the terrible dirge, which lasts two days and nights, during which the female members make cuts in their arms and chest while the men, painted to the hips in vermilion, sing of the virtues of the dead man. The deceased is buried in his best finery along with all his weapons, and the most precious horses, often as many as 20, are slaughtered and their blood must run into the pit prepared on behalf of the dead man.—A remarkable sense of piety drives the Indians to bury the deceased at home; I know of a case where an adopted son held the dead man in front of him on his horse for four days, at the hottest time of the year, to bring him to his tribe.

Games. The passion for games is probably shared by all Indians, and the usual game among the Comanches consists of a mass of sticks, 24 of them, that have different notches and colored symbols; they are taken in the player's hand and thrown onto a longish rock; the sticks that remain lying on the rock are counted, and one of the players wins depending on the amount, the notches and color.

Dance. Dancing is crude and untrained, and is limited to jumping, back to back with another dancer in time with the music, or moving forward very slowly in a long line, with arms closed tightly around the person in front, and stepping forward according to the rhythm.

Music. The instruments are extremely simple and consist of a kind of drum and a small gourd with tiny stones in it; in particular, the rhythm is kept with this while the shrill notes of the women mix with the deeper ones of the men and quite suddenly plunge from the highest to the lowest guttural tones of an Indian throat.—The ones striking the gourds usually sit holding in their left hand an unstrung bow and at the same time a bouquet while accompanying their songs by rattling the gourd with their right.

Lifestyle. The Comanches live in small divisions, because owing to the many horses and mules that each one more or less owns, a large mass of animals cannot be kept together due to grazing; someone who is a brave warrior or a lucky horse thief always owns a large number that can range from twenty to several hundred.

Chiefs. The tribes are ruled by a war and a peace chief; the former honor is hereditary within the family, the latter is elected, and this happens when the tribe is dissatisfied. The power of the chiefs is very limited, since every decision is debated and voted on, where the majority decides. Every family father has a seat and a vote, as do young warriors who have distinguished themselves or have taken at least one scalp.

Polygyny. Polygyny exists and a man's wealth or his worth is to be measured according to the number of his wives. The Comanche always lives only with a favorite, until she is old or doesn't please him any more; then she is demoted and must yield to a younger, more beautiful woman, until she meets the same fate. These demoted wives receive the meat they need to live from their husbands, but they live in a special tent next to his, and maintain their own household with their children. The Indian quite often trades his wife and, if she already has children, gives a few horses and mules into the bargain as compensation.—A girl is bargained for with her father and the usual price for a very pretty one is: two good horses and mules, two wool blankets, and some powder and lead.

Adultery and Marriage. As long as the fair sex is unmarried its members are not accountable to anyone concerning their lives, which freedom is not left unutilized by the red beauties either; however, a correspondingly strict condition becomes operative when she is the wife of an Indian, and a violation is punished by the husband either with death or in most cases by cutting off the nose and one ear, which seems to be practiced frequently, because in every tribe one sees a number who have been operated on in this way. Manhood is evidently attained during the ninth or tenth year for I saw husbands who still seemed to be children.

Activities of Women. The women are in a real sense the beasts of burden and they are responsible for all heavy tasks, while the man only obtains the meat necessary for living. Everything else, such as watching over the herds of horses, the cutting, drying, and smoking of meat, the loading of pack animals, the striking and erecting of the tent, the saddling of horses, even that of the Indian himself, and the replenishing of his weapons, is left up to them, and I have often seen these slight and delicately built beings almost succumb under the weight of the long poles that serve to support the large tent, while the lord and master sat on his buffalo hide quietly smoking his cigarrita watching the vain attempts of his wives to put up the tent without taking any part himself. She also has to take care of tanning the hides and making his leggings, moccasins, etc. and most of them are very skilled at making very pretty embroidery with beads using a simple instrument, the awl, where instead of thread only the dried sinew of a deer is used. Her clothing consists of a dress of blue cloth with an opening for the head usually encircled by a narrow piece of beaded embroidery on red cloth, with wide sleeves that do not quite reach to the elbow, and usually with a broad red stripe inserted on each side of the seams. Moccasins, with close-fitting leather leggings sewn on to them, as well as a mass of brass rings that start at the wrist, complete her costume. A band or string is looped around the hips, where the make-up pouch hangs, which is embroidered with beads on both sides and contains the case for the awl. The hair is worn half long and parted, but not braided, and the face is painted with a vermilion solution, and a red ring, the symbol of the tribe, is drawn around the eyes. Only a few women wear earrings and then only small ones. The eyebrows and eyelashes are not plucked like the men.

We do not yet have a word-list of the Ute language with which we could verify Ruxton's and Hale's claim that they speak a dialect of the Shoshone language. They have their grazing grounds on the salt lake of the great inner basin of Upper California, which for that reason also often carries their name. This lake lies at latitude 41°N. Southwest of it, at latitude 37°N, Frémont shows the grazing grounds of another tribe by the name of Paiute,[q] which is evidently related to those Utes. Gregg estimates the number of Utes (Yutas) at 10,000. They spend the winter in the valleys and hunt buffalo during the summer. Although they maintain peaceful ties to the government of New Mexico, they force all traders and hunters they meet to pay a tribute and often also inflict the most brutal acts of violence on them.[r] The knowledge we can glean from older accounts about the Apaches[s] has recently increased significantly thanks to the advance of the North American people westward; but to date we have not received any information about their language, so that we still find ourselves in the position of having to take on good faith the claims of travelers that the Apaches form a single people with the Shoshones and the Comanches. Those Apaches residing on the east side of the Rio del Norte are usually called Mezcaleros after one of their favorite foods called Mezcal, the baked root of the Maguey—and a similar plant. By far the larger part of the Apache tribe congregates in the western regions, on the other side of the New Mexican mountain range, in the area of the Gila River, and is known by the nickname Coyoteros, supposedly because these Indians eat the meat of the Coyote or prairie wolf. For the tribe names by which the Apaches in New Mexico are known I refer the reader to the work of Wislicenus.[t] The Apaches have repeated their depredations so often and in such a terrible manner that a large number of farmers (rancherios) have been forced to leave their properties (ranchos) and the wide space between New Mexico and the boundaries of the state of Durango is now entirely depopulated and has, as it were, become a desert;—a consequence of the moral degradation and degeneration of the Spanish race in Mexico, where one government overthrow follows another only to serve the selfish purposes of parties and individuals, where everyone wants to rule and nobody wants to be ruled, which has led to a condition of anarchy that the Apaches have well understood how to exploit. Now that New Mexico, California and the lands up to the Rio Gila have passed to the United States, the president of the North American Union has an Augean stable to clean out, which, if the Apaches are to be controlled, must necessarily lead to an increase in the standing army of the Union States.

The river regions of the Rio Gila and the Rio Colorado (of the West) are an ancient seat of semi-civilized Indian peoples, such as the Moquis (Mawkeys, Munchies) and the Navajos (Navajoes, Navijos, Navahoes, Nabajoas), among whom the latter are said to be linguistically linked with the Utes, and therefore with the Shoshones and Comanches. A more exact investigation into the knowledge of the idioms of these and other tribes in the named river regions is a task, the resolution of which the officers and officials of the North American government, who are used in those regions for administrative and military purposes, should preferably see as an obligation.

During the advance of the North American army from New Mexico to California, Emory wrote down a short list of twenty words from the language of the Coco-Maricopas, a tribe settled near the Rio Gila. Concerning this, Gallatin observes that this language has no similarity with any other Indian language known to him. The word for "man" is "Apatsche," from which Gallatin concludes that the Coco-Maricopas are a tribe of the great Apache people, which according to him could not be counted as Shoshone and Comanche. It is, he adds, a peculiar characteristic of several Indian tribes that the name by which they refer to themselves means "man" in their language, by which they mean to assert their superiority in comparison to other tribes. For the Algonkins, the names "Lenno-Lenape" and "Illinois" are quite usual, and suchlike examples are to be found among the Athapascas, the Araucanas and several other American Indian peoples.[u] (In the Delaware idiom of the Algonkin languages Lenno "man" is called Lenape, "an Indian.")

Whether or not the Apaches are related to the Shoshones and Comanches, and research into their languages must decide this, it nevertheless deserves pointing out that all three nations, as far as their geographical situation is concerned, are inland dwellers, like all the great Indian nations of North America, the Sioux, the Athapascas, the Algonkins, of whom none, or only a few in very isolated instances, reach the shores of the Pacific Ocean.[v] These shores shut out all the numerically great nations absolutely, and the entire sea coast from the far north down to the foothills of St. Lucas, and in particular the stretch that lies between latitude 49° and 32°N and forms a narrow coastal band, is occupied by a large number of small tribes who speak in distinctly different tongues.

The Athapascas are an exception here: Dialects of Tahkali, one of their branches, are spoken by two tribes close to the mouth of the Columbia River and by the Umkwas on the southern sea coast at latitude 43°N. These three tribes, small in number, are to be viewed as isolated outposts of the great Athapasca family, from whom they are separated by peoples speaking other languages.[w]

Another exception seems to present itself in the case of the Shoshones. Not far from the California coast and only a short distance from the place where the peninsular separates itself from the mainland (32½°N latitude), there lie two missions close to the foot of the coast range and in its gorgelike valleys: San Juan Capistrano, at 33°35′, and San Gabriel, at 34°12′N latitude. The Indians, whom the priests have brought together in these compounds partly through persuasion and partly by force, in order to teach them agriculture and crafts,—which has always had very dubious success,—speak the Netela language in San Juan and the Kidsch (kij) language in San Gabriel, two languages that Gallatin, having compared them with vocabularies compiled by Hale, is inclined to consider as sister languages of Shoshone.[x] The similarity, so he says, is too great to be attributable to random contact; nevertheless, to classify the Kidsch, and Netela, and Shoshone languages as branches of the same family is doubtful on the basis of the testimony that claims to guarantee and justify this similarity.

In my estimation, this similarity is somewhat far-fetched. Both languages, Kidsch and Netela, have, with the exception of the numerals, only very few words that show similarity, and the similarity to Shoshone words with the same meaning is very distant, which is true even for the numerals.

Even if the Kidsch and Netelas really are branches of the Shoshones, they are not to be viewed as original inhabitants where we find them in the Californian coastal lands, but as strangers; for it is well enough known that the Spanish priests in these parts often brought their neophytes from a very long way away on the other side of the mountain range using the force of weapons, ostensibly to make Christians of them in the missions, but in fact to use the labor of these Indians for self-seeking purposes for the enrichment of an ignorant clergy and a crude pack of soldiers. Within the last 15 years, since 1835, several missions have collapsed and their buildings have been demolished; most of their former Indian residents hang around the presidios and small towns as pathetic day laborers and beggars, and not a few have returned to their wild brothers.

It is said of the people of the interior that they are all advancing in a southerly direction. The Shoshones, now in the area of the Columbia River, at latitude 48°N, used to inhabit the land of the Satsika or Blackfeet that lies in the drainage system of the Saskatchewan, at latitude 49°N. The Cheyennes, the Kiowas and Comanches are given as another example of this southward flow of peoples, which was merely a continuation of the migration of the Tolteks, Chichimeks, Acolhus, Nahuatlaks, Tlaskalteks and Azteks and other Mexican peoples since the middle of the sixth century A.D.

Another noteworthy phenomenon is the separation and distribution of some families. In the Selish family we find the Atnahs and the friendly village at latitude 53°½N, the Flatheads and Piskwas on the upper Columbia, the Niskwally, Cowelits and Tchikalish on its far side, and the Nsiethawus or Killamuks completely separated from the other tribes at latitude 45°N along the coast on the south side of the Columbia estuary.

These occurrences have led people to suspect that the many small tribes along the sea coast are the remains of nations who supposedly invaded Mexico, a hypothesis that Gallatin has called as arbitrary as it is baseless, but which nevertheless appears to be worthy of closer evaluation, when one recalls that in Mexico many more than twenty languages are common, suggesting very diverse origins of its peoples.

Let us hope that the government of the United States will succeed in bringing about peaceful conditions with the warlike nations of the Rocky Mountains and the Californian Plateaus, to create for intelligent observers the opportunity to study these nations according to their customs and usages, their religious views, their languages, legends, and traditions that appear to offer so much material concerning the history of American humanity. In particular, this material may be expected from the Navajos and the Moquis, those peoples who have emerged from the most rough and savage conditions in the river region of the great Colorado of the West. A. von Humboldt has already energetically directed our attention to them,[y] although we are not yet in a position to say whether a close or distant relationship exists between their language and the Mexican tongues.

May those laudable efforts by the North American government not come to grief because of the "camp of the Israelites" that the Mormon sect has set up on the Great Salt Lake of the Californian basin in order to establish on its banks, and in the valleys whose rivers empty into it, a political community, a state, based on religious fanaticism; may the Washington government be in a position to rein in the rejects and refuse of Indo-European peoples, who in their drive to the goldfields of the San Sacramento in the nineteenth century are simply imitating what drew their predecessors to Peru and Mexico three centuries earlier, the gold and silver territories of the New World. If the government does not step in soon with serious measures, then it is to be feared that the small and weak tribes of the Californian aboriginals will soon disappear from the earth brushed aside by the numerous adventurers, thieves, and vagabonds who have made their way to California, and their histories will be lost.

Notes

^a *Die Völker des Erdballs nach ihrer Abstammung und Verwandtschaft u.s.w.* Brüssel und Leipzig, 1845; I, p. 288. [The Peoples of the Globe According to Their Heredity and Relatedness, etc. Brussels and Leipzig, 1845; I, p. 288.]

^b Ethnographische Karte von Nordamerika. Juni 1845. [Ethnographic Map of North America. June 1845.]

^c *Edw. Umfreville, the present state of the Hudson's Bay.* London, 1790; p.198, 199,—*Lewis' and Clarke's Travels from S. Louis by way of the Missouri and Columbia Rivers to the Pacific Ocean*, London, 1809; p. 180. Cf. Adelung and Vater, Mithridates, III, 3, p. 251, 255.

^d *A. de Humboldt, Essai politique sur le Royaume de la Nouvelle Espagne. 2me Edition.* Paris, 1825. I, p. 383ff. Adelung and Vater, Mithridates, III, 3, 172–182.

^e *Violet, Narrative of Travels and Adventures in California.* Edited by Marryat. London, 1843.

^f *Ruxton, Adventures in Mexico and the Rocky Mountains. London,* 1848.— Ausland [= Das Ausland. Ein Tageblatt für Kunde des geistlichen und sittlichen Lebens der Völker], 1848 [should be: 1849] August 20, No. 199, p. 795, 796.

^g The Tlamath, Tlamatl or Clamet, whose actual name is Lutuami, do not form a part of the Shoshone nation but rather comprise a people of their own with their own language which is quite distinct from the Shoshone tongue. To the east they border on the western group of Shoshones, live along the source tributaries of the Clamet River and of the lake of the same name, and are a warlike tribe, who are a danger to the traders that must cross their territory on their way to California. They live in a constant state of feud with their southern neighbors, the Schasties and Palacks, taking slaves whom they sell to the Waiilatpu and Kalapuyas who live to the north of them.—*Hale's Ethnology and Philology. Vol. VII of the U.S. Exploring Expedition; and his Indians of North-West America in Transactions of the American Ethnological Society.* New York, 1848; Vol. II, p. 17, 18.

^h [Berghaus employs the number 8/letter *h* twice, the first time out of order] In *Die Völker des Erdballs* [Peoples of the Globe], I, p. 289, I assigned the Arrapahos, Arrapahoes or Arrapahays to the linguistic family of the Shoshones and Comanches, based on the information provided by Violet (see note 5 [note *e*]) that they speak the same language as these peoples. According to Gallatin, the Arrapahoes, Arrapaoes or Atsina, who are identical with the Rapid or Fall Indians or Fat-Bellies (Gros-Ventres), have a separate language, from which we have only a meager list of twenty-six words. They live between the south arm of the Saskatschewan [*sic*] and the upper Missouri.—*Trans. of the American Ethnol.* Soc. Vol. II, p. XCIX, CVI; 96 and 98.—These Fat-Bellies are not to be confused with the *Gros-Ventres* of the Missouri or the Minetaries. The latter speak Upsaroka or the language of the Crow Indians.—Ibid. p. 21.

ⁱ *Trans. of the American Ethnol.* Soc. Vol. II, p. CVIII, 18, 62.

ʲ Gallatin's own words are: *"This appears to me doubtful, and should be investigated. If found to be true, it would be a most valuable addition to our knowledge of Indian languages."*—Trans. ibid. p. CVIII.

ᵏ How the young emigrant viewed the life of a settler after about one year of his stay there, can be seen from the letters he sent to his mother. On February 14, 1847, he wrote from Fredericksburg, among other things and in a somewhat crude manner, the following:—

From among the thousands who have migrated here (to Texas) you will not find ten who say that it is good here and better than over there; for they all bring the old German sour dough with them, stick to it like glue, and even here allow themselves to be beaten to death like true dumb Germans [the idiom "deütscher [*sic*] Michel" in original] for their former princes. It cannot be denied that the people have been sold a bill of goods about Texas and that hundreds of families have been made miserable here on account of it. For without money you can't do any more here than you can over there, and anyone who is not in possession of at least 1,500 dollars should stay there. One sixth of the immigrants have died, even whole large families have completely died out; and the best advice I can give is, don't even come here at all until 3 years have passed, so that things can get better organized than they are now, especially since the actual Society [Adelsverein] land, across the Llano, consists of pure rock where only a few individual valleys are capable of cultivation, and the impediments of the terrain, as far as making roads is concerned, are almost insurmountable, so that it is almost impossible to settle the grant. My advice for anyone wanting to emigrate is therefore: Stay home and feed yourselves there as well as you can!

At Indianpoint I got to know one of the kindest men [authors' note: probably Meusebach], who is also playing a leading role in the settlement organization here, and from whom I received the offer to take on the leadership of a company to go to the grant. That is what has now happened, and as a result, in two days I am heading into Indian territory, where the watchword is: keep your eyes and ears open and come back from that wilderness, which up to now has never seen the face of a white man, and make sure you bring your scalp with you. When the expedition is over, which might take 6 months, I am thinking of building a cabin near one of the settlements and will have the opportunity by that time to buy a captured Mexican woman from the Indians, which is not at all difficult. Then I'll have a squaw, who can tan and process the hides and can take care of household business and in any case will love me all the more, because she is a true child of nature and her whole desire has been occasional trifling playthings to adorn herself to try and please me. Don't think what I just said are romantic and poetic ideas on my part; I have already tasted reality for too long to maintain such dreams, since heavy northers and the howling and wailing of panthers and wolves are certainly the right thing to drive out any such ideas.

I no longer really have any thoughts of getting married, which, dear mother, you have assumed I have, because bringing a European woman, especially one from the educated classes, into this still very wild country is not a good idea, as hundreds of examples have shown. For the brief, excited fantasy of being happy even in a poor cabin evaporates here very quickly, and even though Texas is described as paradise in all the books, there are really only very few people who are satisfied here, as the large number who are returning to Europe proves; etc.

[l] In the word list comparing the two languages (or daughter tongues of a single mother language), the Shoshone words, in the dialect of the Wihinasht or Western Shoshones, are taken from Gallatin's treatise in the often cited *Trans. of the Am. Ethnol. Soc.*, Vol. II, p. 121.

[m] *Sozonis*: This name for one of the Comanche tribes reminds us so clearly of *Shoshonees*, that it cannot be overlooked; however I must note that my informant was not sufficiently familiar with the ethnography of the rest of North America to know anything about the existence of the Shoshones.

[n] Besides the Comanches, my informant names the following Indian tribes as inhabiting the territory claimed by the State of Texas:—

1. *The Pawnee-(Pahni-)Picts*, a bold tribe of riders, between the Rio Roxo de Natchitoches and the Canadian South Fork.
2. *Tonkaways and Towaconays*, insignificant and impoverished remnants of Foot Indians, who move between the Brazos and the Colorado. They are linguistically similar to the Caddoes.
3. *Karancahuas (Karankaways)*, a tribe of only about 10 or 12 families; impoverished fishing Indians, who stay on the Aransas Bay and the Nueces.
4. *Caddoes, Kikapoes, Choctaws (Tschatahs) and Chickasaws (Tschikkasahs)*, to whom the above mentioned Witschitas belong, are tribes that have immigrated from the United States and who usually move around between the headwaters of the Brazos and Colorado.
5. *Delaware and Shawnees (Schahnies)*, semi-civilized Indians, live in small groups of 20 warriors, stay close to Austin, Antonio, Braunfels, Friedrichsburg, etc., and are often used in the service of the state. Part of the Shawnees are said to have farms on the Canadian River.

[o] The following are to be recommended from among the works that provide accounts of the life of the Comanches:—*Texas. By Mrs Mary Austin Holley. Lexington, Kentucky, 1836.*—*Scenes in the Rocky Mountains, Oregon, California, New Mexico, Texas and Grand Prairies, including descriptions of the different Races inhabiting the, etc. By a New Englander. Philadelphia 1846.*—And especially: *Commerce of Prairies, or the Journal of a Santa-Fe trader during eight expeditions to great Western Prairies. By J. Gregg. 2 Vols. New York 1847.*—My knowledge of the German writings about Texas is very limited, which is scarcely to be avoided given the countless quantities that appear each year. Among the recent publications, an extensive and thorough treatment of the Comanches may be found in:—Vollständige Beschreibung des Staates Texas in historischer, politischer, geographischer und gesellger Hinsicht [Complete Account of the

State of Texas from a Historical, Political, Geographical and Social Perspective] by B. von Ehrenkreüz [*sic*]. Koblenz, 1846.

[p] I have already published this information about the customs and traditions of the Comanches once before in the "Zeitschrift für Erdkunde" ["Journal of Geography"], Vol. X, Magdeburg, 1850; however, since this periodical has only managed to reach a very small readership, it is appropriate to dedicate some space to it here.—(comment dated April 21, 1851).

[q] *Map of Oregon and Upper California. From the Surveys of John Charles Frémont and other authorities. Drawn by Charles Preuss, under the order of the Senate of the United States, Washington City, 1848. Scale 1:3,000,000.*

[r] Gregg, *Commerce of Prairies etc.* New York, 1847.

[s] Older information about the Apaches may be found primarily in A. von Humboldt, *Essai politique sur le Royaume de la Nouvelle Espagne etc.*, and in Pike, *Voyage au Nouveau Mexique par le Major (americain) Pike. Traduit par Breton. Paris, 1812*; 2 volumes in octavo. Cf. Adelung and Vater, Mithridates, III, 3, p. 177ff. Berghaus' Völker des Erdballs [Peoples of the Globe]. I, p. 290.

[t] Wislicenus' Beiträge zur genaueren Kenntniss des nördlichen Mexico [Contributions to the more precise knowledge of northern Mexico], in Geographisches Jahrbuch [Geographic Yearbook], 1850, I, p. 51.

[u] W. H. Emory, *Notes of a Military Reconnaissance from Fort Leavenworth, in Missouri, to San Diego, in California etc. Washington, 1848*; A thick volume in octavo, with a large map and many illustrations.—*Alb. Gallatin, in Trans. of the Amer. Ethnol. Soc.* Vol. II, p. CVIII, CIX.

[v] Several peoples of the Algonkin language family lived on the Atlantic Ocean, but no branch of this, the largest tribe of Indians in North America, has lived on the coast of the Pacific Sea.

[w] *Hale, Ethnology and Philology, Vol. VII of the U.S. Exploring Expedition; and his Indians of North-West America in Trans. of the Amer. Ethnol. Soc.* Vol. II, p. 9.

[x] Ibid., p. 62., 128.

[y] A. de Humboldt, Essai polit. sur le Roy. de la Nouvelle Espagne, 2me édit. T.[Vol.] II, p. 253, 254.

10

Commentary on the 1851 Article

Berghaus's 1851 article is brimming with significant details that shed light on the state of ethnology in his time and on questions of Indian culture that are still relevant. Explication is best served by a running commentary that treats the people, places, and customs he describes, in the order in which he discusses them.

Berghaus's grouping of the Comanches with the Shoshones has been sustained through all subsequent research. Presently Comanche and Shoshone are classified along with Panamint as two of the three component languages of the Central Numic sub-branch of the Numic branch in the Uto-Aztecan language family, a large family spanning the western United States and Mexico and comprising such diverse groups as the Utes, Pimas, Hopis, Yaquis, and Tarahumaras (Goddard 1996a, 7). Comanche and Shoshone are so similar, however, that they have sometimes been classified as a single language (e.g., Miller 1972, 3). The Shoshones and Comanches may be regarded as members of a "single nation," as Violet claimed, only in these general linguistic terms, as the Comanches have had an independent political identity since some time prior to AD 1700 (Hämäläinen 2008, 22–23).

The Apaches are separate from the Shoshoneans on both linguistic and political counts. There are numerous Apachean languages, dialects, and independent polities classified within the Athapaskan subfamily of the Nadene language family, another large grouping spanning the area from Alaska to the US-Mexico border (Goddard 1996a, 5). The Arapahos are separate yet again, with an Algonquian language endemic to northeastern

North America, and are most closely affiliated with the Cheyennes. In an important moment in the evolution of tribal classifications, Berghaus, in his endnote *h*, departs from his earlier adherence to Violet, and, following Gallatin, accepts that the Arapahos have a language that is distinguishable from Shoshone.

While Violet was in error in noting that "they all speak the same language" and have the same customs, in this period there were many cultural resemblances among all four of the named groups, which would have encouraged the assumption of linguistic affiliation. And, in aggregate, the four groups were prominent among those occupying sections of the vast territory that Violet delimits for them. As the study of his map shows (see chapter 13), however, Berghaus reckoned longitude from the Paris rather than Greenwich meridian, so the coordinates he reports must be adjusted. In 1851 Comanches inhabited an area roughly between 104°W and 98°W, as measured from Greenwich.

The term "undulating prairie" (literally "wave-shaped prairie" in German), probably adopted by Berghaus from his translation of Catlin, approximates the term Rolling Plains sometimes applied to the physiographic province lying north of the Edwards Plateau in northwest Texas and adjacent part of Oklahoma, also known as Osage Plains or Lower Plains; this landform is distinguished from the flatter High Plains (e.g., Stephens and Holmes 1989, 4; Johnson 2010).

The population estimates that Violet provided cannot be taken at face value, as these vary widely across sources, and it is not clear who he was counting as "Comanches." Pre-reservation Spanish and American population estimates for the Comanches in total typically range between 6,000 and 20,000 (Gelo 2002, 81; see also Rivaya-Martínez 2006, 395–403). "They were probably never a large tribe, although supposed to be populous on account of their wide range" (Mooney 1907a, 327).

Ruxton's characterization of the Shoshone-Comanche relationship is essentially correct. But as Berghaus clarifies in his endnote *g*, drawing upon Hale, the Klamath ("Tlamath") of southwestern Oregon, while living adjacent to the Numic-speaking Northern Paiutes, belong to the Plateau Penutian language family. Characterization of the Klamath as warlike stems from their habit of raiding neighboring Indian groups to take slaves, though they were never hostile toward whites (Farrand 1907). The "actual" name that Berghaus provides, Lutuami, was applied to both the Klamaths and neighboring Modocs (Kroeber 1976, 318). The

Utes ("Jutas"), having a language classified as Southern Numic (Goddard 1996a, 7), are closely related linguistically to the Shoshones and Comanches and could in some ways be regarded as a geographically and culturally intermediate population. Berghaus discloses the contemporary uncertainty on this point in his endnotes *i* and *j*, citing the contrary positions of Hale and Gallatin on the matter.

There are alternate accounts of the separation of the Comanches from the Shoshones (e.g., Wallace and Hoebel 1952, 9–10; Kavanagh 2008, 188–89). Ruxton did not give a source for his legend, but almost certainly he got it from a white trapper rather than an Indian. The personal names Wakananga, Wakomish, and Asaqua, have not, to the authors' knowledge, been perpetuated elsewhere in oral history. The references to springs are nevertheless consistent with the Uto-Aztecan narrative convention of employing springs as representations of historic and spiritual places (see Gelo 1994). Berghaus uses Ruxton's legend of the springs to locate the place where the Comanches separated from the Shoshones. Taken literally, the area Berghaus identifies as between the headwaters of the South Platte and Arkansas Rivers and adjacent to the flats of South Park lies in the vicinity of Leadville and Alma, Colorado. Actually, Ruxton was describing a site some seventy-four direct miles to the southeast: Manitou Springs, a system of effervescent mineral springs on Fountain Creek, at the eastern foot of Pike's Peak, west of the city of Colorado Springs. Wallace and Hoebel (1952, 9) provide a different separation legend in which the tribes split in a dispute over a slain bear, and this episode is "supposed to have occurred on Fountain Creek north of Pueblo, Colorado." Unfortunately, their citation of this information is imprecise and does not account for the origin of the bear story, while their Fountain Creek reference derives from Ruxton through an intermediate source, Grinnell (1920, 258–59). Other sources have suggested that the Comanches and Shoshones parted company farther north, at South Pass, southwestern Wyoming (e.g., Schoolcraft 1851–57, 1:201).

The tribes Ruxton identifies as neighbors of the Shoshones are known today by alternative names: Waiilatpu are the Cayuse of northeastern Oregon and Southeastern Washington; Lutuami are the Modocs and Klamaths of northeastern California and south-central Oregon; and Palaiks refers to the Palaihnihan or Shastan-speaking groups of northeastern California and adjacent Oregon. The Wihinasht or Western Shoshones, also called Shoshoko, comprise numerous small bands spread across the Great Basin from Death Valley, California, through central Nevada, to northern Utah and adjacent southeast Idaho. The Panasht or Bonnaks, known now as Bannocks, are a segment of the Northern Paiute occupying southern Idaho. The Owyhee River is a tributary of the Snake River flowing through the area where Oregon, Idaho, and Nevada join. As Berghaus recognizes parenthetically in his text, this name is an early spelling of "Hawaii," as the region was first mapped by crews that included native Hawaiians. Upsarokos, now commonly Absarokes or Absáalooke, is the self-designation of the Crows, a Siouan-speaking Plains Indian tribe.

After discussing the Shoshone-Comanche relationship, Berghaus reports the dwelling places and headmen of the Comanches in Texas. His Rio de Puercos is a corruption of Rio de Pecos, which takes its name via Spanish from the Keresan Pueblo village of Pecos in San Miguel County, New Mexico. "Rio Puerco," signifying "dirty river," has long been in use among Mexicans of the region (Hayter 2010). Berghaus may have picked up on the notion of the "river Puerco" as the western boundary of an exclusive Comanche territory from Kennedy (1841, 2:344). Both authors are correct in noting the Pecos River as an approximate boundary of the core Comanche area (e.g., Richardson 1933, 106–7); it flows where the Staked Plains and Edwards Plateau, more hospitable to grazing animals, give way to the Chihuahuan Desert. Comanches did, however, frequently venture much farther west, employing Horsehead Crossing of the Pecos in present northeastern Pecos County, Texas (Gelo 2000, 291; Gelo and Pate 2003, 196–98). Berghaus is also accurate in identifying the Colorado ("red," not "colored," in Spanish; originally applied to the muddy Brazos [Clay and Kleiner 2010]) and Red River drainages as defining the Comanche homeland during this period. As Berghaus describes, Comanches ravaged northern Mexico from the later 1830s through the 1850s, with the most intense devastation occurring during 1848–52. The grim toll on settlements of the region has been ably documented by Smith (1959, 1961, 1970), Viscaya Canales (1968), DeLay (2008), and Hämäläinen (2008), among others.

Santa Anna or Santana was one of the southern Comanche headmen who rose to prominence following the massacre of several leaders in the 1840 Council House fight. He apparently earned his name on forays into Mexico, and was known earlier as Pia Kusa or Big Leggins (*pia*, "big" + *kusa*, "men's leggings") (Rivaya-Martínez 2006, 180; DeLay 2008, 362). Roemer described Santa Anna as "a powerfully built man with a benevolent and lively countenance" (Roemer 1983, 269). In late 1849, he perished in the epidemic of cholera brought to Texas by the '49ers on their way to California (Richardson 1933, 159). (A "notoriously bad Indian by the name of Santa Anna" was subject to arrest in Texas in 1858 [Winfrey and Day 1995, 5:262–263], but this must have been someone who took or inherited the name). Santa Anna's camp has been placed on the headwaters of the Nueces River in 1839 (Rivaya-Martínez 2006, 180), though he is known at times to have camped farther east. His name remains on the Texas landscape at Santa Anna Peaks, east-central Coleman County, a cave-riddled mesa used as a rendezvous and camp site (Harston 1963, 10–11, 44–45, 48, 110–17; Pelon 1993; Gelo and Pate 2003, 127–28; Gelo 2013, 37–38, 63, 103–4).

Berghaus places Santa Anna's grazing lands in an area roughly between Paint Rock, Texas, to the northwest and Mason and Llano to the southeast. His identification of the Concho River (Conjo) as Enehokue is significant. "Concho" is said to derive from the Spanish *concha*, "shellfish," on account of a prevalence of freshwater mussels (Smith 2010). Its equivalent is a Comanche hydronym, reducible to *uнuн*, "animal, creature, critter," and *okweetн*, "creek, stream, small river" (this second element appearing in several early area stream names). The semantic range of *uнuн* is quite broad, as it is often glossed as "bug" or "insect," yet appears in compound for everything from "red ant" (*ekaнuнu*, "red creature") to "elephant" (*esiнuнu*, "gray creature"). In the present case, although Comanche does have a specific term for shellfish that includes mussels (*wa?koo*), it seems likely that *uнuн* refers to the same creatures that the Spanish term commemorates. It follows that the Spanish and English names are derived from the Comanche name. Additional derivations of Spanish and/or English stream names from Comanche are discussed in Gelo (2000). An alternate Comanche name for the Middle Concho was *ebi hunu?bi*, "blue/green stream," preserved in Spanish as Rio Azul (Gelo 2000, 284). Berghaus's map depiction of the Concho is more accurate than those of several earlier maps, which often show "R. Conchas" as a small tributary of the San Saba rather than as a large independent branch of the Colorado.

Pahajoko (Pahayuko) appears frequently in records of the era among the headmen encountered in the Hill Country. His name is usually translated as "Fuck in the Water" (*paa* "water" + *yoko* "sexual intercourse"), although an acquaintance, Indian agent Robert. S. Neighbors, who was familiar with some Comanche words, explained the name as "one who has connexion with his uncle's wife" (i.e., *paha* "father's sister" + *yoko*) (Schoolcraft 1851–57, 2:128). Neither seems intended as a compliment; Comanche personal names were nearly as likely to summon ridicule as admiration, and not infrequently they drew attention to defects and misdeeds. Pahayuko was normally identified as a member of the Hois (i.e., Penateka) division by Anglo-Texan observers. Neighbors listed him as Hois when enumerating "principal chiefs" of the various divisions (Schoolcraft 1851–57, 2:128; see DeLay 2008, 362n24 for other similar contemporary attributions). Kavanagh, however, proposes that he was a Tenewa based on his appearance in and north of the middle Red River domain of that division (Kavanagh 1996, 5, 265); also, it appears that he was camped with Tenewas and members of other northern divisions near the Salt Fork of the Brazos in January 1848 (Kavanagh 1996, 307). This possibility suggests some residual Penateka-Tenewa interaction of the kind earlier pioneered by the Tenewa headman Paruakevetsi, who was active south of the Brazos until his death in 1831 (see Kavanagh 1996, 292–93, 484; Gelo 2013, 8, 85, 107, 148, 150, 226, 229). Pahayuko sometimes remained aloof during Penateka treaty negotiations, and for a period beginning in spring 1844, upon the death of his son on a Mexican raid, he retired in mourning to the Salt Plains of the Arkansas River in northwestern Oklahoma; he camped there again in the winter of 1848/49 (Winfrey and Day 1995, 2:64; Foreman 1939, 90). Nonetheless, Berghaus or his informant saw him as "first chief of all Comanche tribes known in the settlements." Of the leaders Berghaus lists, he was, along with Mupechucope, among the older ones. It is assumed that he died in the mid-1850s (Kavanagh 1996, 5, 484).

Berghaus then conflates two Comanche headmen of the period. Keteumzi or Ketumsee was a local band headman who became the principal Penateka leader during 1855–61 (Kavanagh 1996, 5, 39). He was approximately fifty-three years old when he first encountered the Germans in 1847 (see Schoolcraft 1851–57, 5:682–683). His name has been glossed as "he pays no attention to happenings" (Kavanagh 1996, 304), a suitable characterization for a peace chief, or "one who would not fight" (Harston 1963, 193), which is perhaps a folk etymology related to the preceding gloss. In 2013, in helping to prepare a historical marker identifying the exact location of the February 5, 1847, first meeting of the Meusebach party and Comanches, for placement in Mason, Texas, members of the

Comanche Language and Cultural Preservation Committee determined that the name possibly meant "we don't grow anything," and that it should be spelled Ketumusua (Zesch, e-mail to Gelo, August 14, 2013). In any case the initial element *ke-* for negation at least is apparent in the name. Ketumsee's name lives on in two of the rare Comanche toponyms of Texas. Katemcy Rocks in north-central Mason County is a sheltering granite formation along Devil's Spring, a tributary of the San Saba River. A crossroads hamlet north of the rocks is also called Katemcy. The nearby flats at present Camp Air were known as a Comanche pasture (Gelo and Pate 2003, 100–102; Rhodes 2010). After greeting the German party, Ketumsee participated in the famed treaty council, which took place in his village on the San Saba, though inexplicably he was not among those who signed the treaty. Later he led the Penatekas to settle successively on the Brazos and Oklahoma reservations.

Old Owl is the English name for a different person, Mupechucope (various English spellings; *mupitsi*, "owl," + *tsukupu*, "old man"). He appears as a principal Penateka leader in the 1840s, frequently in coordination with Buffalo Hump, Santa Anna, and to a lesser degree Pahayuko and Ketumsee. He was an ardent negotiator in treaty talks of the period, arguing for a strict boundary to westward settlement as well as for the removal of Lipan Apaches from Comanche territory. Roemer described him as "a small old man who in his dirty cotton jacket looked undistinguished and only his diplomatic crafty face marked him" (Roemer 1983, 269). Like Ketumsee, Old Owl was present at the Meusebach treaty negotiations but did not sign, reportedly wishing to gain approval from his band first (Kavanagh 1996, 305). Whereas Ketumsee has been associated primarily with the San Saba, Old Owl was demonstrably itinerant. His camp was indeed found on the San Saba in the summer of 1845, but in May of that year he had occupied a combined Penateka village on the Little River southeast of present Temple, Texas (Texas National Register 1845; Winfrey and Day 1995, 2:283–84). In January 1846, he and Buffalo Hump greeted the first US delegation under Butler and Lewis at Comanche Peak (Foreman 1935; Foreman 1948). In 1849, Old Owl was camped on the headwaters of the Leon River (Neighbours 1975, 70–73; not "Leon Creek" per Kavanagh 1996, 324). Later that year he, like Santa Anna, died from cholera (Williams 1849).

Buffalo Hump was another celebrated Penateka headman and signatory of the German-Comanche Treaty (Henderson 1959; Schilz and Schilz 1989). The name Buffalo Hump was a Texan derivation that may have been applied to more than one Comanche (see Gelo 2013, 88), but here refers to the individual recorded variously as Potsanaquahip, Po-cho-no-quiet, or Ko-cho-no-quoip. The meaning of the Comanche name is speculative. One interpretation relies on a putative form of the Comanche word *kwahi*, "back," preceded by an otherwise unattested term *potsana*, "male buffalo" (Kavanagh 1996, 252, 505n22). Schilz, however, writes that "Buffalo Hump" was a euphemism and "the [Comanche] name had a phallic significance not precisely recorded" (Schilz 2010). English euphemisms for Comanche names considered distasteful are known in other cases (e.g., Noyes 1999, 62; see also Casagrande 1955, 11).

Roemer described Buffalo Hump as "the genuine, unadulterated picture of the North American Indian," one who, unlike the majority of his tribesmen, scorned European clothing (Roemer 1983, 269). He was prevalent in tribal affairs, first as the war chief who staged the 1840 attacks on Victoria and Linnville, Texas, in revenge for the Council House massacre, then as a diplomat and leader of Mexican raids through the 1840s and 1850s. As his influence waned in competition with Ketumsee and others, he settled his band on the Comanche Reserve on the Brazos in 1856. The band rode as renegades in 1858 and was attacked at Rush Springs, Oklahoma, by Major Earl Van Dorn. In 1859 Buffalo Hump brought his followers onto the Kiowa-Comanche-Apache Reservation in Indian Territory (southwest Oklahoma). He died there in 1870.

Berghaus associates Buffalo Hump with "hunting grounds" (vs. "grazing places") between the San Saba and Concho "but more to the east" (than Santa Anna?). Indeed, in spring 1849 part of his band formed a large multiband camp at the junction of Pecan Bayou and the Colorado River, in the area designated (Neighbours 1975, 72–73). Berghaus's map, however, shows Buffalo Hump's camp on the upper Concho, and it is known that his band was encamped with Santa Anna's on the Clear Fork of the Brazos in spring 1848 (Kavanagh 1996, 310).

Beginning with the stream name Uranazwene, Berghaus names five tributaries joining the Colorado River west of the Concho-Colorado confluence (a sixth tributary, between the second and third, is shown on the map but not named). According to his map, the first four of these streams flow generally from the west or southwest, and the last from the northwest. This is a reasonable general depiction of the upper Colorado watershed, but particularly because of scale distortion in the map, it is not possible to determine with certainty the actual identity of each stream. Undoubtedly one of the streams Berghaus shows is the perennial Beals

Creek, also known as the Salt or South Fork of the Colorado and Sulphur Draw, which rises four miles west of Big Spring, Howard County, Texas (Fisher 1994). The eponymous spring (dry since 1925) and neighboring ones formed a major source of water and game for the Comanches and other tribes (Brune 1981, 237). Also, the stream trending from the northwest, labeled Passiwono, and perhaps others adjacent, represent the farthest upper forks of the Colorado in Borden County, Texas, surrounding the Comanche landmark of Mushaway Peak (cf. Fisher 1994, 8; Gelo 2000, 284, 287–91).

Most of the stream names that Berghaus provides are decipherable. Uranazwene suggests several Comanche cognates (e.g., *ura*, "find," *natsaweni*, "hanger, hook") but remains indefinite. Narohono includes the term *hunu?bi*, "creek, stream" and an indefinite element, possibly *narayʉʉka*, "quicksand," or *narʉ-*, "trade," the latter appearing also in Comanche names for Yellow House Draw (Brazos tributary) and the North Fork of the Red River. Woquequahono combines *wokwe*, "cactus" and *hunu?bi*, showing the common Comanche practice of naming streams by characteristic vegetation. Tagkanohi resembles *tahka hunu?bi*, "ice creek," still in use in modern Comanche for the Colorado River. Gatschet (1884, 108) reported the cognate *Tax'ka húnubh*, "frozen river," for the Arkansas River. Either the name has been applied to more than one stream, or, more likely, the term Gatschet reported was actually or originally the homonymic *tahka? hunu?bi*, "arrowhead creek," a designation for the Arkansas that is common across Southern Plains tribes owing to the abundance of prehistoric projectile points found along the river (Meadows 2008, 24). Pissapejunowa is *pisaapi hunu?bi*, "paint/rouge creek," possibly a reference to the presence of ocher used for painting and anointing, or, it may have been a name for the Concho River recognizing Paint Rock, the long rock face covered with Indian pictographs running along the north bank of that stream. Passiwono is clearly *pasi hunu?bi*, "sand creek," another name the Comanches applied to a section of the Colorado River, as well as to Cache Creek in Oklahoma and the adjoining section of the Red River (see Gelo 2000, 284, 288, 290). This name appears as "R. Pasigono" in several maps from the period 1830–49.

For the people dwelling between the named streams, Berghaus lists a number of ethnonyms, some referring to Comanche political units and others properly to non-Comanche groups. Nokoni is the name of a small Comanche division operant from the 1840s to the 1870s around the upper Red and Pease Rivers (Kavanagh 1996, 485). The name is translated as "they travel around" or "wanderers"; an alternate name for the band was Noyeka. Essekuita is the Comanche word Esikwita ("gray butts"), their name for the Lipan or Mescalero Apache. Puheua most resembles Pohoi, glossed as "wild sage" and generally signifying the eastern or Wind River Shoshones of Wyoming, also known as Washakie's Band (see Gatschet 1884, 121; Hodge 1907, 2: 919–20, 1122; Wallace and Hoebel 1952, 31). Mooney listed the Pohoi, presumably a segment of the Wind River Shoshone, as a Comanche division composed of "adopted Shoshoni," and Gatschet, most likely Mooney's source, indicated the same (Mooney 1907a, 328; Gatschet 1884, 125; Mooney 1896, 1045; Kavanagh 2001, 905; Rivaya-Martínez 2006, 155–56). Ten Kate (1885, 123) also identified the Pohanim as one of "*sept petites tribus*" ("seven little tribes") of the Comanches, though translating the name as "*peuple des collines*" ("people of the hills"). The name is of interest at present in suggesting that Shoshones were camped among the Comanches around Kriewitz's time. Gatschet's later notes further support this possibility (Gatschet 1884, 72–73): "There are a few Snake Indians with the Yäp-pä-reth-kās, enrolled as Comanche, and one very old man, a Shoshone, with the Qua-hād-dā band. Straight Feather, who is about 70 years old, says his father was a Snake Indian and his mother one half Pawnee and one half Penatethka."

Tanemoe is clearly Tanima, a Comanche division name glossed as Liver Eaters. The name resembles another Comanche band name, Tenewa or Down Stream (People), and although many scholars have posed two distinct groups (e.g., Mooney 1907a, 328; Richardson 1933, 20; Wallace and Hoebel 1952, 29), Kavanagh (1996, 483–84) has argued that the two names do not co-occur in original sources, but rather reflect "orthographic confusion" and refer to a single group. The modern tribal dictionary lists Taninʉʉ as the "Liver Eaters Band living south of the Pease River in Texas" (Comanche Language and Cultural Preservation Committee 2010, 189). Pero could be the Spanish word *perro*, "dog," or else Piro, the name of a Puebloan tribe residing on the Rio Grande from central New Mexico to below El Paso. Neither of these possibilities comports with the known ethnology of the area Berghaus is discussing. However, the second term resembles Teua, which follows; this is most likely Tewa, another Rio Grande Puebloan group, suggesting the importation of some more westerly ethnonyms in Berghaus's construction.

Nonenoe most resembles the Comanche band name Itɛta'o or Otʉta?oo? (*otʉ*, "brown" + *ta?oo?*, "pounded meat"), a pre-reservation band of "less importance" whose name meant Burnt Meat (Wallace and Hoebel 1952, 30; cf. Kavanagh 2008, 404). This name does not appear in any other historical sources to the authors' knowledge; this could be its earliest mention. The modern tribal dictionary identifies the similar Ohnonʉʉ as Hill People, a "Comanche clan from the Cyril [Oklahoma] area" (Comanche Language and Cultural Preservation Committee 2010, 189). This band had living membership in the 1980s (Gelo 1982, 29), but it is not clear if its name is a version of the earlier names noted. Another reported band name that somewhat resembles the one provided by Berghaus is No-na-um, said to signify a people living exclusively on the High Plains (Schoolcraft 1851–57, 2:128; see Kavanagh 2001, 905 for two later cognates).

Taeuaraoe may be an attempt at Taovaya, one of several similar renderings of the name of a main Wichita subtribe, called Tawahesh by the Anglo settlers, or else Tawakoni, another Wichita subtribe. Quitarae presents two possibilities. Kwitarai (*kwita*, ref. to buttocks or feces + *tai*, "hole"), is a Comanche name for the Pawnees. A more remote option is Quetahtore (*ke tahtonʉ*, "never wears moccasins"), which is often assimilated with another regional ethnonym, Napuat (*napʉ wahtʉ*, "lacking moccasins"). These two names have been treated as alternate names for a Comanche band (Gatschet 1884, 126; Kavanagh 2001, 905) or more prevalently as Comanche names for the Carrizo, a Coahuiltecan people of northeastern Mexico, who wore sandals rather than moccasins and were well known to the Texas tribes. Japarishka is Yamparika (*yapai*, an edible root + *rʉhka*, "eat"), Root Eaters, the northernmost Comanche band and last to separate from the Shoshones. Quassare could be Kwahada (*kwaharʉ*, antelope), the Antelope Band of the Comanches, a small, late, and combative outgrowth of the prominent Kotsoteka (*kuhtsutʉʉka*, Buffalo Eaters) division frequenting the Staked Plains. If accurate, this would be the earliest attestation of the name; otherwise, Kavanagh (1996, 481) theorizes that the Antelopes did not come into existence "much before the 1860s." Kaesua is most like Kaéso, the Tonkawa version of "Carrizo"; lesser alternatives are Comanche band names *kuˈtsuɛka* (Meat [Buffalo] Eaters; Hoebel 1940, 13) or the obscure Kotsai (untranslated; Mooney 1896, 1045). Manakiko is not even remotely evocative of any known area ethnonym.

Nabachho is most suggestive of Navajo, which appears historically in many spelling variants, designating the Athapaskan tribe of New Mexico

and Arizona. Although Comanche legend relates that Navajos interact-
ed with Comanches during the period 1864–68 when the former were
interned at Fort Sumner, New Mexico, the location of any Navajos near
Comanches in Texas circa 1848 seems highly improbable. Nevertheless
"Nabajoe" were also viewed as part of the regional milieu by Berlandier
in his treatise on Indians of Texas circa 1830 (Berlandier 1969, 136–37).
It could be that Berghaus or his informant conflates Navajo with Nabe-
dache (Navadocho in Spanish) or Anadarko (Nadaco in Spanish, Nadaho
in French), tribes of the Caddo confederacy, particularly since he follows
with names of other Caddoan groups. Kitcha and Keacheyes both appear
to be variants of Kitsai, a small, distinct Caddoan population intermediate
between, and affiliated with, the Caddos and Wichitas. Jonies is Ionies,
the Anglo settlers' pronunciation of Hainai, the name of the principle subgroup of the Hasinai of the Caddo confederacy. In listing these names,
Berghaus records the phenomenon of Caddoan dispersal westward from
the river basins of northeast Texas.

Moving north toward the Brazos watershed, Berghaus lists more stream
names and ethnic groups. Peoan is not a Comanche word, but simply a
transcription error for Pecan (Bayou) appearing both in the text and on
the map. This major tributary of the Colorado, joining from the north, is
thought to be the westernmost stream called "bayou," and was a famous
camp and raid staging area for the Comanches (Gelo 2013, 37, 70, 84, 94,
101, 114; Hanke 2010). Pato Pinto is another error, for Palo Pinto (Creek),
which flows into the Brazos from the southwest. Berghaus also gives a
Comanche name for this stream, Ekaoque or "Red Creek" (*eka*, "red" +
okweetu̱, "creek, stream, small river").

Next are more ethnic groups associated with these waters. Sariteka is
the Comanche term Dog-Eater (*sarii*, "dog" + *ru̱hka*, "eat"). This term
designates the Arapahos among the Comanches, Shoshones, and through
borrowing, among the southern Plains Caddoan speakers (Fowler 2001,
860–61). The name, however, was also applied prior to about 1840 to an
undetermined population of Plains Athapaskans, and this population may
have eventually amalgamated with Apaches and/or Comanches (Thurman
1988). People by this name were reported to have been allowed to dwell
among the Comanches and were encamped on the Pecos and upper Colorado by 1830 (Berlandier 1969, 108–11). Some two hundred warriors
speaking a different language and called Come Perros (Dog Eaters) rode
with Comanche raiders in Mexico in July 1850 (Smith 1970, 40). Given the

time he was writing, Berghaus's Saritekas could have been either Arapahos or Athapaskans. Note that Berghaus mentions the Arapahos by that name in his opening remarks. Either he meant to distinguish the Saritekas from the Arapahos, or else he simply failed to reconcile his own overview of tribes with the details provided by his informant.

Aracho has no exact correlate in the historical sources but appears to be the term used for the Pawnees, rendered Arache, Aguajes, and so forth; the name is of Caddoan origin, perpetuated in French and Spanish sources (Parks 2001, 544). The Pawnees were based on the Platte and Republican Rivers in Nebraska and Kansas, and their presence in Texas was sporadic. Berlandier included the Aguajes among the Indians of Texas in 1830, though noting that they "never come to San Antonio de Bexar" (Berlandier 1969, 103); Berlandier's informant José Ruiz reported that "the Aguaje Indians of New Mexico sell guns made in Great Britain which are preferred by the Comanches. . . . The Aguaje Indians come all the way to the Brazos River to deal with the Comanches. The latter do not visit the Aguaje settlements" (Ruiz 1972, 14).

Tagaroe is most likely a version of the name Tonkawa. On his map Berghaus shows both Tagaroe and Tonkaways at different locations, but this appears to be the result of combining matter from different sources rather than a deliberate record of two distinct ethnic groups. The Tonkawa of north and east-central Texas were reduced and impoverished under Comanche domination and Anglo settlement. Their exact location as a group on the upper Palo Pinto circa 1850 is questionable, though by 1855 they did occupy a reservation village at the junction of the main Brazos and Clear Fork, in the same general vicinity.

Continuing northward, Berghaus notes another major tributary of the Brazos: Tascoque. He does not, however, discuss a connected stream that is shown on his map as Rio Boema. Furthermore, Berghaus's map depiction of the Brazos forks is difficult to match with modern maps (and it is typical of all early maps that the precision of stream courses wanes with distance from the settlements). His Rio Boema, a name with no clear Comanche or Spanish cognate and no other attestation, could be the Clear Fork. Tascoque appears to be the Comanche name *tosa okweet̯ṳ*, "white creek." This name also appears as *tosa hunuʔbi* and was likely the basis for the Spanish name Blanco, which gave rise to the Anglo terms Blanco Canyon and White River still in use (Gelo 2000, 289–90). While this is likely the name employed, the White River is not precisely depicted on the map, and its tributary labeled Red Fork on the map is not identifiable. Red Fork is an old name for the main Brazos above the Clear Fork confluence (e.g., Johnston 1964, 137).

Juchta must refer to the Ute Indians. The Utes were endemic to northern New Mexico, Colorado, and eastern Utah. Although close linguistic relatives and early allies, from the mid-1700s until the 1870s the Utes and Comanches were avowed enemies. Utes are not known to have camped in the Brazos drainage as Berghaus reports. Waqoes is undoubtedly Wacos, the Wichita subtribe that dwelled in a village on the Brazos at present Waco, Texas, from 1779 or earlier to 1830. Since the Wacos had been pushed upstream by 1850 they could be called "[the] Expelled," but their name has never been demonstrated to mean this literally, as Berghaus might seem to indicate.

Two more ethnic groups are located between the Brazos and the Trinidad (Trinity River). Tuachhare is a close approximation of *tawa·khári̇w*, the Wichita designation for their band known to Anglo settlers as Tawakoni (Newcomb 2001, 565). This name has been conflated at times with that of another Wichita band, Tokane (Newcomb 2001, 565–66). The reported position of either group on the Trinity River is accurate for this period. Berghaus is correct in locating the Sozonis (Shoshones) to the north of the other populations, though the main body of the tribe was much farther north than the map indicates. This discrepancy is the source of his puzzlement in endnote *m*. He does not recognize the aforementioned Puheua as a Shoshone band or broach the possible commingling of Shoshone and Comanche bands in Comanche territory.

The Li-pans (Lipan Apaches) and Mezcaleros (Mescalero Apaches) are said to dwell between the Pecos River and Guadalupe Mountains. These were not synonyms as Berghaus indicates, but two distinct Apache tribes that were beginning to meld. Previously, the Lipans occupied South and Central Texas. Today a majority of the remaining people of documented Lipan heritage live on the Mescalero Reservation in southeastern New Mexico. Berghaus's mention of the Comanche word Haiz reveals direct input from someone familiar with Comanche culture, presumably Kriewitz. The term *haitsi̲* may refer to a same-sex cousin but more often refers to an institutionalized form of friendship between two males, something akin to "buddy" or "blood brother" (see word list entry 6). In reality the relationship between the Comanches and these Apache neighbors was variable. Berlandier classified the Mescaleros in 1830 as "enemies of the

Comanches," though noting that "most of them speak Comanche, which has become almost naturalized among them" (Berlandier 1969, 136).

In endnote *n* Berghaus expands on the other tribes living within the state of Texas according to Kriewitz. Here he lists the Pawnee Picts (Wichitas), Tonkawas, Caddos, Kickapoos, Choctaws, Chickasaws, Delawares, and Shawnees. By the time of writing, the Choctaws and Chickasaws were a minor presence, largely expelled from East Texas along with the Chero-kees, who are not mentioned. The Tonkawas had been fine equestrians in the eighteenth century rather than "Foot Indians" as Berghaus states, but they were indeed impoverished of horses and all else by the time Kriewitz came to Texas. His other characterizations of the tribes are accurate, and the information is broadly consistent with his map depiction of the tribes and their locations.

Another testament to Kriewitz's influence is found in Berghaus's col-orful legend of Mission Santa Cruz de San Sabá. Meusebach and Roemer came upon the ruins of San Luis de las Amarillas Presidio set deep in wil-derness on the north bank of the San Saba River, one mile west of present Menard, Texas, on February 18, 1847 (Roemer 1983, 256–60). Kriewitz only joined with the Meusebach party after this episode (Penniger 1971, 48), but no doubt he heard about the mysterious ruins at first meeting and subsequently during his years residing in the area. Roemer initially as-sumed that the presidio and mission were one and the same, then, seeing no evidence of abandoned cultivated land, concluded that perhaps there never was a mission, only a fort. But the mission lay on the south bank of the river four miles east, and apparently had already fallen into obscurity. The actual site was verified by archaeologists only in 1994. Berghaus does not locate the presidio or mission on his map. Nevertheless, the rep-etition of oral traditions by both Roemer and Berghaus make it clear that nearly a century after the destruction of the mission by allied Wichitans, Caddos, Tonkawas, and Comanches, the story of the place still loomed large in the regional imagination.

Details of the mission effort, attack, and aftermath are available in Simpson (1959), Weddle (1964, 2007, 2010b), and John (1975). It will suffice to explain some of the elements in Berghaus's version of the leg-end. First, the sacking took place on March 16–17, 1758, not 1780, and there was no prolonged siege. The mission and presidio had been built in 1757 to Christianize Apaches; their association with Spanish prospect-ing in the area was only coincidental. A few Spanish attempts to mine in the Riley Mountains, south-central Llano County, some forty-three miles south of the mission, spawned persistent tales of lost "San Saba" silver mines and buried treasure, long part of Texas folklore (Kennedy 1841, 1:112–13; Domenech 1872, 125–26; Dobie 1930, 1–61; Patten 1970; Penniger 1971, 37; Berlandier 1980, 2:300; Eckhardt 1982; Roemer 1983, 218, 258–59; Sörgel 1992, 118; Weddle 2010a). The presidio garrison numbered about one hundred soldiers at maximum strength, and there were about two hundred civilians, including six priests, initially staffing the mission. Berghaus's figure of six hundred is actually the number of men said to have participated in Colonel Diego Ortiz Parrilla's fall 1759 punitive expedition against the San Saba attackers (Weddle 2010b).

Modern historical readings do not support the idea that the sacking was prompted by a Spanish attack on innocent Comanches, or that the Comanches were allied with Apaches. Although the Comanches were long blamed in vernacular history, they were in the minority of the force of some two thousand, mostly Wichitans and Caddos, all bent on destroying Apaches and the mission that was attempting to harbor them. Three priests remained at the mission when it was sacked, and only one survived, having wandered outside the burned compound wounded and starving for two days, hence Berghaus's notion of the lone monk. Berghaus then places this character in a novel rendition of another local legend. The name "Brazos" was first applied by the Spanish to the Colorado River, and vice versa, so Berghaus is correct on that matter (Clay and Kleiner 2010; Hendrickson 2010). There are several documented legend versions accounting for the full name El Brazos de Dios, "The Arms of God" (Hendrickson 2010), but these have to do with the deliverance of Spaniards from thirst, not Indian pursuit, and while one version concerns miners from San Saba, none include the Mosaic parting-of-the-waters motif reported by Berghaus.

Berghaus then turns his attention briefly to his Comanche glossary and list comparing Comanche with Shoshone, which are examined in chapters 11 and 12. Berghaus is astute in noting Spanish loanwords and Comanche neologisms. These phenomena are elaborated in Casagrande (1954a, 1954b, 1955), Shimkin (1980), and García Rejón and Gelo (1995). The borrowing of *casa* for "tipi" is not recorded elsewhere, however. Notable instead is the extension of meaning by which *kahni*, originally a brush shelter in Shoshone, is used for "tipi" and also now for modern "house," "room," and "home" in Comanche (Casagrande 1954b, 218; Comanche Language and Cultural Preservation Committee 2010, 32).

Berghaus is appropriately laudatory of Kriewitz's observational skills as he introduces his informant's sketch of Comanche customs. Kriewitz's familiarity with George Catlin and James Fenimore Cooper, current authors of the time, bespeaks a well-read observer. The artist and explorer Catlin's account of Comanche horsemanship appears in his *Letters and Notes* (Catlin 1841, 2:65–66). Kriewitz then refers to novelist Cooper, whose characters Uncas and Chingachgook in the *Leatherstocking Tales* published 1827–41 institute stereotypes of the taciturn Indian. Kriewitz's "general view," which contrasts this stereotype against his own more textured understanding of the Indian temperament, is an early example of the enduring German fascination with literary treatments of the West and Indians (see Calloway, Gemünden, and Zantop 2002). His observations on Comanche civility and joviality during social occasions are confirmed in many sources; for example: "Although a few isolated incidents might seem to indicate that the Comanches are an inhospitable people, they are nevertheless the most hospitable people in all Texas" (Berlandier 1969, 63); "They are formal and suspicious of strangers, but hospitable and social to those they consider their friends" (Schoolcraft 1851–57, 2:132); "The fun is broad, coarse, as might be expected of a savage race; but jollier, more light-hearted, better pleased people I have never seen at any social gathering, and the temper of the whole affair is perfect" (Dodge 1882, 378). Comanche sobriety in earlier times is noted in several sources, including Berlandier (1969, 62); Kennedy (1841, 1:347–48); Burnet (Schoolcraft 1851–57, 1:233); Roemer (1983, 278); Humfreville (2002, 185); Marcy and McClellan (1968, 167); Smithwick (1900, 179); and Wallace and Hoebel (1952, 112). Ironically, according to the Delaware scout John Conner, Penateka Comanches started to become fond of whiskey in the early 1850s, upon visiting the German settlements (Newcomb with Carnahan 1978, 60).

Kriewitz's details about Comanche religion are valuable and supportable, with one exception. He may have been predisposed to identify opposing good and evil gods on account of his European background, or else he may have read Kennedy's report on Texas, which states: "The religious conceptions of the Comanches are very confused; they call God the Great Captain who is in the sky, and they entertain the notion of an evil genius under the earth" (Kennedy 1841, 2:347). But other evidence indicates that traditional Comanche religion does not recognize an evil supreme counterpart to the generally benevolent but largely disinterested creator, manifest in the sun (*Taa? Ahpu̱*, Our Father, and other similar names), except as a late reflex to or adoption of Christian doctrine (e.g., *tuʔkwasitaibo*, "black- [?] tail white man," or *ahkatu ke hinatokwe hanitu tuanoo kwasikatu*, "has horns and a tail, doesn't do anything right" for "devil"). Instead, spirits in the form of animals, miniature people, and ghosts are the main supernatural agents, imparting power (*puha*) to humans with good or bad effect (Gelo 2002, 83). According to Kriewitz's contemporary Robert Neighbors, "They do not worship any Evil Spirit, and are not aware of its existence, attributing everything to arise from the Great Spirit, whether of good or evil" (Schoolcraft 1851–57, 2:131).

Human experts in communicating with the spirits and manipulating power are called *puhakatu*, "power possessor," "medicine man" (or "medicine woman") in English, thus Kriewitz's term Oakatas. More on the social status and methods of Comanche curers may be found in Jones (1972, 1980) and Gelo (1986, 133–36).

A few of Kriewitz's ritual details are not in print elsewhere: the use of the buffalo bladder to transfer therapeutic smoke, and the "instrument" combining what are usually two separate implements, a feather fan and whistle made from a wing bone. The resinous substance worn in a pouch for protection was probably *tupi naatsuu*, "rock medicine," the amber-colored gummy matrix from mason bee nests, synthesized by the bees from pollen and nectar (and thus associated with sacred plants), which Comanches mold into small balls for medicinal use (Carlson and Jones 1939, 534n4; Jones 1972, 63–64). Typically, this substance is burned to make curative smoke; its use in amulets is not otherwise recorded.

The Comanche cultural focus on hunting and warfare that Kriewitz describes has been emphasized by virtually everyone who has ever written on the tribe. Kriewitz alludes to the nascent Comanche class system, in which men strove for wealth in horses and trade items (see Gelo 2002, 83; Hämäläinen 2008, 259–69). He then makes an important and often overlooked point, that "hunting in the grazing places is very poor," necessitating alternate if not competing strategies for bison procurement and horse herd management (see Gelo 1997, 145). He is also astute in linking horse raiding and the taking of captives as two related aspects of the tribal economy. Comanche captivities have received a great deal of scholarly and popular attention; see: Rister (1940, 1955); Smith (1955); Corwin (1959); Harston (1963, 195–98); Greene (1972); García Rejón and Gelo (1995); Brooks (2002); Gelo and Zesch (2003); Zesch (2004);

Rivaya-Martínez (2006); and Barr (2007). For a list of the copious sources about the most celebrated Comanche captive, Cynthia Ann Parker,
see Gelo (2013, 80–81). The specific instance or instances that Kriewitz
mentions of Americans ransoming several Mexican girls circa 1848 are
not readily apparent among the over 1,400 reported captivity cases tabulated by Rivaya-Martínez (2006, 417–519). Given the timing of his stay
among the Penatekas, however, he may well have heard of the recent
ransoming of captive Juana Cavasos by the trader George Barnard on the
Brazos, and subsequent marriage of Cavasos to her redeemer's brother, Charles Barnard (see chapter 7, note 5; Rivaya-Martínez 2006, 438;
Prewett 1910; Nunn 1975; Elliott and Padon 1979; Andrus 1982, 2010;
Orozco 2010).

As the subject turns to dress and material culture, it is noteworthy that
two other members of the Meusebach expedition besides Kriewitz observed
men's use of buffalo hair to lengthen their concha-decorated queues (Penniger 1971, 39), though only the tail tuft hair would be of much use for
this purpose. Other materials more usually mentioned include horse hair
and mules' tails (Wallace and Hoebel 1952, 84) and women's hair, specifically wives' hair (Sibley 1922, 79–80), the hair shorn by women in
mourning (Wallace and Hoebel 1952, 83; Kavanagh 2008, 459), and a
woman's hair worn in the scalp lock as a remembrance (Kavanagh 2008,
459). Kriewitz then refers to the long whitish barrel-tapered beads called
hair pipes, manufactured in Bergen County, New Jersey, from the colu-
mellar lip of the West Indian conch (*Strombus gigas*) for the Indian trade,
and probably first made available to Comanches directly in 1836 (Ewers
1957, 42–49).

Brass or "yellow" wire was a prominent trade and gift material made
available by the Spanish government at Bexar during 1799–1807, the Republic of Texas during 1838–45 (including goods supplied by the Torrey
Brothers, who kept stores at various times at Austin, San Antonio, Fredericksburg, New Braunfels, Waco, Bosque River, and Comanche Peak), and
Warren's Cache Creek trading post during the 1840s (Gelo 2013, 224). In
his later memoir, Kriewitz indicates that the Penatekas he knew at Fredericksburg traded at the Waco post (Penniger 1971, 49). Brass bracelets have
been found in five of the ten recorded probable Comanche archaeological
sites, and brass finger rings at two of these sites (Gelo 2013, 200–201, 203,
207, 220).

By noting "buffalo" soles, Kriewitz identifies stiff rawhide sewn to soft buckskin uppers, which distinguishes Southern Plains Indian moccasins from the soft-soled moccasins of the Woodlands and early Northern Plains. Fringe decoration on moccasins was characteristic of the Comanches, Kiowas, and, to some extent, the Cheyennes (Wallace and Hoebel 1952, 78; Koch 1977, 145–47).

The blanket made of two sections of red and dark blue cloth (*ekasɨkwe*, "red half") remains today as ceremonial regalia. It represents sacred dualities such as day and night. The original material used was stroud trade cloth, abundant in the known lists of Comanche gifts and trade goods (Gelo 2013, 209–11). Comanches made tweezers (*motso noʔi*, "whisker pluck") from bone, shells of freshwater clam, sometimes known locally as "mussel," and later, metal springs; manufactured tweezers are wholly absent from the gift and trade lists.

Kriewitz's sketch of Comanche weapons mostly conforms to other reports. He may have been especially sharp in noting a trend away from shield (*topɨ*) use with the advent of firearms, but other contemporary observers through the mid-1800s emphasized the shield's continued use and efficacy in turning not only arrows but also musket balls and rifle bullets (e.g., Dodge 1882, 422; Wallace 1954, 133). Secoy (1953, 61, 91) posited an increasing role for the shield, as a practical alternative to hide armor, once guns became widespread. All agree that the shield remained important as an emblem of warrior status and locus of protective spiritual power (see also Baylor 1929, 374), as it does today (Gelo 1986, 207). Secoy (1953, 61) theorized that dependency on defensive spirit power would have increased in the face of gunfire. There is no firm distinction between physical and symbolic protection in the traditional Comanche conceptualization of defensive weaponry (Gelo and Jones 2009, 62).

The Comanche term for a war club or battle ax is *wupitapuʔni*. Dodge too noted that this type of weapon, even the fancy manufactured kinds combining pipe and tomahawk, had fallen into disuse except as "a mere ornament . . . they are beginning to be voted a bore by the average Indian" (Dodge 1882, 420). Kriewitz's list places "tomahawk" among ornament terms. The prevalence of (metal) knives is supported by the gift and trade records (Gelo 2013, 216–17).

When Kriewitz notes that "the women ride like the men," he means astride; Roemer also found this custom noteworthy (Roemer 1983, 275). Women's riding postures were ably captured in sketches by Friedrich

Richard Petri (Newcomb with Carnahan 1978, 208–9). Petri, a German settler living outside Fredericksburg during 1852–57, was a professional artist who left a fine pictorial record contemporaneous with the work of Kriewitz (Wickham 1996, 72–74).

Comanche dances would have seemed simple to a nineteenth-century German observer, and Kriewitz is dismissive in writing about them. The two dances he describes are not clearly recognizable. His "jumping" dance could refer to a type of movement seen in what is now called the Gourd Dance, in which men dance in place by flexing their knees in time to the drum beat, though, at least in modern times, not back to back. Also, in 1933 the Comanche consultant Niyah mentioned jumping in his description of a defunct dance called the *otsinɨhka* (knee dance) (Kavanagh 2008, 277). The line dance sounds initially like the Snake and Two-Step dances performed at modern powwows, but these go at a brisk pace, so more likely Kriewitz is referring to something like today's stately processual war dance, which is done in the parade-like grand entry that starts the powwow, and intermittently afterward when individuals are called out and honored. All of these modern dances include women. None involves closing the arms tightly around the person ahead. In the Two-Step, young men and women join hand in hand and lightly embrace like ice skaters; however, this dance is non-Indian in origin, "a simulated waltz first observed at Army posts" (Powers 1990, 69), which only came to Oklahoma from the Dakota Sioux in the years before World War I (Gamble 1967, 103). In all cases the "forward" movement is around a large circle, normally clockwise. In contrast to Kriewitz's hasty treatment, ten Kate provides a fuller list of Comanche dances as of 1883 (ten Kate 1885, 128); the 1933 Santa Fe Laboratory field party interviews provide information on a variety of obsolete Comanche dances (Kavanagh 2008); Gelo (1986, 179–91) gives an inventory of twentieth-century Comanche dances, and Meadows (1999) offers the history and choreography of Comanche military society dances.

Kriewitz is equally condescending about music but still notes some of the essential features of Comanche practice. He mentions the drum and gourd rattle, but does not account for the variety of drum types employed or the use of flutes and whistles. In an unflattering way, he records the women's practice of singing an octave higher than the men, and he describes the typical melodic contour of Plains Indian song, cascading from high to low within an octave. The singers' posture with an unstrung bow and "bouquet" (cluster of sacral gray sage, *pohoobi, Artemisia ludoviciana,* clutched in the left hand horizontally with the upright bow in a cross pattern), and gourd rattle in the right hand, is not found in modern powwow singing but does survive today in the Comanche peyote ceremony. Participants take turns singing while holding the road man's (ritual leader's) staff with sage and rattle in this manner. The staff (*natsihto*) is made from bois d'arc, a wood used in bow making, and is likened to a bow; or else, an actual bow was used as a staff (McAllester 1949, 20; LaBarre 1975, 66–67; Gelo 1986, 161–62).

Returning to "lifestyle," Kriewitz makes another significant observation on ecological limits and their influence on social organization. He notes that the Comanches live in "small subgroups" because extensive grazing would not be available for the large numbers of horses that would accompany larger human congregations. As his phrasing indicates, group size was flexible and changeable, but Kriewitz still draws attention to grazing as a limiting factor. His description of chiefly authority and the duality of war and peace chiefs is substantiated in other writings, although his categorical statement that "every decision is debated" is itself debatable, for charismatic individuals could at times exercise considerable agency.

Kriewitz's observations on marriage and adultery are closely echoed in many other works. As for the punishment of adulterous women, cutting off the nose is commonly mentioned, but Kriewitz's grim recipe of nose plus one ear is unique. His remark about attaining manhood at age nine or ten is misleading, in that the notion of early marriage for males is contradicted in several sources. Kriewitz may have seen some boys who had been promised in arranged marriages (Kavanagh 2008, 42), but while not unknown this was not the typical marriage pattern. During the 1933 field party interviews, Comanche consultant Herman Asenap claimed that "marriage was not at an early age" (Kavanagh 2008, 34) and that girls did not marry until age seventeen or eighteen (Kavanagh 2008, 42). In attempting to summarize the 1933 data, Wallace and Hoebel state that "it was not uncommon for the male to marry at an early age," although they then make it clear that there was incentive for a male to gain prestige and plunder in war and hunting in order to secure a wife, so that the average first marriage age of males was twenty-five to thirty (Wallace and Hoebel 1952, 132–33). More discrepancy would result upon considering plural marriages rather than first marriages; men who took multiple wives usually did so progressively as they aged, and these women could belong to their own or the succeeding generation.

Kriewitz's remarks about the division of labor and women's work are widely corroborated. His best contribution here concerns women's attire. A red and blue dress similar to the one he describes is shown in the watercolor of a Lipan or Comanche Indian girl painted circa 1853 by Petri (figure 6; Newcomb with Carnahan 1978, 141–42, 188). The Comanche woman Nemaruibetsi, aged about seventy when interviewed in 1933, recounted: "The Penanʉʉ, Penatʉhka, in the southeast, were wealthier, and wore fancy clothes. The women wore red [triangular] insets in the sides of their dresses, and had red sleeves, *ekawewek*, which were very fashionable. There were also small bands of red over the shoulder and as sleeve trim: it was very distinctive" (Kavanagh 2008, 458). The sleeve term includes *eka*, "red," and possibly a term related to *wewenuka*, "hanging down." Dresses of this design and coloration have been worn by modern Comanche women during traditional ceremonies (figure 7). Kriewitz then describes the Southern Plains style of women's footwear combining shoe and legging to form a high boot (*kusa napʉ* in Comanche), thought to be a Comanche invention (Evans 1962; Koch 1977, 146). Vermilion was one of the most common materials on the gift and trade lists (Gelo 2013, 199, 224), and red mineral pigments (*ekwipu̱sa*, "rouge") also occur naturally in Comanche territory. The notion that a red eye-ring was a symbol of the Comanche tribe is not noted elsewhere. Face paint designs and colors generally have been regarded as idiosyncratic (Wallace and Hoebel 1952, 83–84), although customary patterns of red near the eyes are noted in several instances (e.g., Kavanagh 2008, 376, 458).

The sketch then resumes in Berghaus's voice as he returns to consideration of tribal classifications. As mentioned, the Utes (Jutahs) and Paiutes (Pah-Jutah) have since been assigned to the Numic group in the Uto-Aztecan language family along with the Shoshones and Comanches. And, as we have seen previously, he was correct to be skeptical about classification of the Apaches, as they belong to the Athapaskan rather than Uto-Aztecan language family and are culturally distinct from the Shoshones and Comanches despite some resemblances. Moquis is an early name for the Hopi, a Puebloan tribe of northeastern Arizona. Their language belongs to the Uto-Aztecan family, though forming a distinct branch at some distance from the Numic branch that includes the Shoshones and Comanches. The Navajos of the Four Corners region, on the other hand, are not linguistically linked to these others, belonging instead to the Athapaskan family with the Apaches. The Cocopahs (Coco) of the Colorado River delta at the junction of Arizona, California, Baja California, and Sonora, and the Maricopas or Piipaash of the lower Gila River Valley in southwestern Arizona belong to two different branches of the Yuman language family, separate from the other language families and ethnic groups mentioned.

Berghaus then follows Gallatin in noting the common phenomenon in which tribal self-names denote "the people" or something similar. The Delaware self-name Leni Lenape [*sic*] has been translated as "real men" (Mooney 1907b, 385) or "men of our nation" (Wright 1951, 145) and Illinois as "men" or "they are men" (Mooney and Thomas 1907, 597; Wright 1951, 157). The Comanche self-name *Numunuu* ("we, our" plural, "our people") also conforms to this practice.

Next Berghaus underscores the great diversity of Native California, with its many small, peaceful, isolated populations, and improbable juxtaposition of groups belonging to different language families. This complex picture warranted designation of California as a distinct culture area (Kroeber 1976). The Takulli (Tahkali) comprise a number of bands located along the upper Fraser River in British Columbia. Their language, of the Northern Athapaskan subgroup, is known as Takulli, Dakelh, or Carrier. Takulli presence per se is not documented as far south as Berghaus indicates, but there is a substantial Athapaskan isolate formed by other tribes such as the Tolowa and Hupa in coastal northwestern California and adjacent Oregon (Kroeber 1976, 121–58). Umkwas in this case refers to the Upper Umpqua on the Umpqua River, southwest Oregon, whose extinct language, recorded by Hale, was part of the same Athapaskan isolate; the Lower Umpqua (Siuslaw, Kuitsh) dwelling downriver spoke an unrelated language, called Yakona or Alsea, with apparent Penutian origins.

The Indians native to the Orange County, California, area where Mission San Juan Capistrano was established, known as Juaneños or Acjachemen, are decidedly of Shoshonean (Northern Uto-Aztecan) linguistic stock. Netela signified "my language" in their idiom (Gatschet 1876a, 555). The Gabrieleños or Tongva associated with Mission San Gabriel Archangel, Los Angeles County, are likewise Shoshonean speakers. The designation Kidsch/kij, also Kizh, appears to be an early self-name, also applied to their language, that resembles and may derive from their term for "houses" (see Gatschet 1876a, 556). Kroeber (1976, 621) reports several other names for the Gabrieleño language(s). The terms Netela and Kizh, introduced to the literature by Hale (1846, 222), had become locally defunct by the 1870s even while linguists were perpetuating them (Loew 1876, 542). Contrary to Berghaus's argument, the integrity of these Shoshonean languages is generally assumed even though the missions also housed neophytes brought from elsewhere. But he was correct in noting the divergent character of the coastal Shoshonean tongues, and they have since been said to compose a Takic group within the Uto-Aztecan family, separate from the Numic group that includes the Shoshoneans of interior California, the Great Basin, and Plains (Goddard 1996a, 7).

Satsika is Berghaus's rendering of *Siksikáwa*, self-name of the Blackfoot tribe (or Blackfeet, as they are known in the United States). His picture of southerly movement by the Shoshones proper, the Cheyennes (Shyennes), Kiowas (Kaiawas), and Comanches, is borne out in later research as a general trend during the Protohistoric and Historic periods, although the Shoshones and possibly the Kiowas had earlier southwestern origins (see Gelo 2012, 29–42). Apacheans also migrated southward during the Late Prehistoric. Berghaus then likens these migrations to those of the various, mostly Uto-Aztecan, ethnic groups that moved into central Mexico from Aridoamerica (present United States–Mexico border region) in Prehistoric times. Modern versions of the names he mentions are: Toltecs, Chichimecas, Alcohuas, Nahuas, Tlaxcaltecs, and Aztecs. While it appears true that all the groups named moved south at some point in their existence, the ecological and political factors spurring their movements were so varied, and the time frame for them in total so great, that these migrations are not presently considered a single phenomenon with explanatory value, as might be inferred from Berghaus's comments.

Pondering further on the distribution of language families, Berghaus refers to the Salishan language family ("Selish") of the Pacific Northwest, with its distinction between coastal and interior language branches and its peculiar distribution pattern, in which twenty-one of the twenty-three constituent languages are contiguous, forming one large area, and the remaining two are outliers. Modern designations and spellings for the groups he mentions include: Shuswap or Secwepemc for Atnahs; Salish for Flatheads; Pisquow; Nisqually; Cowlitz; Chehalis for Tchikalish; and, Nsiethawus and Killamuks are both earlier names for the Tillamook or Nehalem. As Gallatin predicted, the hypothesis of a connection between Salish and Mexico no longer stands, while apropos of Berghaus's attention, the Salishan case has informed other subsequent important theories of language distribution as an indicator of culture history (Foster 1996, 78–81).

Figure 6. *Plains Indian in Red-and-Blue Dress* by Friedrich Richard Petri. Courtesy Katherine Weber.

Berghaus closes with prophetic musings on the effects of settlement in the Great Basin and the California gold rush on Native populations. Cholera introduced by the '49ers passing through Texas had ravaged Kriewitz's Penatekas by the time his vocabulary reached print (Wallace and Hoebel 1952, 149). The rapid extinctions in California that Berghaus foretold took place by the end of the century (Kroeber 1907, 190). The problem was even greater than Berghaus imagined, for gold fever also led to the United States' appropriation of Sioux territory in the Black Hills of South Dakota in 1875–78, giving rise to a reparations case that remains unresolved to this day (Gelo 2012, 351).

Figure 7. Comanche women performing Scalp Dance in red and blue dresses, near Medicine Park, Oklahoma, 1983. Photograph by Daniel J. Gelo.

PART III

The Berghaus Glossary and Map

11

The Glossary: An Overview

As the first substantial published list of Comanche words, the Kriewitz/
Berghaus glossary is a valuable legacy. To render this work most
useful to modern readers, the present edition provides English translations of the original German entries plus comparisons of Kriewitz's
Comanche terms with ones from later vocabularies. This material is arranged in a five-column table of numbered entries showing the German
terms or phrases (with Berghaus's idiosyncratic spellings and use of the
umlaut retained), our English translations of the German, the Comanche
words as published by Berghaus, and our comparisons. The entries in the
original were not numbered and only some verbs were alphabetized. We
tabulated the terms in the order originally published by Berghaus in case
this order revealed anything about Kriewitz's methods or Berghaus's
purposes. We have, however, also created an index of the English terms
to aid research.

For Comanche cognates, this study relies mainly on the latest revision of the dictionary compiled by tribe members (Comanche Language
and Cultural Preservation Committee 2010), and we defer to contemporary tribal scholarship in matters of orthography and definition whenever
possible. Language references elsewhere in the present edition that are
not otherwise cited also come from this source. Another key modern reference is the dictionary issued by the Summer Institute of Linguistics
(Wistrand-Robinson and Armagost 1990). Other older or more obscure
sources, and Miller's and Crapo's dictionaries of Shoshone (Miller 1972;
Crapo 1976), were also used where necessary to shed light on particular
Comanche words as published by Berghaus.

This close look at the Kriewitz/Berghaus effort confirms reasonable degrees of scope, phonological accuracy, and definitional reliability. Value derives from Kriewitz's relatively brief but intensive immersion in the culture and his obvious thoughtfulness in elicitation and recording. We are left to wonder exactly how he prepared for and went about his work, but the results suggest a good basic grammatical education, perhaps some self-study or tutelage in what was then called philology, and a spirit of dedication.

There is no evidence that the items in the list were elicited in the sequence in which they appear. Some of Kriewitz's inquiry, however, appears to have been systematic. The groupings of body part and gun part terms may indicate orderly elicitation, while other terms are not grouped with related entries and seem unlikely as items for scheduled query, and may instead have been jotted down by chance during daily life. Readers may imagine many terms that are "missing" from the evident patterns of elicitation, but Kriewitz still managed to compile a fairly thorough lexical inventory.

Kriewitz's attention to phonology is noteworthy, particularly regarding vowel sounds, including lengthened vowels and voiceless vowels, both important features in Comanche. His entry for "rain" (90), for example, captures proper vowel lengthening. He accounts for voiceless vowels by using parentheses ("hair," 8), by showing voiced vowels ("eyebrows," 14), or through elision ("small buckle," 221). His treatment of medial glottal stops is not consistent, but he sometimes employs *ch* to represent this sound ("cheeks," 16; "stirrup," 254). This is all somewhat difficult territory for the field linguist, since in everyday Comanche and related Shoshonean-language speech, pronunciations tend to become relaxed; noninitial vowels vary, medial glottals and final features are dropped, and so forth (see Miller 1972, 16; Wistrand-Robinson and Armagost 1990, 239; García Rejón and Gelo 1995, xxiv). There are band dialectal differences in terms and pronunciations as well. These phenomena help to explain Kriewitz's attempts at exactitude as well as the occasional variations that are apparent when comparing his entries with those in later vocabularies. The precision in several of his entries seems to indicate that he recorded these terms as emphatic responses during formal interview, while other entries suggest varied or casual pronunciation, informal collecting, summoning from memory, or some combination of these conditions.

Kriewitz was also sensitive to matters of semantic and cognitive precision. For example, he documents a term for the space between the fingers (42) and apparently attempted to distinguish between the front and rear sights of a gun in Comanche, as German does (properly *das Korn* vs. *die Kimme*; cf. 266, 267). His list contains several artifacts that inform interesting semantic questions, such as those surrounding the development of the Comanche vocabulary for animals. Shoshone and Comanche animal terms vary over time, and some semantic replacement occurred, as Comanche forebears adjusted to different faunal environments while relocating from the Great Basin to the Southern Plains. And since animal terms are common in personal names, and the Comanches observed a taboo on speaking the name of a deceased person, neologisms and descriptive circumlocutions (for example, "hair hanging down" or "yellow smeared on snout" for "bear") came into use. Kriewitz's term for "skunk" (113) appears in only one other, very early, source, Berlandier's November 22, 1828, journal entry during an excursion northwest of San Antonio with Comanche hunters (Berlandier 1980, 2:351). The term given, meaning "little brother-in-law" and connoting a potentially annoying or troublesome creature, is used later and today to refer to spiders such as the tarantula, and has also been used as a name for the mink. Kriewitz's term for "deer calf [fawn]" (132) no longer appears in Comanche lexicons but can be found in modern Shoshone, suggesting an old or obsolete Comanche form. The translation of his term for "panther" (110), and the relation of this term to "leopard" (111) remains puzzling. Issues inherent in Kriewitz's collection of animal terms are not unlike those seen in another early Comanche vocabulary, that published by the Mexican philologist Manuel García Rejón in 1865 (García Rejón and Gelo 1995, xviii–xx).

Another semantic field of interest in Comanche studies and beyond is that of color terms. Shoshone-Comanche is notable for its partial conflation of green and blue. The basic term covers blue and green, but there are others in Comanche to specify green when desired. Elaborations are seen by comparing entries 171, 173, 247, and 293; 173 includes a "green" term not documented since the 1890s. Some other old if not obsolete terms are confirmed only in García Rejón's 1865 list, including those that Kriewitz provides for "file" (234), "saddlebag" (253), "scissors" (233), and "no" (303). Another such term common to Kriewitz and García Rejón, for "rifle" (260; *piaet*, literally "big bow"), was recorded again in 1940 (Casagrande 1954b, 219) but appears to have now fallen out of use.

Thus Kriewitz's phonetic and semantic discriminations are refined enough that they should be taken initially at face value and considered in any discussions of Shoshonean language evolution. He may have documented a former tendency to terminal nasalization (see "nostrils," 20) or a sibilant that is no longer heard (e.g., "to eat," 317). On these matters concerted comparisons across the various word lists compiled through time would be beneficial. Further study of his material is also warranted to explore cases of semantic shift, semantic replacement, and neologism, expanding the work of Casagrande (1954a; 1954b; 1955) and Shimkin (1980). Such avenues run beyond the bounds of the present edition, but the relevance of Kriewitz's work to future research seems assured.

Under the circumstances of Kriewitz's "fieldwork," the transmission of his materials to Berghaus, and the printing process, errors were inevitable. Once again it is clear that Kriewitz was sometimes eliciting terms, if only because he reports body part terms with the prefix *nʉa*, "my," and some other terms with the prefix *ma*, "this, that." Speaking of body parts in the personal possessive is customary in Shoshonean languages to begin with. This effect is also evident in the García Rejón vocabulary (García Rejón and Gelo 1995, xxv, 22). Kriewitz's reporting here is mistaken only insofar as he fails to translate the prefix.

One lexical mistake appears when Kriewitz supplies the word for "crazed" instead of "to braid hair" (196). This error may be explained by noting the Plains Indian Sign Language gesture for "crazy": a circular motion of the right hand near the forehead. There is also a sign for "braid" but it involves twisting both hands on the right side of the head (see Clark 1982, 79, 131). One can imagine Kriewitz making something that resembled the first gesture when he inquired about twisted hair, perhaps to Santa Anna himself, and getting the wrong word in response. Something similar must have occurred in the elicitation of "nosebleed" (65), the word for which reduces not to "nose" and "bleed" but "whisker pull."

Some other quite understandable elicitation errors are evident in the terms he provides for "eyelids" (15), "finger" (36), and "fingernails" (43). His elicitation of the phrase "it belongs to someone else" (361) seems to have involved a rifle. There is some confusion between verbal and nounal forms, as seen in the entry for "rain" (90). There are also some errors that can only be explained by carelessness during initial notation or retranscription. Terms for "hail" (see 75) and "snow" (76) have incorrect definitions, and these two "meteorological" mistakes are in sequence. There is also confusion over the words for "sea" (96) and "bat." In three instances (128, 336, 337) Berghaus clearly misread Kriewitz's notation, as revealed by the Comanche terms supplied. In one entry, "feet" (55), Kriewitz or Berghaus indicates well-founded uncertainty about the Comanche word by adding a question mark.

There are a few places where Kriewitz records the same Comanche word under more than one German definition, and appears unaware of doing so: compare "small pouch" (211) and "leather bag" (213) or "knife" (223) and "large knife" (225). In these instances, and in some other places (e.g., "horse's hoof" [126] and "horse's tail" [127]) he uses different spellings for the same Comanche word. These features suggest that Kriewitz recorded his entries over an extended time period and that they were published without much study by either Kriewitz or Berghaus of the list as a whole. Also, the differing spellings, which are often near if not adjacent to each other, would likely have come to Kriewitz's attention had his manuscript employed the same order of entries as the print version, and therefore it appears that Berghaus had some hand in reordering the entries for publication.

The documentation of pronouns (304–9) does not accurately account for various forms, which in Comanche distinguish singular, dual, plural and, in the third person, indicate spatial distance from the speaker, as well as nominative, accusative, genitive, and coreferential cases (see Wistrand-Robinson and Armagost 1990, 301–5). Also, the first and second person singular pronouns in both nominative and possessive forms are confused (304, 309), likely a result of elicitation error. Similarly, the Comanche phrase "you eat" is given for the German "I eat" (318). The Comanche terms for "you [second person plural familiar]" and "she" are transposed (307–8).

Several of the terms begin with the element *ma(-)* (7, 36, 67, 186, 189, 261, 263, 266, 288, 312, 316, 329, 330, 332, 334, 337, 351, 356). This element has been characterized in various ways in the grammatical literature. It has been called an indefinite object prefix (Charney 1993, 128), a demonstrative root (Charney 1993, 90–92), an instrumental prefix signifying "hand" (Miller 1972, 18; Crapo 1976, 9; Crum and Dayley 1993, 106) or a combination of these possibilities, that is, an unspecified object indicator having to do with hand activity (Wistrand-Robinson and Armagost 1990, 272). In keeping with these analyses, *ma* has also been defined as a third person pronoun and the transitive verb "holding" (Wistrand-Robinson and Armagost 1990, 39; Comanche Language and Cultural Preservation Committee 2010, 17). Consequently, the element has been translated as "he, she, it," "this or that," or "someone," as well as "hand," "with the hand" or "with the open hand." In the present analyses, we interpret the element according to its semantic context; for example, as "with the hand" when it prefixes verbs having to do with manual operations. In contrast, the term "to shoot" (316), for example, might admit of a prefix denoting "it" "someone," or "with the hand." Readers should be aware that there is sometimes uncertainty or ambiguity in the interpretation of this element.

Several faults in the Comanche terms at the phonetic level appear to have been introduced during the original editing, as one might expect upon reading Berghaus's disclaimer about his informant's handwriting. A few of these errors may have resulted from Kriewitz's mis-recording initial or medial consonants (see the term for "brass" [102] or "fringes" [185]), but the majority of these errors seem to have resulted during transcription. These mistakes become obvious once modern Comanche terms are compared, and they are so common that they would clutter the term table, so they are listed here instead. In some places the letter *"b"* is read by Berghaus or his printers as an "1" (see terms for "nose" [12], "eyebrows" [14]); *"h"* is misread as "b" (224), "k" (25, 279, 339), or "n" (165); *"k"* is taken as "n" (335), "s" (129), "t" (174, 235, 237), or "w" (207); *"m"* is taken as "n" (10); *"n"* is taken as "m" (49, 145, 313, 337, 339, 351); *"p"* is taken as "k" (343) or "r" (287); *"r"* taken as "b" (297) or "m" (252); *"s"* is taken as "o" (165); *"t"* is taken as "b" (312) or "k" (142); *"w"* is taken as "m" (170, 343) or "n" (221, 238); and *"y"* is taken as "g" (111, 126, 341) or "p" (297, 365). In addition, it is conceivable that the aforementioned Comanche term for "feet" (55) includes a *"k"* for "n" and *"g"* for "p", and that the question mark indicates Berghaus's struggle to make out Kriewitz's handwriting. Similarly, comparison of Berghaus's term for "iron wire" with a Shoshone word for "barbwire" (219) possibly reveals misreading of *"h"* for "n" and *"y"* for "g" (219).

Berghaus intrudes in one place in the glossary, commenting via his endnote (originally note 14, the second of two so numbered) that the term reported by Kriewitz for "bull," *padoko*, resembles the ethnonym Padouca (various spellings). The latter is an early Siouan designation for the Plains Apacheans, and subsequently the Comanches, that appears in several French sources (see Grinnell 1920; Secoy 1951; Comanche Language and Cultural Preservation Committee 2010, 43). Kriewitz's entry (109) is a collapsed rendering of the term that literally means "cow male" and its resemblance to the ethnonym is coincidental.

Ultimately some of Kriewitz's entries remain unclear. An entry is marked "unattested" if it exhibits one or more of the following characteristics: (1) it cannot be found to exist as a discrete term or semantic entity in other published sources; (2) it is not an obvious compound or phrase conforming to the usual Comanche grammatical rules; and, (3) it is not recognizable as a corruption of a documented term, obvious compound, or obvious phrase. Some 45 (12 percent) of the entries are so designated. In these cases when possible we provide as comparative material one or more alternate common Comanche terms and one or more speculative cognates or terms that appear to contain cognate elements (see, for example, "feet" [55], "to rain" [91]).

Beyond its enduring value for those studying Comanche, the Berghaus/ Kriewitz word list informed Berghaus's systematic comparison of Comanche with Shoshone to verify the historical relationship between the two peoples. He presented this exercise in a separate table in the 1851 article, following his Comanche word list, and this table is also relocated to chapter 12 and translated, following the glossary and its index. Berghaus does not get into the particulars of the comparison in his article, but, as he probably supposed, the basis for his determination that the two languages are related is obvious from the table he provides.

The table contains 55 Shoshone terms. The terms are basic ones, like "mother" and "water," words that are less likely to change under the influence of time or neighboring languages. These terms are specifically from Wihinasht (Berghaus spells it Wihinascht in his table, though not in his text) or Western Shoshone, the language of the small bands ranging from California to Idaho, which, along with Northern and Eastern Shoshone, is one of three distinct dialects of Shoshone (Goddard 1996a, 7). The terms, according to Berghaus's note 1, are taken from Gallatin's 1848 report to the American Ethnological Society. Berghaus was then able to provide 36 matching terms from Kriewitz's Comanche list. Here a few of the deficiencies of Kriewitz's list become apparent, as there are no Comanche terms for numbers or some other basic concepts, and the Comanche pronouns are confused; also, inaccuracies in the Berghaus/ Kriewitz phonology or transcription are suggested once comparative material is brought to bear, as in the case of the word for "blood." At the same time, a mistake in Gallatin's list is also revealed—he gave the Shoshone word for "cloud" as "rain." Despite these imperfections, at least four cognate relationships are patently obvious, and, as Berghaus explains, several others are perceptible upon closer examination. The only remaining mystery is a little crescent moon symbol placed in parenthesis next to the Comanche term for "moon" in the original table (not reproduced in the present edition). The term given is for "moon" in general, not "crescent moon" in particular, so the purpose of this nicety eludes us. In all, Berghaus's Shoshone-Comanche comparison confirms Horatio Hale's declaration that the two languages were undoubtedly "intimately related," and thus serves as one of the wellsprings for the modern classification of the Numic branch and Uto-Aztecan language family.

12

Comanche Glossary

	German	English	Comanche (Berghaus)	Comanche (Later/Modern)*
1	*Vater*	father	*achpe*	*ahpʉ* father, father's brother (CLCPC 1)
2	*Mutter*	mother	*pia*	*pia* mother, mother's sister (CLCPC 45)
3	*Frau*	woman	*weishpe*	*waiʔiʔpʉ* (CLCPC 84)
4	*Knabe*	boy	*tuinipp*	*tuinʉhpʉ* young boy (CLCPC 73)
5	*Kleines Kind*	young child	*ounha*	*onáa* baby (CLCPC 96)
6	*Vetter (Freünd)* [*sic*]	[male] cousin (friend)	*haiz*	*haitsi* man's male friend (CLCPC 4)
7	*Kopfhaut (Skalp)*	scalp	*makoichzischka*	*ma* this, that + *kuʔekwisi* scalp lock, pony tail (CLCPC 13, 17)
8	*Haare*	hair	*pap(i)*	*paapi* (CLCPC 128)
9	*Zopf*	ponytail	*nekoiz(i)*	*nʉʉa* my + *kuʔekwisi* scalp lock, pony tail (CLCPC 13, 36)
10	*Seitenzöpfe*	pigtails	*newapoiuchta-na*	cf. *nʉmʉ* we, our [Indian] + *papi wʉhtamʉ* braided hair (CLCPC 37, 43)
11	*Stirn*	forehead	*kai, nekaii*	*nʉʉa* my + *kaʔi* forehead (CLCPC 36, 123)

	German	English	Comanche (Berghaus)	Comanche (Later/Modern)*
12	*Nase*	nose	*muule*	*muubi* (CLCPC 22)
13	*Augen*	eyes	*puile*	*pui* eye, eyes (CLCPC 51)
14	*Augenbraunen* [sic]	eyebrows	*kaile*	*kai?ibʉ* (CLCPC 9)
15	*Augenlider*	eyelids	*puursi*	*pu?tsi* eyelash (CLCPC 51); cf. *pui naruso̱* eyelid [eye sack] (WRA 88)
16	*Backen*	cheeks	*schoo*	*so?o* cheeks of face (CLCPC 56)
17	*Backenknochen*	cheekbones	*nezoob*	*nʉa* my + *so?o* cheeks of face (CLCPC 36, 56); cf. *so?o tsuhni* cheekbone (CLCPC 56)
18	*Bart*	beard	*motz*	*motso̱* whiskers, beard (CLCPC 21)
19	*Lippen*	lips	*tupe*	*tʉpe* mouth, lips
20	*Nasenlöcher*	nostrils	*nemobitain*	*nʉa* my + *mubi* nose + *taina̱/tainʉ* rectum, cave hole, room, cluster of trees; cf. *mubita?i* nostril [nose hole] (CLCPC 22, 36, 62)
21	*Zahn*	tooth	*netam*	*nʉa* my + *tama*, tooth (CLCPC 36, 175)
22	*Zähne*	teeth	*tama*	*taama̱* (CLCPC 59)
23	*Zahnfleisch*	gums	*nerochk*	*nʉa* my + *tuuku* flesh (CPCLC 36, 74); cf. *tamaruhka* gums of teeth [tooth flesh] (CLCPC 62)
24	*Zunge*	tongue	*ehk*	*eko* (CLCPC 174)
25	*Speichel*	saliva	*koschip*	*hʉtsipʉ* (CLCPC 7)
26	*Brust*	chest	*nanema*	*nʉnapʉ* (CLCPC 38)
27	*Brüste*	breasts	*pitzi*	*pitsi* breast of woman (CLCPC 48)
28	*Brustwarze*	nipple	*apizii*	cf. *pitsi* breast of woman (CLCPC 48); ĕk'-ĕr-vĭtch-ĭ-sē'-àh-kŭt nipples (D94 79)

	German	English	Comanche (Berghaus)	Comanche (Later/Modern)*
29	*Kinn*	chin	*paritz*; *nebaduez*	*nʉa* my + *parʉtsʉ* chin (CLCPC 36, 43)
30	*Hals*	neck	*toichk*; *neroig(h)*	*nʉa* my + *totʉ* neck (CLCPC 36, 66)
31	*Schlund*	throat	*nekuz*	*nʉa* my + *kuitsʉ* throat (CLCPC 12, 36)
32	*Ohr*	ear	*nak(i)*	*nak̲i̲* (CLCPC 25)
33	*Arm*	arm	*pur(e)*; *neana*	*puura* upper arm, forearm (CLCPC 53); *nua:* my + *ama* arm (CLCPC 1, 36)
34	*Ellenbogen*	elbow	*kip*	*kiipʉ* (CLCPC 10)
35	*Hand*	hand	*mashpa*	cf. *moʔo* (CLCPC 21)
36	*Finger*	finger	*massit*	*masiito* finger nail (CPCLC 20)
37	*Daumen*	thumb	*biomogto*; *nebiamachtoko*	*nʉa* my + *pia* big + *matookóo* thumb [hand grandfather] (CLCPC 20, 36, 45)
38	*Zeigefinger*	index finger	*nerechzigzoka*	*nʉa* my + *tʉtsisuka* index finger [ref. to pointing] (CLCPC 36, 81)
39	*Mittelfinger*	middle finger	*nemachbina*	*nʉa* my + *matʉbinaa* middle finger [hand middle] (CLCPC 36, 142)
40	*Goldfinger*	ring finger	*nemachtaka*	*nʉa* my + *moʔotsinika* ring finger [ring] (CLCPC 36, 157)
41	*Kleiner Finger*	little finger	*nemachtoa*	*nʉa* my + *matua* little finger [hand son] (CLCPC 20, 36)
42	*Fingerspalte*	space between fingers	*nemanisisk*	cf. *nʉa* my (CLCPC 36) + *màn'-sēēk* space between knuckles (D94 80)
43	*Nägel*	fingernails	*techzezuke*	*tʉtsisuka* index finger [ref. to pointing] (CLCPC 81); cf. *masiito* finger nail (CPCLC 20)
44	*Herz*	heart	*nebigk*	*nʉa* my + *pihi* heart (CLCPC 36, 46)

	German	English	Comanche (Berghaus)	Comanche (Later/Modern)*
45	*Bauch*	stomach	*nesap*	*nɨɨa:* my + *sapɨ* stomach (CLCPC 54)
46	*Bauchwarze*	navel	*nessiik(o)*	*nɨɨa* my + *sikoo* navel (CLCPC 36, 55)
47	*Rippen*	ribs	*newuachzo*	*nɨɨa* my + *waatsɨ* rib (CLCPC 36, 84)
48	*Bein*	leg	*newichkap*; *ohm*	*nɨɨa* my + *(ta)ʔwiiitsa̱* calf of leg (CLCPC 36, 64); *oomo̱* leg (CLCPC 40)
49	*Knie*	knee	*tamap*	*tanapɨ* (CLCPC 63)
50	*Kniescheibe*	kneecap	*nerannup*	*nɨɨa* my + *tanapɨ* (CLCPC 36,62); cf. *tanakue* [knee hill] (CLCPC 63)
51	*Biegung im Knie*	bend of knee	*nenazimina*	*nɨɨa* my + *natsimina* joint (CLCPC 32)
52	*Unterbein*	lower leg	*neohn*	*nɨɨa* my + *oomo̱* leg (CLCPC 40)
53	*Wade*	calf	*nerauiz*	*nɨɨa* my + *taʔwiiitsa̱* calf of leg (CLCPC 36, 64);
54	*Spanne*	instep / arch of foot	*nervam*	*nɨɨa* my (CLCPC 36) + [ʔ]; cf. *tabu̱tsubɨ, takɨtsuki̱* instep (CLCPC 134)
55	*Füsse*	feet	*koegen (?)*	[unattested] cf. *naape* foot; *tapikoo, tahpi̱koa* heel of foot (CLCPC 29, 63)
56	*Fusssohle*	sole of the foot	*neragpan*	*nɨɨa* my (CLCPC 36) + *tah-páana̱* sole of foot (WRA 101)
57	*Hacken*	heel	*neragpiko*	*nɨɨa* my + *tapikoo* heel of foot (CLCPC 63)
58	*Zehe*	toe	*tassewueke*	*tasuwɨki* toes, all toes (CLCPC 63)
59	*Grosse Zehe*	big toe	*biaragtoke*	*pia* big + *tahtokóo* big toe [foot grandfather] (CLCPC 45, 61)
60	*Blut*	blood	*poschp*	*pɨhpi* (CLCPC 52)
61	*Eingeweide*	entrails/ intestines	*zap*	*sapɨ* stomach [organ] (CLCPC 54); cf. *tuʔkohi* intestine (CLCPC 75)

	German	English	Comanche (Berghaus)	Comanche (Later/Modern)*
62	*Kopfweh haben*	to have a headache	*nochzikuagh newap*	*nɨɨtsikwarṵ* to have pain + *nua:* my + *paapi* head, hair (CLCPL 36, 39, 41); cf. *papikamaitɨ* have a headache (WRA 75)
63	*Brustweh haben*	to have pain in the chest	*nochzikuagh worainah*	*nɨɨtsikwarṵ* to have pain (CLCPC 39); cf. *amawɨnɨtɨ* suffer chest pain (CLCPC 1)
64	*Leibweh haben*	to have a stomach ache	*nochzikuagh cochicam*	*nɨɨtsikwarṵ* to have pain, body pain (CLCPC 39, 100) + *kohikamɨtɨ* abdominal pain (CLCPC 10)
65	*Nasenbluten*	nosebleed	*mochtochtan*	[unattested] cf. *motso* whiskers, *tsaʔnoʔinɨ* pull; *mubi* nose, *pɨɨokwetɨ* bleed (CLCPC 21, 22, 53, 70) [elicitation error?]
66	*Kleine Wunde*	small wound	*uaz*	*ɨʔaʔ* wound, sore (WRA 143)
67	*Sehen*	to see	*mabuni*	*ma* it + *puninɨ* see, look at, watch (CLCPC 17, 51)
68	*Hören*	to hear	*manakan; neminakat*	cf. *nɨ* I; *ma* it; *nakaarɨ* hear, listen (CLCPC 17, 26, 36); *tɨmahyokɨrɨ* listen to someone (WRA 131)
69	*Riechen*	to smell	*okuin; multare*	*ɨkwitɨ* smell (v.) (CLCPC 82); cf. *murawe* point with the lips or nose (CLCPC 23)
70	*Niessen* [sic]	to sneeze	*aux*	*akwɨ̱si* (CLCPC 1)
71	*Gähnen*	to yawn	*echtaman*	*ɨɨtama* (CLCPC 83)
72	*Schielen*	to squint	*muraunar*	cf. *muruahwɨnɨtɨ* point with the lips or nose (CLCPC 23)
73	*Husten*	to cough	*ornip*	*ohni* (CLCPC 40)
74	*Schlafen*	to sleep	*mishpo; uchpoiton*	cf. *mitsokokɨkatɨ̱*, sleepy (WRA 45); *uhpɨitɨ* (WRA 142)
75	*Schläfrig sein*	to be tired	*pahobe*	cf. *nananɨɨmaitɨ* tired; *pahoobi* hail (CLCPC 28, 42) [recording error?]

	German	English	Comanche (Berghaus)	Comanche (Later/Modern)*
76	*Träumen*	to dream	*taksip*	cf. *nabisiʔaitᵾ* dream (v); *takabi* snow, ice (CLCPC 62, 117) [recording error?]
77	*Weinen*	to cry	*jake*	*yaketᵾ* (CLCPC 90)
78	*Singen*	to sing	*toniog*	*tᵾnikwᵾ* (CLCPC 79)
79	*Sonne*	sun	*tabih*	*tabe* watch, clock, day, sun (CLCPC 60)
80	*Erde (Planet)*	Earth (planet)	*chokoo*	*sokoobi̱* land, earth (WRA 94)
81	*Halber Mond*	half moon	*mea*	*mᵾa* month, moon (CLCPC 23)
82	*Stern*	star	*tazinupp(ig)*	*tatsinuupi̱* (CLCPC 64)
83	*Tag*	day	*tabikan*	cf. *tabe* watch, clock, day, sun (CLCPC 60); *tabeʔikarᵾ* (Wianʔnᵾᵾ band dialect) (adj.) evening, sunset, sundown (WRA 100)
84	*Morgen*	morning	*pötzk*	*pᵾetsᵾku* (CLCPC 52)
85	*Mittag*	midday	*tokuichtawene*	*tokwetabeni* noon, midday (CLCPC 145)
86	*Abend*	evening	*jehume*	cf. *yᵾinakwᵾ* evening, dusk, sunset (CLCPC 91)
87	*Asche (des Feuers)*	ash (of the fire)	*etschip*	*etsipᵾ* ashes, coals (CLCPC 4)
88	*Rauch*	smoke	*quip*	*kwipᵾ* (CLCPC 16)
89	*Wasser*	water	*pa*	*paa* (CLCPC 41)
90	*Regen*	rain	*omaart*	cf. *ᵾmaarᵾ* rain (v); *ᵾmapᵾ* rain (n) (WRA 143)
91	*Regnen*	to rain	*naridiad*	[unattested] cf. *umaarᵾ* rain (v) (WRA 143); *pawiiH* to rain [Shoshone] (M 148]
92	*Blitzen*	lightning	*ekapuschtke*	cf. *ekakwitseʔe* lightning flash (WRA 14)
93	*Donnern*	thunder	*tomojake*	*tomoyaketᵾ* (CLCPC 66)
94	*Wolken*	clouds	*tommohab(ig)*	*tomoobi̱* (CLCPC 66)
95	*Wind*	wind	*neait*	*nᵾetᵾ* (CLCPC 36)

	German	English	Comanche (Berghaus)	Comanche (Later/Modern)*
96	Meer	sea	honobish	cf. pia paa ocean, large body of water (CLCPC 46); jonopitz bat [animal] (GRG 18); hono-pittseh bat (the animal) [Shoshone] (M 109) [recording error?]
97	Warm	warm	uduik	yuʔai (CLCPC 91)
98	Kalt	cold	etscho	cf. ʉtsʉʉ ouch (cold) said when cold or touching something cold; ʉtsʉʔitʉ cold, it's cold (CLCPC 83)
99	Gold	gold	oaoch	cf. ekawi gold color, shiny; ohahpuhiwi̱ gold (yellow metal) (CLCPC 3, 39)
00	Silber	silver	tochzaui	tosahwi̱ (CLCPC 67)
01	Blei	lead	nabahaak	nabaaka̱ bullet, lead (CLCPC 103)
02	Messing	brass	nadino	cf. tʉtʉma wire (CLCPC 81) [brass wire was a trade commodity]
03	Stahl	steel	cozo	cósob steel (for starting fires) (GRG 45); kaw'sawo flint and steel, to light fire with (D95 112)
04	Salz	salt	onahap	onaabi (CLCPC 40)
05	Büffel	buffalo	pimmoroo, kuchz	pimaróo cow, cattle; kuutsu cattle, buffalo (CLCPC 13, 47)
06	Büffelfell	buffalo skin / pelt	nachozuma	cf. ne'mĕ kú 'htcha pĕ' buffalo skin (G84 122)
07	Büffelhaare	buffalo fur	kuchzunapo	kuutsu cattle, buffalo (CLCPC 13) + jenepoá skin (GRG 43); cf. hʉnʉpoʔa human skin (WRA 22)
08	Büffelkalb	buffalo calf	ekakogzo	eka red + kuutsu cattle, buffalo (CLCPC 2, 13); cf. eka kuura baby buffalo (CLCPC 2)
09	Stier	bull	padoko†	pimoróoʔa kuhma̱ (CLCPC 47)

	German	English	Comanche (Berghaus)	Comanche (Later/Modern)*
110	*Panther*	panther	*keberakuazie*	cf. *kabɨrɨɨ* sheep, goat [from Spanish *cabra*] + *kwasi* tail; *toya tuhku, tɨmakupa* panther mountain lion (CLCPC 8, 15, 67, 78)
111	*Leopard*	leopard	*naboragaroque*	*nabo?royaruku, naboo toyaruhku, naboohroya tuhku* leopard, tiger, mountain lion (CLCPC 78, 137)
112	*Wilde Katze*	wildcat	*machzope*	*matsoope* bobcat, wildcat (CLCPC 20)
113	*Stinkthier*	skunk	*teguez*	*teharitsit* [*tïeretsi* little brother-in-law] (B 351); cf. *pisuni* (CLCPC 48), *pohni?atsi* (archaic) (WRA 84)
114	*Bär*	bear	*ochzo*	cf. *wasápe* (CLCPC 85)
115	*Hund*	dog	*zari*	*sarií* (CLCPC 54)
116	*Braunes Pferd*	brown horse	*ekakoma*	*ekakɨma* bay horse (reddish brown male) (CLCPC 3)
117	*Schwarzes Pferd*	black horse	*hochpier*	[unattested] cf. *tupɨsi kuma* black male horse; *hooki* hog, *piabɨ* female animal (CLCPC 6, 46, 74)
118	*Blässe*	horse with blaze (white streak between eyes)	*tochzako*	cf. *tosa?* white horse (WRA 111); *tosa-* (pfx) white, silver (WRA 110), *koobe* face (CLCPC 11)
119	*Schimmel*	gray or white horse	*tochza*	cf. *tosa?* white horse (WRA 111); *esi pia* gray mare (CLCPC 4)
120	*Rothschimmel*	sorrel horse	*ixenebok*	ĕk'-àh-tsà-nŏb-ād red-spotted [horse] (D94 96)
121	*Scheck (Pferd)*	pinto, piebald horse	*tochzanabo*	*tosanaboó* calico horse (spotted on the hips) (CLCPC 67); *tosa naboo?* calico, paint horse (WRA 110); *tō'-tsà-nŏb-ād* black-spotted [horse] (D94 96)
122	*Grosser Scheck*	large pinto, piebald horse	*essarawa*	cf. *esi-* (pfx) gray (WRA 16), *nabóo* painted, spotted, striped, marked (CLCPC 24)

	German	English	Comanche (Berghaus)	Comanche (Later/Modern)*
123	*Hengst*	stallion	*kobi*	*kobe* wild horse [from Spanish *caballo*] (CLCPC 10)
124	*Fohlen*	foal	*pukkuroa, matoa*	cf. *pukurua* colt (literally "horse child"); *marʉa* herd (CLCPC 20, 51)
125	*Pferdemähne*	horse's mane	*nabinikka*	cf. *ania* horse mane (CLCPC 1)
126	*Pferdehuf*	horse's hoof	*theogoth tossit*	*tʉhʉya* horse, *tasito* hoof (CLCPC 63, 76)
127	*Pferdeschweif*	horse's tail	*tichoa quash*	*tʉhʉya* horse, *kwasi* tail (CLCPC 15, 76)
128	*Rüstern [transcription error: Nüstern]*	horse or cattle nostrils	*mamobita*	cf. *ma* this, that; *mubitaʔi* nostril (CLCPC 17, 22)
129	*Pferdebrand*	horse brand	*manasochpo*	cf. *ma* this, that; *nakohpoo* brand (cattle) (CLCPC 17, 26)
130	*Gallen beim Pferde*	horse's swelling (of joint, etc.)	*mamachta*	[unattested] cf. *pekwitʉ, pekwipʉ* swell, swollen (CLCPC 45); *mamada* suck, sucking [Spanish; ref. to sucking cure for swelling?]
131	*Hirsch*	deer/stag	*arika*	*arʉka* deer; cf. *arʉkáa kuhma* buck (CLCPC 1)
132	*Hirschkalb*	deer calf	*ewua(b)*	*aiwa* fawn (M 94)
133	*Hirschhaare*	deer fur/pelt	*some*	cf. *tsomo* beads (CLCPC 71)
134	*Puter*	turkey [male]	*kujonie*	*kuyunii* turkey (CLCPC 13)
135	*Fische*	fish [pl.]	*bek (uih)*	*peekwi* (CLCPC 45)
136	*Laus*	louse	*puchzie*	*pusia* head lice (CLCPC 51)
137	*Kleine Made*	small maggot / grub	*tochzaama*	cf. *tosa-* white, silver (WRA 110); *woʔaabi* worm (CLCPC 86)
138	*Klapperschlange*	rattlesnake	*nuicha*	cf. *nuhye* snake; *kwasinaboo wʉhtitsuʔtsuʔikatʉ* rattlesnake (CLCPC 16)
139	*Biss derselben*	bite thereof	*kichzian*	*kʉhtsiarʉ* bite (used in speaking of dogs or babies who bite) (CLCPC 14)

	German	English	Comanche (Berghaus)	Comanche (Later/Modern)*
140	*Fliege*	fly	*turuaed*	[unattested] cf. *ture* leech; *animui* fly, house fly (CLCPC 1, 74);
141	*Holzbock*	tick	*michta*	[unattested] cf. *karaʔaa* tick (insect) (CLCPC 174)
142	*Heüschrecke* [*sic*]	grasshopper	*kome*; *achtak*	cf. *tuhmeko̲* cricket (WRA 123), *tu meso* cricket (CLCPC 31); *aatakii* grasshopper (CLCPC 1)
143	*Seemuschel*	seashell	*uak*	*waʔkoo* (CLCPC 85)
144	*Ameise*	ant	*hanikochzi*	*anicútz* large red ant (GRG 17); cf. *anikuura* ants (CLCPC 1)
145	*Gras*	grass	*zomip*	*sonipʉ* grass, hay (CLCPC 56)
146	*Zweig*	twig	*kanipp*	[unattested] cf. *sʉʉki̲* twig, switch; *puhipʉ* leaf, brush, grass, weed (CLCPC 50, 58)
147	*Rinde*	bark	*hopichtapoa*	*huupita poʔa* tree bark (CLCPC 6)
148	*Eiche*	oak	*hop(ch)*	cf. *huupi* tree; *paʔsa ponii huupi* oak tree (CLCPC 6, 45)
149	*Eichenblatt*	oak leaf	*pachzaponin*	cf. *pasaapuni* oak tree (CLCPC 45)
150	*Maisblatt*	corn leaf [husk]	*temaquatubok*	*tʉmakwatui*, *tʉmʉkʉtubi* plant used for cigarette wrappers [corn husk so used] (CLCPC 78)
151	*Trocknes Blatt* [*sic*]	dried leaf	*passa puni puhip*	cf. *pasaapuni* oak tree + *puhipʉ* leaf, brush, grass, weed (CLCPC 45, 50)
152	*Aeste*	branches	*passa poni*	cf. *pasaapuni* oak tree (CLCPC 45)
153	*Brot*	bread	*shimmita*	[unattested] cf. *naruku̲*, *nohkopʉ*, *paanʉ*, *tohtiya*, *tohtiiya* bread (CLCPC 35)
154	*Fleisch*	meat	*teschkap*	*tʉhkapa* food, meat (CLCPC 76)
155	*Sehne*	sinew	*tamm*	*tamu̲* (WRA 103)

	German	English	Comanche (Berghaus)	Comanche (Later/Modern)*
56	*Zucker*	sugar	*pigna*	*pihnáa* sugar, honey (CLCPC 47)
57	*Mexikanisch. Zucker*	Mexican sugar	*mox*	[unattested] cf. *pihnáa* sugar, honey (CLCPC 47); *pihnab* raw sugar loaf [*piloncillo*] (G 46)
58	*Kaffee*	coffee	*tuchpa*	*tuʔpa* (CLCPC 6)
59	*Honig*	honey	*powikkina*	[unattested] cf. *pihnáa* sugar, honey; *ʉnʉ piná*, *ʉnʉ pihnáa*, *ʉnʉ bihnáa honey* (CLCPC 47, 83)
60	*Taback*	tobacco	*pa(hm)*	*pahmu* (CLCPC 42)
61	*Sumach, wilder Tab.*	sumac, wild tobacco	*temagia*	*tʉmaya* (CLCPC 78)
62	*Rosinen*	raisins	*nachzabukum*	cf. *natsamukwe* grape; *natsamukweʔa pasapʉ* (CLCPC 32)
63	*Syrup*	syrup	*pina*	cf. *pihnáa* sugar, honey; *huupihnaa* syrup. molasses; *huʔpina*, *tusonipihna* molasses, syrup (CLCPC 6, 7, 47)
64	*Branntwein*	spirits, liquor	*boschawa*	*posa paa*, *posaba* (CLCPC 49)
65	*Fleischbrühe*	meat broth	*oanap (ich)*	*saʔhuʔpa* soup (CLCPC 54)
66	*Weisser Zwieback*	white cracker	*techzachta*	cf. *tosa tohtiya* cracker (CLCPC 66)
67	*Kleine Bohnen*	small beans	*hochzistabacki*	[unattested] cf. *tʉtaatʉ* little; *pihúura* beans [from Spanish *frijole*]; *hʉitsi*, *hʉitʉhtsi* small amount of something; *huutsúʔa tʉʉkapʉ* sumac [lit. bird food; children ate the fruits of smooth sumac] (CLCPC 7, 47, 80)
68	*Milch*	milk	*opitschzi*	*pitsipʉ* (CLCPC 48); *pitseni* milk, breast (G95 13)
69	*Medizin*	medicine	*natscho*	*natsu* (CLCPC 33)
70	*Baumwollen Zeüg [sic]*	cotton cloth	*manap*	cf. *wanapʉ* cloth; *yuʔwanapi* cotton cloth (CLCPC 84, 91)

	German	English	Comanche (Berghaus)	Comanche (Later/Modern)*
171	*Blauer Blankett*	blue blanket	*echptosawoka*; *ewoichtossos-aboke*	[unattested] cf. *ebi*, *ebibi̲tʉ* blue or green; *sabara/sabara* bedsheet, sheet for bed, also sash wrapped around waist in peyote ceremony (CLCPC 2, 54); *tosa-* (pfx) white, silver (WRA 110); *ecatzasabocá* red blanket (GRG 19); *wika* blanket [Shoshone] (M 148]
172	*Rother Blankett*	red blanket	*echkatatosa-woka*	*ecatzasabocá* (GRG 19)
173	*Grüner Blankett*	green blanket	*kuewowanna*	cf. *kōrōpōĭp* green (D95 112); *patuiwiya* green; *wa'na* blanket [notations for "blanket, dark green"] (G84 78); *patiwiaketʉ̲* green (CLCPC 188)
174	*Halstuch*	scarf / bandanna	*toanatorochk*	cf. *tuu-* black, *wana-* cloth, *korohko̲* neck tie (WRA 29, 123, 145); *wʉtsokʉ̲kʉna* bandanna, scarf (CLCPC 89)
175	*Schuhe*	shoes	*nap*	*napʉ̲* shoe, shoes (CLCPC 29
176	*Schuhsohle*	shoe sole	*tachtezako*	cf. *tasʉyuki* shoes, traditional [men's moccasins]; *napʉ̲ tahpaana̲* shoe sole (CLCPC 29, 64)
177	*Hemd*	shirt	*quazo*	*kwasu* dress or shirt (traditional) (CLCPC 16)
178	*Gürtel*	belt	*nazanishki*	*nʉʔʉhnehki* belt, plain (CLCPC 98)
179	*Mütze*	cap	*uichtoabab*; *wichtoawab*	cf. *wihtua* bucket, pot; *paapi̲* head, hair (CLCPC 41, 86); *Bōm'-ēh'-páh* cap; *tsōn'-ĭ-kà* cap or hat (D94 82, 193)
180	*Hosen*	pants	*pitzo*, *pitksokh*	*pitsohko̲* pants, trousers (CLCPC 48)
181	*Läggins (Reithosen)*	leggings / riding pants	*uhs*	cf. *cus* pants (GRG 38); *pikakʉsu* chaps (leather leggings) (CLCPC 47)
182	*Tuchläggins*	cloth leggings	*kuss*	cf. *kōse* leggings (D95 113); *cus* pants (GRG 38)

	German	English	Comanche (Berghaus)	Comanche (Later/Modern)*
183	*Die Lappen daran*	cloths on them	*tuwuanap*	cf. *tu-* prefix to an unspecified object (CLCPC vii); *wanapʉ* cloth, clothes, trade goods (WRA 146)
184	*Handschuhe*	gloves	*moonarsoh*	*moʔo narʉso* glove, mitten (CLCPC 21)
185	*Franzen* [sic]	fringes	*tassek(h)*	*nasʉkia* fringe (CLCPC 31)
186	*Lederne Franzen* [sic]	leather fringes	*manaschaki*	cf. *ma* this, that; *nasʉkia* fringe (CLCPC 17, 31)
187	*Ohrringe*	earrings	*nakzim; tochpiti*	*naki tsaʔnika* (CLCPC 26); [second term unattested]
188	*Halsschmuck*	neck jewelry	*zonip*	cf. *tsunipʉ* bone [i.e., bone bead necklace?]; *tsoomo korokọ* necklace of beads; *korohkọ* neck tie, necklace (CLCPC 11, 71, 72)
189	*Handring*	hand ring	*mabizo*	*maʔwihtsohkọ* bracelet, wristband (CLCPC 21)
190	*Armring*	arm ring	*hizawepua*	[unattested] cf. *pʉʉra* upper arm, forearm (CLCPC 53)
191	*Fingerring*	finger ring	*moziika*	*moʔotsiʔnika* ring (CLCPC 22)
192	*Schminke*	makeup / cosmetic	*pissap*	*pisaapi* paint, rouge, compact powder (CLCPC 148)
193	*Schminktasche*	makeup / cosmetic bag	*pissanasch*	cf. *pisaapi* paint, rouge, compact powder; *narʉso* bag, purse, sack (CLCPC 86, 148)
194	*Schminktäschgen* [sic]	small makeup / cosmetic bag	*pissanapsch*	cf. *pisaapi* paint, rouge, compact powder; *narʉso* bag, purse, sack (CLCPC 86, 148)
195	*Haarpinsel*	hair brush	*natzistuge*	*natsituʔye* hairbrush, comb (CLCPC 32)
196	*Haare flechten*	to braid hair	*possikett*	cf. *poósabʉhkaitʉ* berserk, crazed, have an evil spirit (CLCPC 49); *kwisikatʉ* (v) tangle, braid (WRA 38) [elicitation error]

	German	English	Comanche (Berghaus)	Comanche (Later/Modern)*
197	*Tomahawk*	tomahawk	*tohihowan*	cf. *to?i* pipe used for smoking; *huu aawo* mortar, barrel, wooden vessel; *tᵾetᵾᵾka* hatchet; *wᵾpitapu?ni* war club, battle axe with flint stone handle (CLCPC 6, 67, 76, 179) [reference to pipe bowl? manufactured combination pipe-tomahawks were a common trade item]
198	*Spiegel*	mirror	*naboni*	*nabuni* (CLCPC 24)
199	*Zelt*	tent	*tozak*	*tosakani̠* tent, canvas (CLCPC 67)
200	*Büffelzelt*	buffalo tent	*casa*	*casa* house [Spanish]; cf. *kahni* house, tipi, room, home (CLCPC 8)
201	*Ein Zelt bauen*	to erect a tent	*top kareich kan*	*toh-* prefix referring to push; *karᵾkᵾᵾtᵾ* put up; *kahni* house, tipi, room, home (CLCPC vi, 8, 9)
202	*Schüssel*	bowl	*techzoon, tessoon*	cf. *tĭd'àh-ū-ny* mortar; *pē'-àh=sō-kō-ōw* bowl [wooden] (D94 90, 91)
203	*Angel*	fishing pole	*hoea*	*hᵾahuupi̠* fishing pole (CLCPC 7)
204	*Holzdeckel*	wooden lid / cover	*woko*	*wᵾkᵾnarᵾ* (CLCPC 87)
205	*Fernglas*	telescope	*ohap*	cf. *ohapitᵾ* yellow (color) (CLCPC40) [ref. to brass?]; *tebujuaé* spyglass (GRG 45)
206	*Kohle*	coal	*kotop(h)*	*kutᵾhuubi* (CLCPC 13)
207	*Pritsche*	straw / plank bed	*pokuowuchpei*	[unattested] *sonipᵾ, sonipᵾ* grass, hay; *woobi* board, lumber, wood; *kahpe, norᵾnapᵾ* bed; *puku* horse (CLCPC 9, 56, 76, 100)
208	*Seife*	soap	*woanakoze*	*wanako?tse* (CLCPC 84)
209	*Koffer*	trunk / suitcase	*wobiojot*	*wobi aawo* trunk, box, chest, container, barrel (CLCPC 86)

	German	English	Comanche (Berghaus)	Comanche (Later/Modern)*
210	*Eiserner Ring*	iron ring	*wuekonne*	cf. *waikina* wagon (CLCPC 84) [reference to iron wagon wheel tire?]
211	*Kleiner Beütel* [*sic*]	small pouch	*woss*	*wosa* bag, purse, sack (CLCPC 86)
212	*Regenschirm*	umbrella	*hok(h)*	*hʉki* umbrella, parasol, arbor, porch (any kind of shade) (CLCPC 7)
213	*Lederne Tasche*	leather bag	*wosch*	*wosa* bag, purse, sack (CLCPC 86)
214	*Mexikan. Decke*	Mexican blanket	*huichki*	*wokorai* serape, painted bunting (bird) (CLCPC 86)
215	*Henkel*	handle / hook	*piuachnachzaga*	cf. *puhiwi* money, gold, metal, dollar; *natsayaa* handle (CLCPC 32, 50)
216	*Zunder*	tinder	*nawuach*	*nauatz* (GRG 48)
217	*Schwammtasch*	tinder pouch	*cochzo*	[unattested] cf. *kohto* build a fire (CLCPC 10)
218	*Büffelhornspitz*	buffalo horn point	*nartoko*	[unattested] cf. *naʔaa* buffalo horn case (CLCPC 33); *tahkaʔ* arrowhead (WRA 100); *tokoʔ* maternal grandfather, man's uterine grandchild, as in *mahtokooʔ* thumb (lit. hand grandfather), *tahtokooʔ* big toe (lit. foot grandfather) (WRA 40, 101, 109)
219	*Eisendraht*	iron wire	*naxagugé*	[unattested] cf. *yuʔpuhiwi̱* iron; *tʉtʉma* wire (CLCPC 81, 91); *soni wʉhtʉmaʔ, soni tʉhtʉma* baling wire, wire (WRA 94); *mowetsoca* brass wire (G84 85); *hy'y-wajyh* barbwire (from English *wire*) [Shoshone] (Cr 35)
220	*Kleine eiserne Ketten*	small iron chains	*nabochza*	*nabusaʔ* chain (WRA 50)
221	*Kleine Schnalle*	small buckle	*nechtopka*	*wʉtʉpʉka* buckle (CLCPC 89)

	German	English	Comanche (Berghaus)	Comanche (Later/Modern)*
222	Kleine Pfeife	small whistle	muijaka	cf. muyake music, musical instrument, phonograph, organ; tsuni muyake whistle (an object made of bone or wood); huhkụ muyake whistle (made of collarbone; used by medicine men) (CLCPC 6, 23, 72)
223	Messer	knife	huig	wihị knife, awl (CLCPC 85)
224	Kleines Messer	small knife	habi	har-he pen knife (G84 83); cf. tā'-nàh-hō pocket knife (D94 192)
225	Grosses Messer	large knife	wui	wihị knife, awl (CLCPC 85)
226	Grosse Axt	large ax	huuchwanni	[unattested] cf. wụpitapuʔni war club, battle axe with flint-stone handle [head] (CLCPC 88); táh'-pōn-ē war-club (D94 88); tụụkaʔa axe, hatchet (CLCPC 81); huu- tree, wood (WRA 20)
227	Beil	hatchet	howon	cf. preceding entry
228	Hammer	hammer	techanni	tụhanaitụ hammer, pound, sledge (CLCPC 80)
229	Kleine Schellen	small bells	pissagone	pisayuʔne tin, tin can, canned goods, shiny metals used as jingles (CPCLC 48)
230	Grosser Kamm	large comb	nazistoge	natsituʔye hairbrush, comb (CLCPC 32)
231	Kleiner Kamm	small comb	nabuseaka	cf. nụpusiakenụ search for head lice, delouse; pusia head lice; pusiʔa natsihtuʔye fine-toothed comb, literally "head lice comb" (CLCPC 51)
232	Silberner Kamm	silver comb	pohiwonazis-toge	puhiwi money, gold, metal, dollar + natsituʔye hairbrush, comb (CLCPC 32, 50)
233	Scheere	scissors	nechziske	néhtzisque (GRG 41)
234	Feile	file	puiwuichtichka	puihgüitzisca (GRG 27)
235	Nähnadeln	sewing needles	wonachzach-tana	wanatsahkụna needle (CLCPC 84)

	German	English	Comanche (Berghaus)	Comanche (Later/Modern)*
236	*Behälter dazu*	container for needles	*wuginachz*	*wiyu* awl, sharp instrument + *narɨso* bag, purse, sack (CLCPC 86)
237	*Fingerhut*	thimble	*mositon*	*moʔorɨtsakɨna* (CLCPC 22)
238	*Schnalle*	buckle	*nechtopka*	*wɨtɨpɨka* buckle (CLCPC 89)
239	*Hacke*	hoe	*muchpe*	*muhpe* (CLCPC 22)
240	*Kaffeekanne*	coffee pot	*puhihab*	cf. *puhi huubaa* liquid tea (CLCPC 50)
241	*Kleines Futteral*	small case, sheath	*uihinaz*	[see "container for needles" (236) above]
242	*Cigarre*	cigarette / cigar	*temaquatobibb*	cf. *tɨmakwatui, tɨmɨkɨtubi* plant used for cigarette wrappers (CLCPC 78)
243	*Cigarren wickeln*	to roll cigars	*teomaqueta*	cf. *tɨmakwatui, tɨmɨkɨtubi* plant used for cigarette wrappers (CLCPC 78)
244	*Perlmutterschaale*	mother-of-pearl shell	*nachzim; nakzim*	cf. *naki tsaʔnika* earring [see entry 187 above]; *wakoorɨ* mother of pearl (CLCPC 26, 84)
245	*Rothe Perlen*	red beads	*ecachzomo; ekasomo*	*eka* red (color) + *tsomo* beads (CLCPC 2, 71)
246	*Weisse Perlen*	white beads	*tochzachzomo; tochzazomo*	*tosa-* white, silver (WRA 110) + *tsomo* beads (CLCPC 71)
247	*Blaue Perlen*	blue beads	*uichzomo; puichzomo*	cf. *puhi* leaf [green]; *puhi ebipitɨ* green; *tsomo* beads (CLCPC 50, 71, 188)
248	*Kleiner Schleifstein*	small grindstone	*topp(h)*	cf. *tɨpi* rock; *tɨpi tɨmatsune* whetstone, sandpaper; *tɨsoyuni* grinding stone (CLCPC 79, 80)
249	*Pfeife (Tabacks-)*	(tobacco) pipe	*toich*	*to'sh* tobacco pipe (G93 8); *toʔi* pipe used for smoking (CLCPC 67)
250	*Zinnkopf*	tin/metal cap	*huiahk*	[unattested] cf. *hɨki* umbrella, parasol, arbor, porch (any kind of shade) (CLCPC 7)
251	*Sattel*	saddle	*narino; nadegon*	*narɨnoo, naraʔnoo* (CLCPC 30)

	German	English	Comanche (Berghaus)	Comanche (Later/Modern)*
252	*Sattelknopf*	saddle horn	*namunup*	*narᵾno?ba?pi̠* pommel (CLCPC 31)
253	*Satteltasche*	saddlebag	*piksohr*	*pigusoa* (GRG 41); cf. *tᵾnoo* saddlebag (CLCPC 79)
254	*Steigbügel*	stirrup	*narachtoki*	*nara?tᵾki* (CLCPC 30)
255	*Steigbügelriemen*	stirrup straps	*naramushk*	*narumuca* (G84 91); cf. *nŏts'-àh-mŭhk-káh* girth (D94 192)
256	*Sporn*	spur	*naziwueka*	*natsiwekwa* spurs, rowel (CLCPC 33)
257	*Pferdegebiss*	bit	*ashra*	*áh'ráh* bridle or bridle-bit (D95 1); cf. *arai* bridle; *tᵾpe tsa?nika* bridle bit; *tᵾhᵾyᵾ matsorainᵾ* bridle bit (hand-made) (CLCPC 1, 77, 79)
258	*Zügel*	reins	*nachtuko*	[unattested] cf. *àh'-ráhs* bridle (D94 192); *áh'ráh* bridle or bridle-bit; *áh'ráh nŏd dy mōk* bridle reins (D95 1); *nochoretsoneca* halter (G84 90)
259	*Jagdtasche*	hunting bag	*ahinachzevanié*	[unattested]
260	*Gewehr (Feüer-) [sic]*	rifle	*piai*	cf. *piaet* rifle, carbine (GRG 40); *tawo?i* gun (CLCPC 64)
261	*Gewehrlauf*	rifle barrel	*mashkanboni*	[unattested]
262	*Pistole*	pistol	*subuichbieta*	[unattested] cf. *natsahkwinu̠?e* revolver; *natsahkwine* automatic pistol (CLCPC 32); *piaet* rifle, carbine (GRG 40)
263	*Mündung des Gew.*	muzzle of the rifle	*mateb*	[unattested] cf. *ma* this, that; *tᵾpe* mouth, lips (CLCPC 17, 79)
264	*Pfannendeckel*	powder pan cover	*piatenak*	[unattested] cf. *piaet* rifle, carbine (GRG 40); *nakutsi̠* gunpowder (CLCPC 26); *tᵾrohtᵾma* lid (CLCPC 80)
265	*Schraube daran*	screw on it (the powder pan cover)	*pietenaravuen*	[unattested] cf. *piaet* rifle, carbine (GRG 40)
266	*Visir [Visier]*	gunsight	*mawua(ib)*	[unattested]

	German	English	Comanche (Berghaus)	Comanche (Later/Modern)*
267	Korn	front sight	nanaboni	cf. nanabuni window [literally "look through"] (CLCPC 28)
268	Feüerstein [sic]	flintstone	narak	tetecae flint (GRG 28)
269	Ladestock	ramrod	nenarezenni	cf. tʉtsiwai ramrod (CLCPC 81)
270	Kugelform	ball (bullet) mold	nabakaui	cf. nabaka̱ bullet, lead; aawo cup, container (CLCPC 1, 24)
271	Kugellöffel	shot dipper	naauch	[unattested] cf. preceding entry; aikwaci spoon (older speakers) [Shoshone] (Cr 28)
272	Pulver	powder	nahrkoz	nakutsi̱ gunpowder (CLCPC 26)
273	Pulverhorn	powder horn	nachtoko; kuchzuna nahrkoz	cf. entry "buffalo horn point" (218) above; kuutsu cattle, buffalo; aa horn; nakutsi̱ gunpowder (CLCPC 1, 13, 26)
274	Pulvermaass	powder measure	naritze	[unattested] cf. 271 above
275	Bogen (zum Schiessen)	bow (to shoot)	eth	eetʉ (CLCPC 2)
276	Bogensehne	bowstring	pakkauz	bŏk'-ŏx bow-string (D94 88); pa'ka-ush (G84 67)
277	Pfeile	arrows	paak	paaka̱ (CLCPC 41)
278	Pfeilspitze	arrowhead	tachk	tahka? (WRA 100)
279	Köcher	quiver	kokun	hukuhna (CLCPC 6)
280	Lanzenschaft	lance shaft	wuhinahop	cf. wĭh'-tàh-náh-hōōfp knife-handle (D94 91)
281	Lanzenspitze	lance point	zick	tchi'k spear, lance (G84 79, 81); tʉtsuwai lance, spear (CLCPC 81)
282	Degenscheide	scabbard	wuichtanarsch	cf. wĭhk saber (D94 193); narʉso bag, purse, sack (CLCPC 96)
283	Buch	book	tiwoub	tʉboopʉ book, letter, paper (CLCPC 75)
284	Papier	paper	tiboub	tʉboopʉ book, letter, paper (CLCPC 75)

	German	English	Comanche (Berghaus)	Comanche (Later/Modern)*
285	*Schreiben (verb.)*	to write	*tiboub*	*tɨboopɨ* book, letter, paper; *tɨboorɨ* write (CLCPC 75)
286	*Trompete*	trumpet	*piawoin*	*piaguoin* bugle (GRG 21)
287	*Blasen darauf*	to blow on it (a trumpet)	*reagaket*	cf. *pia* big, large, loud (WRA 79); *yakeetɨ* cry (CLCPC 90)
288	*Knoten*	knots	*mawuchpara*	[unattested] cf. *ma-* with the hand; *wɨpitoorɨ* tie a child to one's back (CLCPC v, 88)
289	*Kleines Loch*	small hole	*tait*	*taaitɨ* cave, hole in the ground, rectum (CLCPC 59)
290	*Roth*	red	*ecksa; ecach*	*eka* red (color) (CLCPC 2)
291	*Schwarz*	black	*tochobz*	*tuhupitɨ* black (color) (CLCPC 99)
292	*Weiss*	white	*tochza; tochzach*	*tosa-* white, silver (WRA 11)
293	*Blaue Farbe*	blue color	*puichb*	cf. *puhipu, puhipɨ* leaf, brush, grass, weed [i.e., "leaf-colored"]; *puhi ebipitɨ* green [lit. "leaf blue/green"] (CLCPC 50, 188) ["blue" and "green" terms can overlap in Comanche]
294	*Gelbe Farbe*	yellow color	*equipza*	cf. *ekwipɨsa* rouge on cheeks, red rock used for makeup; *ohapitɨ* yellow (color) (CLCPC 3, 40)
295	*Karminrothe Farbe*	carmine red color	*ecksap*	[unattested] cf. *eka* red (color); *ekasaapana* soldier [lit. "red stomach," ref. to sash] (CLCPC 2, 148)
296	*Rothe Farbe*	red color	*pissap*	*pisaapi* paint, rouge, compact powder; cf. *eka* red (color) (CLCPC 2, 148)
297	*Gut*	good	*apanachke*	*hayarokweetɨ* four (CLCPC 5) [sacred number, used in Comanche to express "okay" or "perfect"]
298	*Sehr gut*	very good	*zaart*	*tsaatɨ* good, fine, pretty (CLCPC 67)

	German	English	Comanche (Berghaus)	Comanche (Later/Modern)*
299	*Nicht gut*	not good	*techzek*	*tʉtsʉ* cruel, mean, ugly, bad; cf. *aitʉ* not good, no good (CLCPC 1, 81)
300	*Schlecht*	bad	*wuapo*	*guapo* angry [Mexican Spanish]; cf. *ai, aiku, aitʉ* bad, wrong (CLCPC 1)
301	*Schnell*	fast	*namachzo*	*namʉsi, namʉsohitʉ* (CLCPC 121)
302	*Ja*	yes	*ha*	*haa* (CLCPC 4)
303	*Nein*	no	*neatz*	*niatz* (GRG 37); cf. *kee* no (CLCPC 9)
304	*Ich*	I	*un*	cf. *ʉnʉ* you; *nʉ* I (CLCPC 36, 83) [elicitation error?]
305	*Du*	you	*unoso*	cf. *ʉnʉse* and you, you too (CLCPC 83, 198)
306	*Er*	he	*ennes*	cf. *urʉ* he, she, it, that, that one (CLCPC 82)
307	*Ihr*	you [second person plural familiar]	*en*	cf. *mʉnʉ* you (pl.); *ʉnʉ* you [sing.] (CLCPC 23, 83)
308	*Sie*	she	*ojet*	cf. *oyetʉ* all; *urʉ* he, she, it, that, that one (CLCPC 41, 82)
309	*Mein*	my	*imma*	cf. *ʉmi* second person singular accusative emphatic (WRA 303); *emmi* second person singular objective; *emmen* second person singular possessive; *nʉ/nʉe* I, me, my, mine; *nʉa* my (CLCPC 36) [elicitation error?]
310	*Abziehen*	to pull off	*techlat*	*tokarʉ* pull off, knock off (CLCPC 65)
311	*Aderlassen*	to let blood	*tasuibab*	[unattested] cf. *tasiʔawʉsiwʉpʉ* vaccination (lit. smallpox cut open); *pʉʉokwetʉ* bleed, hemorrhage (CLCPC 53, 63)
312	*Ausgiessen*	to pour out	*mabuuchtia*	cf. *ma-* with the hand; *tokwʉria* pour out (CLCPC v, 65)

	German	English	Comanche (Berghaus)	Comanche (Later/Modern)*
313	*Ausziehen (Schuhe)*	to take off (shoes)	*nemapagzag-koegen*	cf. *nɨa* my; *napɨ* shoe, shoes; *tsahkɨarɨ* pull up, force out, take out; *tahkweʔyarɨ*, *tahkweʔyuʔi* take off a shoe (CLCPC 29, 36, 61, 68)
314	*Brechen*	to vomit	*oito*	*oitɨ* throw up (CLCPC 40)
315	*Bringen*	to bring	*terrajia*	[unattested] cf. *ta(h)-* (pfx.) with the foot or leg [used in compounds having to do with bringing or carrying] (CLCPC vi)
316	*Erschiessen*	to shoot (dead)	*mateshkan*	[unattested] cf. *ma-* (pfx) demonstrative or indefinite object, "it," "someone" (C 91, 128); *ma-* with the hand; *tsahkwɨti, wɨhkikatɨ, tsatukanɨ, tsatukarɨ, kwɨhtɨku, kwɨtikukɨrɨ, kwɨɨtikukɨrɨ, kwɨtikɨrɨ* shoot (CLCPC v, 68)
317	*Essen*	to eat	*teschkaro*	*tɨhkarɨ* eat, table, fork (CLCPC 76)
318	*Ich esse*	I eat	*unteschkaro*	cf. *ɨnɨ* you; *tɨhkarɨ* eat, table, fork; *nu* I (CLCPC 36, 76, 83)
319	*Du issest*	you eat	*unosoteschkaro*	*ɨnɨ* you; *-tsa* topicalizing suffix; *tɨhkarɨ* eat, table, fork (CLCPC vii, 76, 83)
320	*Er isst*	he eats	*ennesteschkaro*	*urɨ* he, she, it, that, that one; *-tsa* topicalizing suffix; *tɨhkarɨ* eat, table, fork (CLCPC vii, 76, 130)
321	*Ihr esset*	you [second person plural familiar] eat	*nessateschkaro*	*mɨnɨ* you (pl.); *-tsa* 'topicalizing suffix; *tɨhkarɨ* eat, table, fork (CLCPC vii, 23, 76)
322	*Sie essen*	they eat	*osetteschkaro*	*orɨɨ* those, they; *-tsa* topicalizing suffix; *tɨhkarɨ* eat, table, fork (CLCPC vii, 40, 76)

	German	English	Comanche (Berghaus)	Comanche (Later/Modern)*
323	Ich habe gegessen	I have eaten	unmatebi-manuish kom mateschkaro	[unattested] cf. nʉ I 133 tʉhkarʉ eat, table, fork (CLCPC 76)
324	Essen (mit dem Löffel)	to eat (with a spoon)	nebajuneme	[unattested] cf. tʉewoo, tʉawoo, tʉeʔawo̲ spoon (little cup); tʉhka, tʉʉka, tʉhkarʉ eat, table, fork (CLCPC 76)
325	Fischen	to fish	tuinishpe	cf. tuinʉhpʉ young boy (CLCPC 73); hʉarʉ to trap, to fish; tsahpiʔerʉ fish, pull out (fish) (WRA 22, 114); né hö'apenit I fish with the line; né höan úmakᵘ pía hö'amak I fish with the net (G84 123) [transcription error?]
326	Heben	to lift	tuquamene	tohimarʉ (pl) adopt a child, lift up, carry in arms (WRA 112)
327	Kommen	to come	nariskoe	cf. naʔakʉtʉ meet, come together (WRA 62); naraakitʉ come running; kima come (CLCPC 10, 29)
328	Kratzen	to scratch	machziik	máhtsōw'wōnĭt (D95 128); cf. matsitoo fingernail (CLCPC 20)
329	Laden (ein Gewehr)	to load (a rifle)	marribakioo	cf. ma- with the hand (CLCPC v); tʉbakitʉ (pl obj), norʉbakit̲ʉ (sg obj) load items (as into wagon, gun, sack) (WRA 127)
330	Losdrücken (desgl.)	to fire, pull trigger	manawuishki	cf. ma- with the hand (CLCPC v); wʉhkikatʉ shoot a gun, let an arrow fly (WRA 151)
331	Nachsetzen	to add, replenish; reload [?]	ichap matide	[unattested]
332	Nähen	to sew	mazachke	cf. ma- with the hand; tsaakunarʉ sew (CLCPC v, 68)

	German	English	Comanche (Berghaus)	Comanche (Later/Modern)*
333	*Rauchen (Taback)*	to smoke (tobacco)	*pamotubon*	cf. *pahmu* tobacco; *pahmuʔitu* smoke a cigarette (CLCPC 42)
334	*Reiben*	to rub	*mabizzuckin*	cf. *ma-* (pfx) with the hand; *pisunarʉ*, *pisunetu̱* drag something on a flat surface; *pisuʔnetu̱* rub against something scratch rear or back against something (CLCPC v, 48)
335	*Reiten*	to ride	*nominaroe*	cf. *nomohkarʉ* hitch up horse and buggy (CLCPC 35); *kʉayʉkaʔetʉ* (Wiaʔnʉʉ dialect), *tʉhʉya karʉ* (Kwahare dialect) ride horseback (WRA 34, 129)
336	*Schiffen (durchschiffen)* [transcription error: *Schleifen*]	to drag	*poich*	*piwokarʉ* to drag something (CLCPC 48)
337	*Schiessen* [transcription error: *Scheissen*]	to defecate	*machkuschtine*	*nakwitanʉ* defecate on oneself (CLCPC 26)
338	*Schlagen*	to hit	*nare*	cf. *naropai* hit one another (CLCPC 30)
339	*Schleichen*	to creep / to crawl	*temakimaar*	cf. *ta* (unspecified subject or possessor) (WRA 99); *mahuʔinoorʉ* crawling along (CLCPC 18)
340	*Schneiden*	to cut	*nenochkian*	cf. *nʉ* I; *nʉʉkiʔa* cut yourself accidentally (CLCPC 36, 39)
341	*Stopfen (Tabackspfeife)*	to fill (a pipe)	*tomagiah*	cf. *tʉmayaa* sumac [literally "mix together"; smooth sumac (*Rhus glabra*) bark and leaves used in smoking mixture]
342	*Tauschen*	to trade	*temaowegk*	cf. *tʉmʉ* buy, sell, trade; *tʉmʉʉrʉ* buy, sell; *tʉmʉʉkunʉ* buy, already bought; *narʉmʉ* trade, exchange (CLCPC 31, 78)

	German	English	Comanche (Berghaus)	Comanche (Later/Modern)*
343	Tödten	to kill	habechkaro; machukke	cf. pehkarʉ kill; wasʉpu kill (pl.) (CLCPC 45, 85)
344	Treten (sich etwas in den Fuss)	to step (on something)	narazoem	cf. na- (prefix, reflexive); tasaa step over something (CLCPC v, 63)
345	Trinken	to drink	hibig	hibi (CLCPC 5)
346	Umhängen	to sling / to put on	woawuchtoppo	[unattested] cf. woʔa- (pfx) wormy; wʉhtopoʔnitʉ wind into a ball; wʉhtopʉʔnoorʉ tie in round bundle or round knot (WRA 150, 153)
347	Werfen	to throw	kesch	[unattested] cf. wihi, wihi̱ throw; tohpetihtʉ throw around; tahtʉkwarʉ, tah-paʔitʉ throw at something; takwʉkitʉ throw at the foot of something, throw at a line; tsayumarʉ throw down; tsahkwaʔnuʔitʉ throw down a person; kuhtsawitʉ throw into the fire, burn something up; marátʉbaitu, takwʉkitʉ throw it; wihitʉ throw overhand (CLCPC 11, 19, 61, 62, 65, 68, 70, 85, 86)
348	Werfen (mit d. Cop)	to throw [?]	wuip	wihi throw; wihitʉ throw overhand (CLCPC 85, 86)
349	Wegnehmen	to take away	anemazokan	[unattested] cf. yaakʉrʉ take away (CLCPC 90); tahtʉkitʉ take away something live; tsahkʉarʉ pull up, force out, take out (WRA 102, 113)
350	Wiehern (des Pferdes)	to whinney (a horse)	ochattscha-wawo	[unattested] [echoic? cf. kokoraa chickens; waʔóo cat; wowoki dog, to bark (CLCPC 11, 85, 86)]
351	Zustecken	to pin up	machtomaziin	cf. tsihtʉpʉkarʉ pin together, pin up using a pin; ma- with the hand (CLCPC v); tonarʉ (v) insect sting, stab, pierce (WRA 110)

	German	English	Comanche (Berghaus)	Comanche (Later/Modern)*
352	*Wo?*	where?	*hak*	*hakʉ* (WRA 18)
353	*Komm!*	come!	*kim*	*kima* come (CLCPC 10)
354	*Gehe weg!*	go away!	*miaro*	*mairʉ* go, walk (CLCPC 21)
355	*Höre!*	listen!	*karbun(e)*	cf. *tʉnaka, tʉnakarʉ, tʉnakiitʉ* listen, pay attention, hear something, obey orders (CLCPC 78); *puni* look, see (CLCPC 51); *buuni?* see (WRA 262)
356	*Gieb her!*	give it to me!	*majakim*	cf. *ma-* (pfx) with the hand; *yaa* take; *utu* give (CLCPC v, 82, 90)
357	*Da nimm!*	here, take!	*eh(e)*	cf. *yaa* take; *utu* give (CLCPC 82, 90)
358	*Gib mir die Hand!*	give me your hand!	*nomahiik*	cf. *nʉ* I, me, my mine (CLCPC 36); *maka* give (C 218)
359	*Setzt Euch!*	you (all) sit down!	*care*	cf. *kŏt* or *kŏd* "sit down" a request; to sit (D95 116); *karʉ* sit down (singular); *kaarʉ* sit, sit down (CLCPC 8, 9)
360	*Was wollt Ihr?*	what do you want?	*himme en sowui*	*hina* what (obj.); *ʉnʉ* you; *suʔwaitʉ* want (CLCPC 5, 57, 83)
361	*Es gehört einem Andern*	it belongs to someone else	*atrin piaet*	[unattested] cf. *atʉrʉʉ* others; *piaet* rifle, carbine (GRG 40); *hipʉkatʉ, hipʉkatʉ* own, possess; *taʔurʉkatʉ* own something; *namahku, namahkui* personal belongings (CLCPC 5, 27, 64)
362	*Es ist das Meinige*	it is mine	*naimatz*	cf. *nʉe* I, me, my, mine; *ma* he, she, it, this, that; *-tsa* topical suffix (CLCPC v, 17, 36)
363	*Es ist das Deinige*	it is yours	*esse ochkahip*	cf. *itsa* this is; *ohka* his, hers, its, that one (CLCPC 8, 40)

	German	English	Comanche (Berghaus)	Comanche (Later/Modern)*
364	Wir gehen Morgen [sic]	we go tomorrow	miaro poitzka	mairʉ go, walk; pʉetsʉku tomorrow, in the morning (CLCPC 21, 52)
365	Sie kommen an-geritten	they're ap-proaching on horseback	onarin e kima taohpa	cf. orʉʉ those, they (pl.); kima come; tʉhʉya horse (CLCPC 10, 40, 76)
366	Er kommt an	he comes	pennashpe	[unattested] cf. urʉ he, she, it, that, that one; kima come (CLCPC 10, 82)

Citation key: B = Berlandier 1980; C = Charney (1993); CLCPC = Comanche Language and Cultural Preservation Committee (2010); Cr = Crapo (1976); D94 = Detrich (1894); D95 = Detrich (1895); G84 = Gatschet (1884); G93 = Gatschet (1893); GRG = García Rejón and Gelo (1995); M = Miller (1972); WRA = Wistrand-Robinson and Armagost (1990). Orthographies from these sources are all preserved in their original forms. Brackets indicate commentary by Gelo and Wickham.

[Berghaus's second endnote 14 in the original] The word "padoko" resembles the name Paducas, mentioned 1724 by Bourgmont, and is supposedly the name by which the Comanches are known among the Pahni nation. Adelung and Vater, Mithridates, III, 3, p. 174. Berghaus' Völker des Erdballs [Peoples of the Globe], I, 289.

Index of English Terms

Index of English Terms *cont.*

dog	115	grass	145
dried leaf	151	grasshopper	142
ear	32	green blanket	173
earrings	187	gray or white horse	119
Earth (planet)	80	gums	23
elbow	34	gunsight	266
entrails/intestines	61	hair	8
evening	86	hairbrush	195
eyebrows	14	half moon	81
eyelids	15	hammer	228
eyes	13	hand	35
fast	301	hand ring	189
feet	55	handle/hook	215
file	234	hatchet	227
finger	36	he	306
finger ring	191	he comes	366
fingernails	43	he eats	320
father	1	heart	44
fish [pl.]	135	heel	57
fishing pole	203	here, take!	357
flintstone	268	hoe	239
fly	140	honey	159
foal	124	horse brand	129
forehead	11	horse with blaze	118
fringes	185	horse's hoof	126
front sight	267	horse's mane	125
give it to me!	356	horse's swelling	130
give me your hand!	358	horse's tail	127
gloves	184	hunting bag	259
go away!	354	I	304
gold	99	I eat	318
good	297	I have eaten	323

Index of English Terms *cont.*

index finger	38	medicine	169
instep/arch of foot	54	Mexican blanket	214
iron ring	210	Mexican sugar	157
iron wire	219	midday	85
it belongs to someone else	361	middle finger	39
it is mine	362	milk	168
it is yours	363	mine	309
knee	49	mirror	198
kneecap	50	morning	84
knife	223	mother	2
knots	288	mother-of-pearl shell	244
lance point	281	muzzle of a rifle	263
lance shaft	280	navel	46
large ax	226	neck	30
large comb	230	neck jewelry	188
large knife	225	nipple	28
large pinto, piebald horse	122	no	303
lead	101	nose	12
leather bag	213	nosebleed	65
leather fringes	186	nostrils	20
leg	48	nostrils, horse or cattle	128
leggings / riding pants	181	not good	299
leopard	111	oak	148
lightning	92	oak leaf	149
lips	19	panther	110
listen!	355	pants	180
little finger	41	paper	284
louse	136	pigtails	10
lower leg	52	pinto, piebald horse	121
makeup/cosmetic	192	pistol	262
makeup/cosmetic bag	193	ponytail	9
meat	154	powder	272
meat broth	165	powder horn	273

Index of English Terms *cont.*

powder measure	274		shot dipper	271
powder pan cover	264		silver	100
quiver	279		silver comb	232
rain	90		sinew	155
raisins	162		skunk	113
ramrod	269		small beans	167
rattlesnake	138		small bells	229
red	290		small buckle	221
red beads	245		small case, sheath	241
red blanket	172		small comb	231
red color	296		small grindstone	248
reins	258		small hole	289
ribs	47		small iron chains	220
rifle	260		small knife	224
rifle barrel	261		small maggot/grub	137
ring finger	40		small makeup/cosmetic bag	194
saddle	251		small pouch	211
saddlebag	253		small whistle	222
saddle horn	252		small wound	66
saliva	25		smoke	88
salt	104		soap	208
scabbard	282		sole of the foot	56
scalp	7		sorrel horse	120
scarf, bandanna	174		space between fingers	42
scissors	233		spirits, liquor	164
screw on the lid	265		spur	256
sea	96		stallion	123
seashell	143		star	82
sewing needles	235		steel	103
she	308		stirrup	254
shirt	177		stirrup straps	255
shoe sole	176		stomach	45
shoes	175		straw/plank bed	207

Index of English Terms *cont.*

Index of English Terms *cont.*

to take off (shoes)	313	warm	97
to throw	347	water	89
to throw [?]	348	we go tomorrow	364
to trade	342	what do you want?	360
to vomit	314	where?	352
to whinney (a horse)	350	white	292
to write	284	white beads	246
to yawn	71	white cracker	166
tobacco	160	wildcat	112
(tobacco) pipe	249	wind	95
toe	58	woman	3
tomahawk	197	wooden lid / cover	204
tongue	24	yellow color	294
tooth	21	yes	302
trumpet	286	you	305
trunk/suitcase	209	you (all) sit down!	359
turkey [male]	134	you [all]	307
twig	146	you [all] eat	321
umbrella	212	you eat	319
very good	298	young child	5

Comparative Word List of the Shoshone and Comanche Language

English	Shoshone (Western)	Comanche	English	Shoshone (Western)	Comanche
man	*nána*	–	fire	*koso*	*cochzo* (tinder pouch)
woman	*moghoni*	*weishpe*	water	*pa*	*pa*
father	*una*	*achpe*	rain	*tomoa*	*tomojake* (thunder) *tomohab* (clouds)
mother	*pia*	*pia*	snow	*niwaari*	–
son	*itue*	–	earth	*tiip*	*chokoo*
daughter	*tauakhki*	–	river	*anahukwa*	–
head	*tsopigh*	–	stone	*tipi*	–
hair	*ijuo*	*pap(i)*	meal	*atuku*	*teschkaro* (eat)
ear	*inaka*	*nak(i)*	dog	*soghouuk*	*zari*
eye	*pui*	*puile* (plural)	beaver	*kohi*	–
nose	*moui*	*muule*	bear	*padua*	*ochzo*
mouth	*tupa*	*tupe* (lips)	bird	*kuinaa*	–
tongue	*egho*	*ekh*	fish	*aghai*	*bek(uih)*
teeth	*tama*	*tama*	big	*pavaiu*	–
hand	*imái*	*mashpa*	cold	*izils*	*etscho*
finger	*mái*	*massit*	white	*tohakwitya*	*tochza*
feet	*kuki*	*koegen* (?)	black	*tuhukwitya*	*tochobz*
blood	*apui*	*poschp*	red	*atsakwitya*	*ecksa, ecach*
house	*noui*	–	I	*ni*	*un*
ax	*wuwiani*	*huuchwanni*	you	*i*	*unoso*
knife	*wihi*	*huig; roui*	he	*oo*	*ennes*
shoes	*moko*	*nap*	one	*singweiu*	–
sky	*pataskia*	–	two	*wahaiu*	–
sun	*taoa*	*tabih*	three	*pahaiu*	–
moon	*musha*	*mea*	four	*watsikweyu*	–
star	*patuzuva*	*tazinupp(ig)*	five	*napiu*	–
day	*tavino*	*tabikan*	six	*natakskweyu*	–
night	*tokano*	–	ten	*singwaloyu*	–

13

Historical Analysis of the Berghaus Map

Berghaus's map of the Comanche hunting grounds in Texas (map 1), a region he never surveyed or visited himself, is quite original and holds a unique place among the generally incestuous corpus of early Texas maps. As an eminent cartographer Berghaus would have been familiar with many or all previous maps of the region, and yet his is distinct in that it clearly depends on the reports of Kriewitz and is intended to record the full array of Native ethnonyms and locations as well as the German presence. The attribution along the bottom edge of the map indicates that it was "drawn by Theodor Schilling from the handwritten communications of an immigrant." Schilling was a prominent cartographic artist associated with major German atlas publications of the era, such as the Stieler Atlas and atlases of August Petermann. It is impossible to assess what role Schilling might have played in decisions concerning the final look of Berghaus's Comanche map. However, the map clearly met with Berghaus's approval as it was he who submitted it to the publisher Perthes with a cover letter dated April 20, 1851, in which he refers to it as a "map that I have made." A review of preceding maps illustrates Berghaus's debt to earlier mapmakers as well as the novelty of his 1851 work.

The first printed map to include a form of the place name "Texas" and offer appreciable detail of the region is Guillaume Delisle's 1718 *Carte de la Louisiane et du cours du Mississipi* [*sic*] (Delisle 1718; Martin and Martin 1999, 25, 98–99). Although widely plagiarized across Europe, this work seems to have exerted little if any direct influence on Berghaus. Its breadth and scale do not admit of the level of detail seen in later maps of Texas specifically, and the river courses, while improved over earlier maps (and better than some later ones), do not approach the degree of accuracy found in Berghaus. The map is notable for its attention to Native populations; locating the tribes would become a convention in Texas mapmaking. Delisle shows various Caddoan villages at their then-easterly locations, some Jumanos, and coastal "man-eaters," presumably the Karankawas. None of these groups have readily apparent correlates with those shown in Berghaus's map. Generally north and west of Texas, on the headwaters of the Missouri, Kansas, Arkansas, and Red Rivers, Delisle locates the villages and territory of the Apaches and Padoucas, the latter name sometimes used for Comanches, as explained in chapter 11. Also shown within Texas are the Nacanné, a name once equated with the Comanche band name Nokoni (Mooney 1907c, 388), which does appear in Berghaus's discussion and map; this equation, however, has since been implicitly discounted (Kavanagh 1996, 485; 2001, 904), and the Nacanné (as Nocono) are considered to have been a Caddoan population (e.g., Perttula 1992, 151, 219, 220). One more interesting feature of Delisle's map is his indication of "Mines de Plomb" on the southwest bank of the Trinity River. Fables of lead first drew Moses Austin's attention to the Spanish Southwest (Gracy 1987, 53), which set in motion the development of Austin's Colony and thus subsequent colonization efforts, including those of the Adelsverein. Mapmakers were keen on charting mineral resources, an interest that persisted through the cartography of Alexander von Humboldt and Stephen Austin and beyond, and which found expression in Berghaus's allusion to the San Saba mines legend, though he did not locate the mines on his map.

In 1810, with the appearance of English mapmaker Aaron Arrowsmith's "New Map of Mexico and Adjacent Provinces," some reasonable detail of the region north and west of San Antonio became available (Arrowsmith 1810; Martin and Martin 1999, 29, 112–13). Arrowsmith synthesized fresh accounts from the American military explorer Zebulon Pike and Alexander von Humboldt, adjusting for their errors where necessary. This map shows Comanches dwelling on the Pecos River and marks San Saba. Also, it positions the "Yamparicas" to the northwest of the Rio Grande headwaters in present Colorado. The Yamparikas were the last Comanche division to separate from the Shoshones and migrate southward. At this time, it was reasonable to treat "Yamparicas" and "Comanches" as ethnically as well as physically separate populations. The Yamparikas (as Japarishka) are included among the Texas tribes in Berghaus's 1851 article and map.

Pike's own "Map of the Internal Provinces of New Spain" had appeared earlier the same year, variously within or supplementing the book recounting his reconnaissance of the Arkansas and Red River headwaters, during which he was arrested by Spanish troops and escorted home through Texas (Pike 1810; Coues 1895, 2:690–717, 3:955; Jackson 1966, 3:178; Martin and Martin 1999, 110–11; an adaptation of the map also appears in Quaife 1925, xxvi). The first American description of Texas of any length, Pike's book was immediately valued, and within three years had been edited and republished in England, and from that version translated into Dutch, French, and German (Jenkins 1988, 435–42; see Pike 1813 for German edition). Pike's Texas map documents several river courses, locates San Saba and the far northwestern Yamparikas, and places the Ietan Indians on the upper Pecos while also denoting the upper Red River as "Ietan Country," using an early name for the Comanches.

Humboldt's "Map of New Spain" had existed in draft form since he concluded his year of study in Mexico in 1804 (Martin and Martin 1999, 108–9). During his trip home, while visiting President Thomas Jefferson in Washington, DC, he made a copy for US government use, and thus it became available to Pike. The published version was printed presumably on its imprint date of October 25, 1810, for inclusion in Humboldt's *Essai Politique sur le Royaume de la Nouvelle-Espagne* (*Political Essay on the Kingdom of New Spain*), available in both French and English editions (Humboldt 1811). Like both its successors, Humboldt's plat locates San Saba, the Yamparikas far to the northwest, and the Comanches on the Pecos. Humboldt rightly and publicly accused both Pike and Arrowsmith of pirating his map, and Jefferson wrote an apology to Humboldt on Pike's behalf in 1813. Ultimately, however, the Humboldt map was inferior to its imitations in its detailing of Texas. Given Berghaus's relationship with Humboldt, and his citation of Humboldt's 1811 *Essai* as well as the 1812 French edition of Pike's journal in note *s* of his 1851 article, it is a virtual certainty that he knew all three of these maps well and that they conditioned his understanding of relevant places and peoples.

Two more maps that were definitely known by Berghaus, since he translated the book in which they appeared from English into German, were those provided in George Catlin's *Letters and Notes*. Catlin's "Outline Map of Indian Localities in 1833" (Catlin 1841, 1:viii) shows Comanches on the upper Red River and middle Rio Grande. His "U. States' Indian Frontier in 1840" map (Catlin 1841, 2:viii) focuses on the eastern removed tribes and rivers and tribes of the Central and Northern Plains, and provides no detail for Texas, except to show Comanches on the headwaters of the Red and (unnamed) Colorado Rivers. These maps lack any other detail on the order of that provided in Berghaus's map.

Maps devoted specifically to Texas became prevalent once the independent state was formed in 1836 and during the two decades approaching Berghaus's 1851 publication date. These maps, with their enhanced detail of Texas river courses and Comanche river names, appear to be the direct models for Berghaus's map. All of these maps seem to be elaborations of one composed by Stephen F. Austin and published by H. S. Tanner in 1830 (Austin 1830; Martin and Martin 1999, 120–21). Austin had promised to produce a reliable map of the province when he obtained confirmation of his land grant for the Austin Colony from the Mexican government. Through the 1820s he collected information from travelers and surveyors and consulted Mexican sketch maps. During these studies, he may well have run across drawings by the last Spanish Indian emissary from Béxar, Francisco Amangual, army engineer Juan Pedro Walker, or the friars José Maria Puelles and José Antonio Pichardo (see John 1988; Martin and Martin 1999, 28–29). His father referred him to John Melish's popular United States print map, issued in numerous revisions between 1816 and 1823, which depicted Texas among "Other Countries-Spanish Possessions" (Melish 1816; Gracy 1987, 194–95; Martin and Martin 1999, 114–15). He acquired the careful astronomical readings of various Texas locations taken by General Manuel de Mier y Terán during his 1828 inspection tour (Jackson and Wheat 2000, 13). He must have also seen the published maps of Arrowsmith, Pike, and Humboldt.

Many of Austin's own sketches from the period are found among his papers. For example, there is his 1822 drawing with good detail of coastal Texas, a Comanche trail, and "Comanches" inscribed in big letters across the northwest, though yet devoid of upstream details or any other Comanche names or locations (Austin 1822; Barker 1925, following p. 52). The most intriguing of these prototypes is one Austin inked in 1827 as part of his unfulfilled plan to attack the Central Texas tribes, which exists in at least two versions (map 2; Austin 1827a, 1827b; Castañeda and Martin 1930, 49–51; McLean 1974–93, 3:46–47, 266–67; Gelo 2013, 14–16, 69–70, 74). Apart from revealing Austin's ruthless attitude toward

Native populations, the campaign map includes numerous geographic details that are repeated in his published map and its successors. Here we see the advent of a series of stream names ending in the elements *-junova* and *-oque*, which are Hispanicized versions of Comanche words for "stream," *hunuʔbi* and *okweetᵻ*, and other features that would become conventional, such as the Waco Indian village on the Brazos River, Presidio San Saba, and an unlabeled mountain that probably represents Enchanted Rock.

Although a notation on one version of the campaign map states that it was "made . . . from actual observations," inaccuracies in the location of several landmarks and a general distortion toward the west betray that not all of the observations were Austin's own, and that he was more familiar with eastern Texas and relied more on secondhand information when mapping the upriver reaches (Gelo 2013, 15). And while Austin's later maps are generally replete with features relevant to the Comanches, it has been suggested that he manipulated the number and position of Indian populations in particular renditions depending on the intended audience, magnifying the apparent Indian threat when he was seeking protection from the Mexican government for his colony but downplaying it when advertising for new colonists (Jackson and Wheat 2000, 220–21n71; Gelo 2013, 69).

In any event, several reissues and derivations of Austin's 1830 map followed, usually touting the most current survey and grant boundary data and documenting the transition of Texas from Mexican state to independent nation to United States annexation. Typical of the American and English maps following Austin's are those by Burr (1833, 1846; Martin and Martin 1999, 122–23); Bradford (1835, 64.A–64.C; Martin and Martin 1999, 124–25); Hooker (1836); Young (1836); Austin (1836); Hunt and Randel (1839); John Arrowsmith (1841 [see also map 3]; Martin and Martin 1999, 126–27); Day and Haghe (Maillard 1842, 512ff.); Emory (1844); Greenleaf (1845); Wilson (1845; Martin and Martin 1999, 132–33); Disturnell (1846); Tanner (1846); and the Society for the Diffusion of Useful Knowledge (1846). To these examples may be added one published in Brussels by Marche (1835). Similar Texas maps under different nominal authorship also appeared in numerous world atlases of the era, while the Austin details were also adopted in several wall maps of the greater southwest (e.g., Brue 1845). Only with the appearance of land agent Jacob De Cordova's *Map of the State of Texas* (1849; Martin and Martin 1999, 140–41) is there concerted modernization and departure from the Austin formula. About the same time, in association with the Mexican War and the first string of US Army frontier forts, military surveyors brought their superior mapping skills to the region (e.g., Bureau of the Corps of Topographical Engineers 1850).

German publishers were ready to join the Austin-inspired map industry and address the growing interest in Texas in their own country. Stempfle's 1841 *Karte von Texas* (Stempfle 1841), accompanying George Scherpf's book describing this new nation in America (Scherpf 1841), was an acknowledged copy of Hunt and Randel's 1839 map. Its legends and place names are in English. The German nobles who founded the Adelsverein relied on Scherpf for his thorough and optimistic report. Other Hunt and Randel derivatives soon circulated for the audience of potential settlers and, like their American counterparts, included updates on grant titles and boundaries. One with German wording (Anonymous 1845; map 4) appeared both separately and in two influential books, the German translation of William Kennedy's *Texas* (Kennedy 1845) and the Adelsverein's own guide to Texas (Adelsverein 1845). Another very similar *Spezial-Karte* was included in the back of Baron von Ehrenkreutz's immigration manual (Ehrenkreutz 1846). Ehrenkreutz's handbook is cited by Berghaus, so we can be sure he knew this map (Berghaus 1851, 61n15[o]). Besides these Hunt and Randel offspring, Carl Flemming's 1844 map (Flemming 1844) is a German-language version of Arrowsmith 1841, while Joseph Meyer (Meyer 1846) copied Emory's 1844 work.

Also noteworthy are two folding maps included with the distinctly straightforward immigrant's guide written by Adelsverein leader Prince Carl of Solms-Braunfels (Solms-Braunfels 1846a, 1936). These maps were prepared with help from John Coffee "Jack" Hays, a legendary Texas Ranger who engaged in surveying along with his militia duties (Jenkins 1988, 505; Weiss 2010). The first map (Solms-Braunfels 1846b), a full one of Texas and adjoining areas, is fairly ordinary but for its German legends, updates of the various colony boundaries, and robust inclusion of tribal names and locations. This inclusion of tribal names and locations may reflect Hays's background as an Indian fighter as well as the prince's candid approach to reporting local conditions or his sympathetic stance toward the Natives as expressed in his published observations. The second map (Solms-Braunfels 1846c), in English, is unusual and quite possibly a direct precursor to Berghaus's map, as it focuses on the region northwest of

San Antonio. No doubt recording Hays's familiarity with the Hill Country, the second map labels San Saba Fort and nearby "Mineral Region," the lands of the "German Emigration Company," and the site of the yet-to-be-built town of Fridrichsburg [*sic*] south of "Enchanted Rocks." It carefully depicts area streams with their Spanish or English names and the Pinta and Bandera Indian trails, but gives no Indian group names or locations.

The geologic map drawn by Ferdinand von Roemer to accompany his scientific treatise on Texas (Roemer 1849b) reverts to the Austin format, with direct acknowledgment of Wilson 1845, though with German legends and particular heed to stream headwater details, topography, and vegetation. The original version featured hand coloration to indicate geological formations, which is not reproduced in the reprint version. The Comanches reside just northwest of the Fisher-Miller grant. This prettily rendered map and Roemer's descriptions were assuredly known to Berghaus. Also appearing in 1849 was Julius Bädeker's map for prospective immigrants (Bädeker 1849), found in some copies of the original edition of Viktor Bracht's immigration guide (Bracht 1849) or separately. Bädeker's map is drawn again on the Austin—John Arrowsmith—Emory model, but busy with the most current updates regarding the European settlements. Thus along with inset town plans of New Braunfels and Castroville, Bädeker locates the young commune of Leiningen on the Llano River; all three of these settlements are shown in Berghaus's map. The position of the Comanches is announced in large letters, but safely to the west of the Hill Country settlements, as if to calm prospective settlers, in the best Austinian tradition.

Berghaus himself had already published maps on which the territory inhabited by the Comanches is represented, even if not identified as such. The first edition of Berghaus's innovative Physical Atlas appeared in fascicles released between 1845 and 1848. An inset to his global map showing settlement distribution of Germans in both hemispheres of the earth (Berghaus 1852, VIII, map 3, dated "Gotha, bei Justus Perthes, 1846") is titled "Distribution of the Germans in North America" ("Verbreitung der Deutschen in Nordamerika"). The accompanying note incorporated into the map states that the total US population in 1846 is estimated at twenty million. We may assume that Berghaus's map relates to estimated population distributions in that year. A statistical table, initialed by Berghaus, shows the estimated figure 5,233,000 as the total population of Germans in the United States and is dated "Potsdam, December 31,

1845." The inset map includes numerals after state and some city names to show approximate percentage of Germans among the population, and stippling to represent the same information visually. The name "Texas" is followed by a question mark, suggesting Berghaus does not have data for the German population density for the republic/state of Texas at this time, however the density of the stippling suggests 0–20 percent. The inset map does not mention Comanches, though it includes general locations for some tribes, including "Assiniboins, Minataries, Mandaner, Ricaries, Sioux, Puncahs, Pahnies, Omahas und Ottos" in the West. It also includes a list of tribal names, underlined in purple at the approximate location of present-day Oklahoma, of relocated "Algonkin-Lenape and Florida tribes": "Kickapuhs, Delawares, Konzas, Shahnies, Peerias und Kaskaskias, Piankeshahe und Weah, Oncidas, Tuscaroras, Senecas, Shahnies, Tschirokees, Crieks, Seminolen, Tschoktahs, Tschickasahs." The mix of English- and German-based spellings suggests Berghaus was using sources in both languages, or he Germanized the orthography (*tsch, sch, puh*) in some names where he was aware of accepted German spellings.

A second map (no. 17) in the ethnographic section of the Physical Atlas, dated "Potsdam, June 1845," and based, according to an annotation initialed by Berghaus, on information from "Alb. Gallatin, A. von Humboldt, Clavigero, Hervas, Vater, etc.," shows the number 19 under the name "Texas." The map's key of "Language and Tribal Families of Indians" shows 19 to refer to Shoshones and Comanches. The corresponding map in the 1852 (second) edition of the Physical Atlas shows more detail, and instead of the simple colored areas identified by numerals of the 1845–46 edition, includes tribal names entered at particular, generalized locations. Here, one year after the Berghaus article and map in the Yearbook appeared, we see, in addition to the number 19, in an arc stretching from north of the Canadian River southeast to a point west of Galveston, the words "Kamantschen oder Comanches." To the west of this arc are "Li-pans" and "Apaches." The extensive ethnographic annotations printed below the 1852 version of map 17 do not include any reference to Berghaus's 1851 Yearbook map; however, the text of the Physical Atlas in the 1852 edition does refer to the 1851 article and Berghaus's own proof of the linguistic relationship of the Comanches to the Shoshones (Berghaus 1852, 8:57), though not to the map of the Comanche hunting grounds.

Berghaus is credited, along with Solms-Braunfels and "other travelers," as a source in the title of another German Texas map of the period, an extremely rare one drawn for the Adelsverein audience by Walter Farmer (Farmer 1847). This appears to be the only instance in which Berghaus is noted as an influence on his contemporaries in Texas mapmaking. It is difficult, however, to see any effect from Berghaus's work in this map, and perhaps Farmer simply sought credibility by citing the name of a notable cartographer. His map outlines the Verein's grant in green, with the legend "Indianer Jadgrevier" (Indian hunting area) running just northwest, but it contains neither the ethnological information nor statistics on German settlement that distinguished Berghaus's work, and its scope and details leave it very much in the Austin mold.

The final preceding maps for consideration are two issued by the Adelsverein itself in 1850 and 1851. The first of these (Willke 1850; map 5), drawn by Hermann Willke, an engineer and surveyor for the Verein who accompanied Meusebach on the treaty expedition and thereafter worked out of New Braunfels, is a meticulous rendering of the area from San Antonio to the Colorado River. This is a very rare item, intended for inclusion in a pamphlet advising immigrants (Adelsverein 1851) and found within or separately. As a reference for settlers, Willke's map does not show Comanches, but amid all the land sections surveyed around New Braunfels, "Friederichsburg," and on into the Fisher-Miller grant are found some salient features. These include the Old Spanish Fort on the San Saba, and several trails of undoubted Indian origin, including ones named for Meusebach and "Schubart" (Adelsverein settlement leader Dr. Friedrich A. Schubert) and the "Camino Pinta." Also included are the Comanche landmarks Enchanted Rock and House Mountain, and Bullhead Mountain. The second Adelsverein map of interest covers the entire state (Verein zum Schutze deutscher Auswanderung 1851; Wurster 2008, 66–67). It shows no Comanches or other Indians whatsoever, but instead highlights the route that German immigrants would use in traveling to the interior, from Indianola, through Victoria, Gonzales, New Braunfels, and Fredericksburg. The route continues beyond Fredericksburg and terminates just north of the Llano, at three dots labeled "Deutsche Niederlassungen" ("German settlements"), obviously representing the recent colonies of Castell, Bettina, and Leiningen that are labeled individually on the Berghaus map. In other respects, this map is similar to its contemporaries. Drawing on information from the prior few years, the Adelsverein maps were the most up-to-date in detailing the extent of settlement. It is possible though not certain that Berghaus saw them on the eve of his own 1851 publication.

With these German editions joining those from the United States and England, Berghaus and perhaps Kriewitz too would have had ample exposure to the cartographic conventions set in place by Stephen F. Austin and refined by his followers. It then fell to Berghaus to adopt or reject the various common details while adding others to produce his unique picture of the Comanche hunting grounds.

Berghaus's sweeping legend indicating *Jagd-Gebiet der Komantschen* ("Comanche Hunting Grounds") in the northwest, and a lesser one locating the Delawares and Shawnees in the southeast, imitate earlier maps, except in prior cases such legends often referred to animals and vegetation. The practice was old and virtually required, stemming at least from Thomas Jeffrys's 1775 chart of coastal Texas, which announces "VAST PLAINS which are a continual Savanna intermixed with Woods and full of Wild Beeves; They are Inhabited by the Canokosses, Ebahamas, Caouaches, Quelameloueches, Teaos and Several other Tribes of Wandering Indians" (Jeffrys 1775, DE.2; Martin and Martin 1999, 102). Subsequent maps reported in similar fashion as the gaze moved to the interior: "Immence Plains, where the Bisons feed (Cibola)" (Humboldt 1811; Martin and Martin 1999, 108); "Immense Herds of wild Horses" (Pike 1810; Martin and Martin 1999, 110; and Pike's expedition narrative is obsessive about sightings of wild herds and their trails); "IMMENSE DROVES OF WILD HORSES," "Large Droves of Wild Cattle and Horses" (Austin 1830; Martin and Martin 1999, 120); Roemer includes "COMANCHE INDIANER" between the smaller legends "MEZQUITE PRARIEN" and "GROSSE BÜFFEL HERDEN" (Roemer 1849b).

There are no similar animal and vegetation legends in the Berghaus map. By including three major Indian tribe names using the lettering style more usually employed for flora and fauna, Berghaus, like Jeffrys and Roemer, appears to assimilate Indians to other "natural" features found on the landscape, but he goes a step further, reorienting totally from natural resources to ethnology and thus redefining the purpose of the Texas map. He also sets up a contrast between the nomadic Comanches and the two relocated eastern tribes who were at that time allied with the settlers, working as scouts. He even adds a long dotted line between the two Indian groups signifying the boundary between the settlements and Comanche territory. The legend for Delawares and Shawnees therefore should not be taken as a traditional territory or range but rather as an indication that they were associating with the settlements.

From an ethnological standpoint, the recording of Comanche stream names is Austin's greatest mapmaking contribution. His earliest sketches employed only Spanish (and one English: Noland) names, but by the time of his 1827 attack plans, intent on defining a Comanche heartland, he began using a series of names of definite or possible Comanche origin. Initially he assigned one or two of these names to the Wichita River drainage, four to the Brazos, and three to the Colorado. By the appearance of the famous 1830 Tanner map, Austin had made a few spelling changes (notably, Guischaballa became Wisshauea), moved the two names he had assigned to the Wichita drainage into the upper Brazos, and added others, totaling eight in the Brazos drainage and five in the Colorado (table 1). These names, with the exception of Wisshauea, which was nearest the settlements and thus perhaps obsolete early on, were then perpetuated with little variation in the many derivative maps.

Table 1. Comanche stream names in Austin (1830)

Brazos River Drainage	Colorado River Drainage
Ocoque C.	Wisshauea C.
Ontejunova C.	Piaroya C.
R. Tahcajunova	R. Pasigono
R. Taray	Muchique C.
R. Incoque	R. Pisapejunova
R. Tosahunova	
R. Timpisarahca	
R. Keriachehunova	

Berghaus's map and text make equally distinctive contributions on this subject, as he provides nine Comanche stream names, only three of which can be matched to those on preceding maps (table 2).

Table 2. Comanche stream names in Berghaus (1851)

Brazos River Drainage	Colorado River Drainage
Tuscoque, Rio Bosque, Bushy Cr.	Enehokue, Conjo
Ekaoque, Pato Pinto [*sic*]	Uranazwene
Tuscoque [repeated on different stream]	Narahono
	Woquequahono
	Tagkanohi
	Pissapejunova*
	Passiwono

* mentioned in text only; not on map

Berghaus's unique spellings for the three river names that correspond to those on earlier maps, and his misspellings of Palo Pinto and Pecan, possibly misreadings of Kriewitz's handwriting, amount to evidence that Berghaus was working with independently generated information about Comanche geography that most certainly originated with Kriewitz. There is no reason to think that Kriewitz would have been able to survey all the watercourses himself during his spell with the Comanches, but he may have traveled along many of them. Moreover, his linguistic studies show a sophisticated approach to questions of ethnographic detail, and it seems highly likely that he would have inquired about stream names, particularly in the context of where various bands were camping. Berghaus does an additional service by providing alternative names for two of the Comanche ones, for the Bosque and Concho Rivers. It is otherwise notoriously difficult to match up some of these Comanche names with stream courses as they are later known. Berghaus's contribution is not perfect, however, as he uses one name, Tuscoque, to label two different streams; Comanche stream names were sometimes used for multiple streams, but Berghaus does not confirm the practice in this instance. More interpretation of the Berghaus stream names is provided in the text commentary.

The main reason it is hard to connect some Comanche stream names with known watercourses is because the upstream reaches, deep in Indian country, were drawn on speculation, and thus imprecisely, on all the early maps. Solms-Braunfels, writing circa 1845, gives us some insight into the origins of the problem: "The accuracy of most surveyors' maps depends on the human eye alone. A few tracts have been surveyed with the aid of a chain. Neither a surveyor's table, a sight-vane, a sextant, nor any other surveying instrument has yet been used in Texas. Much less has anyone thought of applying trigonometry in measuring the area of the state" (quoted in Jenkins 1988, 505). There is also the persistent gross error of showing the Colorado River headwaters as curving southward as one moves upstream, when they actually trend mostly northwest. Even as finely crafted a work as John Arrowsmith's 1841 map, with beautiful illustration of the regional hydrography, perpetuates these errors, and they are repeated too in German maps such as Bädeker's and Roemer's. For some reason, Burr (1833) and Emory (1844) were able to do a better job on some of the stream courses, but De Cordova's 1849 map, breaking with the Austin template, provides the earliest overall improvement.

Remarkably, Berghaus's hydrography appears to have been independently conceived, and he avoids the error of headwater direction, though he introduces his own errors of proportion. In actuality the Llano River is longer than the Pedernales and the San Saba, but it is foreshortened on Berghaus's map, and the San Saba is most pronounced. One would learn from his map that the sources of the San Saba and the main Colorado were adjacent, when in fact the San Saba rises in the Hill Country, and the Colorado all the way west around the New Mexico border. It may be speculated that the San Saba loomed large in Kriewitz's personal reckoning of Comanche country, and therefore it was enlarged on Berghaus's map. Indeed, an exaggerated impression of the San Saba area must have prevailed among the Adelsverein settlers and in German consciousness generally at this time. In his 1841 historical novel describing German immigration to Texas, H. E. R. Belani has his freshly arrived immigrants stand on a rise north of the city of San Antonio glimpsing the Gulf of Mexico in the east, the plateaus of Mexico to the south, and the "Sierra de San Saba" to the north (Belani 1841, 1:3–4). None of this is physically possible given the distances. It is evident that the author had a map showing the San Saba range at his disposal but was entirely ignorant of its scale. Berghaus's drawing of the San Marcos River is likewise inaccurate. This stream, even including the unlabeled tributary Blanco River as Berghaus seems to show, still begins a good thirty-eight miles east of the source of the Pedernales, but the map has them both starting at nearly the same longitude. Berghaus also foreshortens the entire Brazos system. Because of these distortions, his hydrography is not an unqualified improvement over earlier drawings.

Why did Berghaus labor over stream courses at all for an ethnographic map? He clearly understood the Comanche concept of territory, in which rivers quite naturally played a major role. This understanding is evident in his text. The Comanche migration southward through Colorado, New Mexico, and Oklahoma may be understood as the progressive usurpation of drainages from earlier, mainly Apachean, occupants. Within Texas a similar pattern is evident, as Comanche divisions displaced or allied with Apaches, Wichitans, and Tonkawas and moved progressively into the up-per Red, Brazos, Colorado, Guadalupe, and Nueces watersheds. And they were eyeing opportunities in the lower Colorado and Brazos, the Trinity watershed, and along and beyond the Rio Grande when Anglo-American settlers came pushing in the opposite direction. When Berghaus associates various bands with streams in his narrative, he is recording a snapshot of this migration dynamic as well as defining supposed band grazing areas.

Another standard feature of Texas maps of the era was the depiction of mountain ranges, including some in Central Texas. Austin's 1830 map showed narrow ranges spreading like varicose veins through the middle of the state, between the rivers, and some unnamed peaks, one of which is clearly Comanche Peak on the Brazos River in present Hood County. In 1835 Bradford's map identified the "San Saba Hills," a designation re-peated in Ehrenkreutz's 1846 map as "San Saba Geb." (San Saba Moun-tain Range). Arrowsmith (1841), in addition to showing linear ranges like Austin, marks Comanche Peak as "High Peak" and also marks Enchanted Rock, the distinctive pink granite dome north of Fredericksburg. Solms-Braunfels was one of several writers to mock the Texans' proclivity for labeling mesas and hills like those found in the San Saba vicinity as "mountains" (Jenkins 1988, 505; Gelo 2013, 22n8).

Berghaus avoids this cartographic conceit, showing no mountain ranges. But he does carry on by marking Enchanted Rock, using the German direct translation *Bezauberter Felsen*; and in addition to Enchanted Rock, Berghaus depicts the next major prominence to the west, House Mountain ("House mount"). While Enchanted Rock became a celebrated landmark for non-Indians, House Mountain did not, though both were important places for the Comanches. In fact, Enchanted Rock is arguably the inferior landmark, as it lies in an erosional depression and is not so visible from all directions and such distances as is House Mountain. Ranger Jack Hays reportedly engaged Comanches in a fight on top of Enchanted Rock in fall 1841 (Wilbarger 1985, 74–75; Sowell 1986, 334–35), and Comanches used the rock as a rendezvous site, as witnessed by the captive Dolly Webster in 1843 (Dolbeare 1986, 21). Another captive, Herman Lehmann, a German boy from Fredericksburg who rode with raiding Comanches in the 1870s, tells of using House Mountain as a lookout and resting place (Greene 1972, 24–25). Berghaus's inclusion of House Mountain along with Enchanted Rock probably reflects Kriewitz's close knowledge of Comanche navigation. But it may have been especially amusing to Berghaus to add this site because its name in German is a reversal of his own. And if so, perhaps then it was uncharacteristic modesty that moved him to provide the name in English instead of German, as he does for Enchanted Rock.

The prevailing attention to mountains, however humble, probably relates to the abiding interest in mineral resources. In the classic Texas maps, silver mines are typically associated with the so-called San Saba Mountains and the abandoned San Saba presidio. The hoary legend associated with this cluster of map features is explained in chapter 10. Some German mapmakers were happy to hint at treasures untold; thus, Ehrenkreutz's reference to the "zerstörte spanische Mission u. Ft" ("destroyed Spanish mission and fort"), and below that, "alte Minen" ("old mines") (Ehrenkreutz 1846). Roemer, however, simply locates the Spanish fort without any reference to mines or mountains (Roemer 1849b). Trained as a paleontologist and having served as geologist and naturalist with the Meusebach party, he had actually visited the presidio and vicinity and, concluding that no silver was present, discounted its importance (Roemer 1983, 258–59). In doing so, he confirmed doubts voiced by fellow naturalist Berlandier upon his excursion northwest of San Antonio in 1828 (Berlandier 1980, 2:343, 350).

Since Kriewitz met up with Roemer upon the latter's return from his survey, Kriewitz may have learned, even before the publication of Roemer's book, about the absence of silver and transmitted this finding to Berghaus, or else Berghaus learned by reading Roemer directly. Although he mentions "the very rich silver mines that were said to be nearby" in his essay, Berghaus, like Roemer, downplays the possibilities on his map, merely marking the "Alter [*sic*] Fort" ("Old Fort") on the San Saba River. We know nevertheless that the presidio ruins were significant in Comanche geography; they used them as a landmark and camping place along the well-defined trail system connecting San Antonio de Béxar and New Mexico via the Hill Country. Comanche guides led the Béxar Indian envoy Francisco Amangual to the abandoned presidio on both his outbound and return trips in 1808 (Loomis and Nasatir 1967, 466, 531). According to Berlandier, who traveled part of the same route with Comanches twenty years later, the Comanches referred to the ruins as Casas Viejas ("Old Houses"). They called the San Saba River *tsuku kahni hunuʔbi*, "old house river," mirroring the Spanish name in their own language (Berlandier 1980, 366; Gelo 2000, 296).

Trails are altogether absent from Berghaus's map even though they had become a standard feature in earlier maps. The route between Béxar past San Saba to New Mexico comprised the Pinta Trail connecting San Antonio with the Fredericksburg area, portions of which were used by Meusebach and Roemer as well as Amangual and Berlandier in their travels (Morgenthaler 2010; 2015). This route is portrayed on the maps of Hunt and Randel (1839), John Arrowsmith (1841), Wilson (1845), and Ehrenkreutz (1846). Another prominent Indian path connected with this route, one shown by John Arrowsmith as "Comanche Road" (Arrowsmith 1841), ran north–south through the Bandera area and the Sabinal River canyon (Cañon de Ugalde) (see also Williams 1979, 32–33; Berlandier 1980, 2:360–62; Tubbs 2010). Both routes, as previously noted, are also shown by Solms-Braunfels (1846c). Day and Haghe's "New Map of Texas, 1841" (Maillard 1842, 512), the most peculiar of those spawned by Austin, shows a north–south "Comanche Trail" running from a Co-manche village on Red River to beyond the Nueces River, completely bisecting the area covered by Berghaus.

Other trails, attributed variously to the Comanches or Wichitan groups, ran east–west, linking the domains of both. Austin shows a "Road to the Cumanchy," running from the upper Brazos drainage deep into East Texas, on his earliest sketch map (Austin 1822), and John Arrowsmith includes it on his printed map as "Comanche Trail" (Arrowsmith 1841). A roughly parallel track called the "Comanche Trace" crossed the middle Brazos near the old Mexican Fort Tenoxtitlán, a site indicated on Berghaus's map. All told there existed a well-defined system of main stems, alternates, and local branches (see Gelo 2013, 39–47). By the early 1850s the Indian paths with-in the Hill Country were being superseded by settlers' roads that often took the same general course over gentler, more wagon-friendly terrain (see Morgenthaler 2010; 2015), and recording the old trails was unlikely to have been deemed an essential contribution. But surely Kriewitz knew something of the customary travel routes, and it is unfortunate that Berghaus does not provide us with a picture of them, which would further underscore the Native heritage of Central Texas.

Berghaus was more diligent, if not entirely accurate, in locating the main non-Indian towns and settlements of the era. Judging from its position at the junction of the Brazos River, Bosque River, and Aguila (that is, Aquilla) Creek, the town name "Wasserville" corresponds to present-day Waco. The town was built on the site of an abandoned Waco Indian village, which is indicated on most of the early Texas maps. In 1851, the town was known as Waco Village. There is no other evidence that the place was named "Wasserville" or the English equivalent, Waterville. Downstream, Berghaus locates the Mexican Fort Tenoxtitlán ("Tenoxitlan"), which lasted from 1830 to 1832 and sheltered some Anglo-American settlers, and its nearby successor, settled by Anglo-Americans, Nashville-on-the-Brazos ("Nashville"). On the Colorado are found the towns of Austin, Bastrop, and La Grange ("la Grande"). Austin's status as the state capital is not readily apparent from the map. Bastrop began as a German settlement, and La Grange had gained many German settlers by 1851. New Braunfels (Neu-Braunfels), the first Adelsverein town and one that figures so prominently in Kriewitz's life as a Texan, is located on the Guadalupe River, along with Seguin and Gonzales. The old Spanish provincial capital of San Antonio de Béxar is shown, and to its west, the young Alsatian settlement (since 1844) of Castroville.

Approaching Comanche country, on the Pedernales and Llano Rivers, are four of the six Adelsverein settlements that were founded beyond New Braunfels. Signifying its importance from the German perspective, or perhaps its new status as county seat of Gillespie County, Fredericksburg ("Friedrichsbg") shares a larger title and symbol with the erstwhile and current capitals of San Antonio and Austin. Like New Braunfels it was central in the saga of German frontier settlement and the operations of Meusebach and Kriewitz. Fredericksburg was only five years old in 1851, but had already appeared on the maps of Solms-Braunfels (1846b, as "Fridrichsburg"), Ehrenkreutz (1846; as "Friedrichstadt"), De Cordova (1849), Roemer (1849), and Bädeker (1849). Berghaus is not precise in locating the town, which is not near the junction of the Pedernales and Colorado as he shows, but many miles upstream, nearer the source than the mouth. It should be almost directly south of the *Bezauberter Felsen*. This error seems careless because Roemer (1849) had already rendered the correct position along the river. Also, Fredericksburg does not lie east of San Antonio as the map shows (there is no compass rose, but the longitude lines indicate an intended north–south alignment); here once again the distortion of the river courses may come into play. The correct modern coordinates are 29.4°N, 98.5°W for San Antonio, 30.3°N, 99°W for Fredericksburg. Note, however, that the Greenwich meridian was only established as a prime meridian in 1851 and not widely adopted until 1884, and Berghaus reckons longitude from the Paris meridian instead; hence, San Antonio lies beyond the 101st meridian west on his map.

To the northwest of Fredericksburg, on the north bank of the Llano River, are three colonies that were settled from Fredericksburg in 1847: Bettina, Castell, and Leiningen (Biesele 1930, 152–57; Morgenthaler 2007). They lie on the southern edge of the unlabeled Fisher-Miller grant spanning the country between the Llano and Colorado Rivers, which the Adelsverein had contracted for in 1845, and, they were beyond the pale of US military protection, represented by Fort Martin Scott two miles southeast of Fredericksburg, established in 1848. Castell is the only one of these communities that survives today, though it was relocated to the south side of the river, outside the Fisher-Miller grant, in the 1870s. John Meusebach selected the town site at Catfish Ford, a Pinta Trail crossing, and Emil Kriewitz guided the first settlers. Kriewitz resided here in later years, serving as a store owner, county justice, and postmaster. Castell was named for Adelsverein business manager Count Carl Frederick Castell-Castell. Leiningen was laid out a few miles downstream by Kriewitz expressly for some Lutheran immigrants. This small settlement, named after Adelsverein cofounder and first president Prince Carl of Leiningen, appears to have lasted until at least 1853.

Bettina was the commune founded not by the Adelsverein directly but by "The (Darmstadt) Forty," idealistic young professional freethinkers. They too were guided to their townsite by Kriewitz. The location, however, was not upstream of Castell as Berghaus indicates on his map, but "about a mile below Castell" at the Elm Creek confluence (Biesele 1930, 156). Its inhabitants included the remarkable Dr. Ferdinand Herff, who performed successful cataract surgery on a Comanche man, and a female Mexican Comanche captive was gifted in return for the operation (Herff 1973, 1:14–15; Morgenthaler 2007, 80–81). Despite such friendly interactions and the official German-Comanche accord, peace along the Llano was tenuous at best. Indian horse thievery and a few murders, likely perpetrated by Lipan Apaches or Wacos, as well as the looming threat of outright warfare, only encouraged abandonment. Bettina lasted less than a year.

Two more settlements on the north bank of the Llano, Meerholz and Schoenburg, were pioneered out of Fredericksburg, but never took hold—Meerholz near Bettina and Schoenburg just downstream of Leiningen. Neither appears on Berghaus's map. Nor do two communities founded outside of the Adelsverein's auspices, and hence outside of Kriewitz's direct experience: Sisterdale, settled in 1847 by Nicolaus Zink from New Braunfels, and Tusculum (now Boerne), settled from Bettina in 1849 (Morgenthaler 2007, 88–89, 108–9). Berghaus still provided the most thorough mapping of the Adelsverein settlements to date. But some of his locations are inaccurate, and his presentation is outdated to the extent that it suggests stable towns on the Llano, for according to the 1850 census only thirty-two people were still living in any of these settlements (Biesele 1930, 153).

Berghaus's signal contribution to Texas mapmaking is his documentation of tribal names and locations. He locates twenty-seven named populations using triangular tipi emblems to indicate dwelling places. Each of these names is listed with almost complete consistency in Berghaus's essay. Four of the names, Santa Anna, Pahajoko, Buffalo humb (Hump), and Kateumzi, are the names of headmen, and the rest are names for Comanche divisions or various non-Comanche groups. There is some inconsistency between the locations of the four headmen's populations as marked on the map and described in the essay. Further details about each of the names and locations are provided in the text commentary.

Berghaus's map employs gradations of calligraphy that reflect his erroneous supposition that all of the twenty-seven populations are Comanche. Their titles are all on the same scale, and, curiously, consistent with those of the small German settlements on the Llano. Eight other tribal names are distinguished with larger, parenthesized legends, indicating "non-Comanche" groups: the aforementioned Delawares and Shawnees, plus Chickasaws, Choctaws, Caddoes, Tonkaways, Kikapoes (Kickapoos), and Pawnee Picts (which is actually another name for Wichitas), included among the twenty-seven.

Berghaus was not the first mapmaker to locate Comanche camping places. Delisle (1718) showed Padouca (possibly Comanche) villages represented with small tipi figures on the upper reaches of four Plains rivers. Day and Haghe (Maillard 1842, 512) portray a Comanche village on the Red River using a small legend and a "Comanche Chief Town" in bold lettering south of the San Saba–Colorado River confluence, and Wilson (1845) marks a "Great Comanche Village" along the upper Colorado, again with small tipis, a device adopted by Berghaus. Berghaus's more ambitious accounting of the grazing grounds of specific bands is interesting but must be viewed with caution. No doubt Kriewitz provided the positions and names as he was aware of them during his sojourn with the Comanches. And as has been noted, the principle of locating bands between drainages is consonant with other pictures of Comanche territoriality. We also know, however, that the bands were highly mobile. Documentation of some alternate camping places during the German settlement period is provided in the text commentary (and for an earlier picture of Comanche camp locations, see those plotted from Spanish reports for the period 1786–1808 by Kavanagh [1996, 136–37]). Berghaus's specificity about band locations reflects an overriding desire for exactitude. This desire was born not out of arrogance but the style of scholarship (and mapmaking) prevalent at the time. Berghaus was simply intent on providing the best information available at the moment. He had utmost faith in the scientific process of continuous research and revision, and he expected that his information would be improved upon. This outlook is embodied in the very form of publication he chose, the "yearbook."

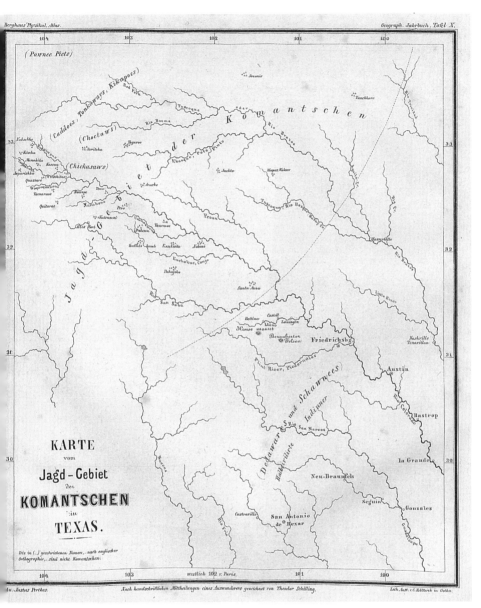

Map 1. Berghaus's map of the Comanche hunting grounds. Courtesy Forschungsbibliothek Gotha der Universität Erfurt, Sammlung Perthes.

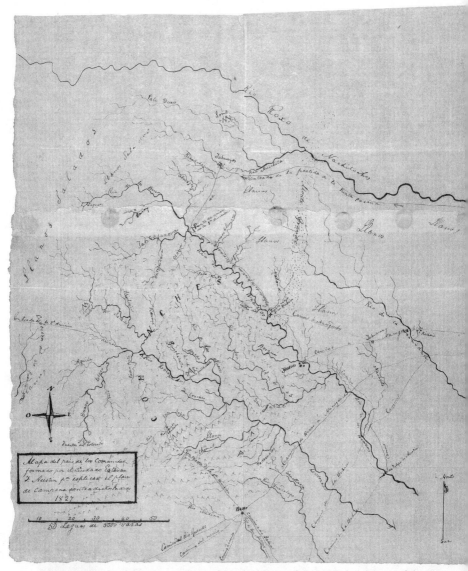

Map 2. One of two known versions of Stephen F. Austin's 1827 sketch map of the Comanche region of central Texas. Courtesy Beinecke Rare Book and Manuscript Library, Yale University.

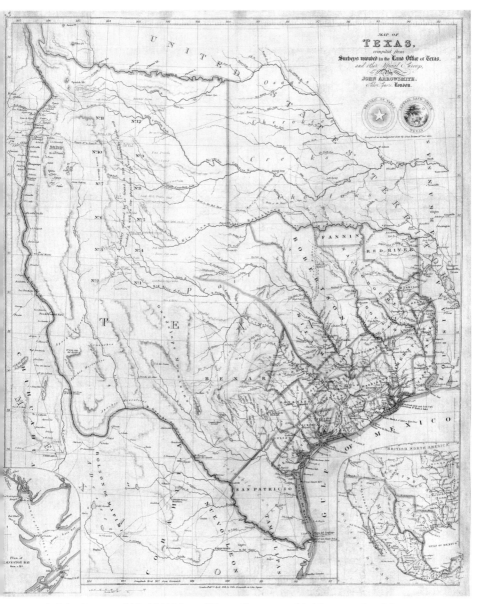

Map 3. John Arrowsmith's 1841 Map of Texas. Image provided by www.RareMaps. com—Barry Lawrence Ruderman Antique Maps Inc.

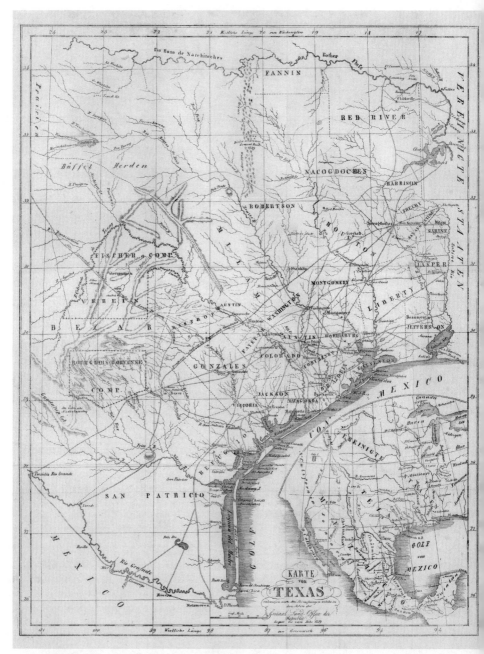

Map 4. Anonymous, Karte von Texas, 1845. Image provided by www.RareMaps.com—
Barry Lawrence Ruderman Antique Maps Inc.

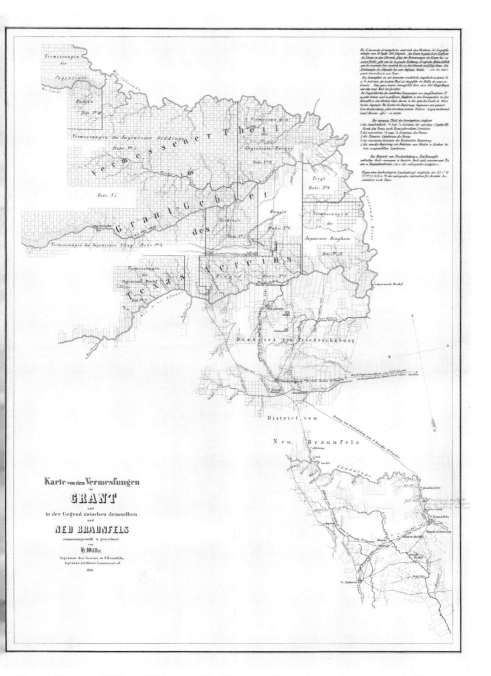

Map 5. Hermann Willke's 1850 map of the German settlement areas. Image provided by www.RareMaps.com—Barry Lawrence Ruderman Antique Maps Inc.

NOTES

Preface

1. Examples of the scholarship we have in mind include Schiedt (2011); Penny (2013); Calloway, Gemünden, and Zantop (2002); Usbeck (2015); and Vermeulen (2015).

Introduction

1. In his political history of the Comanches, Kavanagh (1996, 268, 271) fails to recognize Old Owl's reference to the junction of the Llano and Colorado Rivers, or to account for the effect of mapping error, and therefore states erroneously that Houston's treaty draft included a line drawn "to the San Saba River," which followed "Mupechucope's [Old Owl's] advice from the year before."

2. Varied perspectives on Adelsverein history may be found in recent scholarship, including Hatzfeld (2015), Kearney (2010), Morgenthaler (2009), Tippens (2010), and Strubberg (2012).

3. In his 1927 article, Biesele numbers the colonists at "approximately 700," but in his 1930 book he counts 439, of whom, he speculates, about 200 made the initial trip to New Braunfels.

4. The exact number is reported differently in the various secondary sources; the *Handbook of Texas Online* gives 5,257; Benjamin 5,247 (1910, 49); Morgenthaler "more than 5,000" (2007, 5).

5. In contrast to Schubert's alleged multitude, estimates from preceding years had counted no more than five hundred Texas Kickapoo families (see Berlandier 1969, 128).

6. For a list of books that participated in this debate, see James Kearney's "Chronological Bibliography of Nineteenth-Century German Works That Discuss or Mention Texas" (Dunt 2015, 175–82).

Chapter 1

1. This article is also available online at http://reader.digitale-sammlungen.de/de/fs1/object/display/bsb10812789_00051.html, in German.

Chapter 3

1. Berghaus had taken responsibility for editing the *Zeitschrift für Erdkunde* in 1847 and attributed the demise of the journal to the political climate surrounding the March Revolution of 1848, which resulted in the first all-German parliament. His published correspondence with Humboldt includes a note stating, "all literary activity ground to a halt; the whole world was giddy with politics and was working to reform the fatherland and establish a German empire. Who could be concerned about what was happening far away on the broad fields of geographic discovery and the triumphs on the immeasurable territory of geographic knowledge? Month by month the journal, which was already struggling, sank further and further. Magdeburg was also not the ideal place to publish a journal of this kind. . . . German consumers of intellectual publications want their needs to be met by businesses of solid reputation in well-known centers of the publishing trade [such as Leipzig]" (Berghaus 1863, 100; Beck 1956, 7).

2. Curiously, in his otherwise meticulously researched biography and evaluation of Berghaus's work, Engelmann fails to mention the article when he lists contributions authored by Berghaus in the Yearbook. "Berghaus' eigene Beiträge bezogen sich auf Afrika (1850), Innerasien (1850, 1852) und das arktische Amerika (1852)" (Engelmann 1977, 127). ("Berghaus's own contributions [to the Yearbook] had to do with Africa [1850], Inner Asia [1850, 1852], and arctic regions of America [1852].")

Chapter 4

1. Georg Forster (with James Cook) from Australia and the South Pacific, Humboldt and Bonpland from Venezuela and the New World, Karl Philipp Martius and Johann Baptist von Spix from Brazil, Adelbert von Chamisso from Hawaii and the Pacific, Paul Wilhelm von Württemberg from North America, Maximilian zu Wied-Neuwied from Brazil and, later, the Missouri region of the Midwest, among others.

2. Berghaus is mistaken in classifying Arapaho with Shoshone and Comanche. Such errors are discussed in chapter 10.

3. In his translation (Catlin 1851) Berghaus renders Catlin's letters numbered 39 and 40 as his chapter 36; Catlin's letter 41 becomes Berghaus's chapter 37; and letter 42 becomes chapter 38.

4. An unbound exemplar of this fascicle is housed in the Sammlung Perthes [Perthes Collection] of the Universitäts- und Forschungsbibliothek Erfurt/Gotha, Schloss Freudenstein, Gotha [Signatur: SPA 4° 000693 (03)].

Chapter 5

1. The personal file on Berghaus maintained by the Prussian government (Acta Personalia Berghaus) contains the official correspondence with Berghaus on this and other matters. It is archived at the Landeshauptarchiv Brandenburg in Potsdam under call number Rep. 2A I Pers. Nr. 326.

2. For example, Scherpf (1841), Wrede (1844), Raumer (1845), Kennedy (1845), Schultz (1845), Ehrenkreutz (1846), Mühlenpfordt (1846), Behr (1847), Walther (1848), Roemer (1849a), Steinert (1850), Ross (1851), and Schlecht (1851).

3. Berghaus provides the following information about the publication of Wislizenus's original text in his footnote 4: "[Wislizenus's] memorandum, which was not made available through public distribution, bears the title: 'Memoir of a tour to Northern Mexico, connected with Col. Doniphan's Expedition, in 1846 and 1847. By A. Wislizenus, M.D. With a scientific Appendix and three Maps. Washington: Tippin and Strepper, Printers, 1848.' 141 pages in octo.—It was printed on the order of the Senate, in accordance with a resolution of January 13, 1848, in 5000 copies for the use of the Senate and 200 copies for the traveler himself" (Berghaus 1850a, 53).

4. At this point, Berghaus inserts a footnote (5): "Almost simultaneously with Wislizenus, namely in March 1848, I expressed similar views in a critical treatise on the American isthmus, which is printed in the *Zeitschrift für Erdkunde*, vol. IX, No. 4, Magdeburg 1849, p. 270–321. The relevant passage is on p. 319 and 320" (Berghaus 1850a, 53).

Chapter 6

1. The unpublished manuscript of the curriculum vitae is located in the Brandenburgisches Landeshauptarchiv, Potsdam, call number: Rep. 2A I Pers. Nr. 326. See also Engelmann 1977, 164.

2. In the 1990s several publications appeared acknowledging Berghaus's importance for cartography, among them Camerini (1993 and 2000), Espenhorst (2003), Christy and Lowman (1998), and later Kozák and Vaněk (2002). His role in the development of ethnology is only recently and briefly recognized in Vermeulen (2015, 338, 423).

Chapter 7

1. Berghaus's endnote *p* refers to his publication of Kriewitz's comments on Comanche traditions, knowledge, and cultural practices, "Sitten und Gebräuche der Comanches in Texas. Von Emil Kriwitz." *Zeitschrift für Erdkunde* 10 (Berghaus 1850c, 401–9). These comments are included with only minor editorial emendations in the 1851 article.

2. Knopp suggests that the initiative for Kriewitz's stay with the Comanche came from Meusebach: "Meusebach convinced Kriewitz to seek permission from the chiefs to live among them and to make sure that both sides not only kept the provisions [of the] treaty but exceeded the terms as much as possible" (Knopp 1999, 3). The source of this claim and others made by Knopp relating to Kriewitz's activity with the Comanche is unclear.

3. There appears to be no Comanche word approximating "commissioner" or "diplomat" beyond the term *itsina*, adopted from the English "agent" and signifying an Indian agent. The notion of incorporating individuals from other

social groups, however, is embedded in the terms *nʉkwʉpʉ* "captive, slave," and *kwʉhʉ*, "wife," both derived from *kwʉhʉpʉ*, "caught," albeit the incorporation alluded to in this terminology is forced rather than voluntary (Comanche Language and Cultural Preservation Committee 2010, 8, 17, 37, 93, 105, 164, 181).

4. Kavanagh (1996, 252) erroneously locates Coleman's Fort in Bastrop County and Muguara's camp in Burleson County.

5. The trader's name has been reported as Barnett (Kriewitz, in Penniger 1971, 49) or Dietter Barnett (Hadeler 2010; n.d.). Given the unlikely German-sounding first name and the apparent absence of this person from other Texas annals, this name may have been an error begun by Kriewitz and perpetuated in local history. The similarly named George Barnard was the proprietor of the Torrey Brother's trading house on Tehuacana Creek, a tributary of the Brazos eight miles southeast of present Waco, at the time the German treaty was negotiated.

Chapter 8

1. Subsequently, when approached for a testimony to encourage Prussian government investment in the Adelsverein project, Humboldt advised against subsidies to support German emigration to Texas (Kearney 2010, 56, 119).

2. See Vermeulen (2015, 430–36) for a similar appraisal of Boas's role in the German ethnographic tradition and genesis of modern anthropology.

REFERENCES

Adelsverein. 1845. *Gesammelte Aktenstücke des Vereins zum Schutze deutscher Einwanderer in Texas*. Mainz: Victor von Zabern; Bonn: F. P. Lechner.
―――. 1851. *Instruction für deutsche Auswanderer nach Texas*. Wiesbaden: Selbstverlag des Vereins-Comite's. Rpt., Berlin: Reimer, 1983.
Andrus, Pearl. 1982. *Juana: A Spanish Girl in Central Texas*. Burnet, TX: Eakin Press. Rpt., Waco, TX: Texian Press, 1986; Clifton, TX: Bosque Memorial Museum 1994, 2007.
―――. 2010. "Barnard, Charles E." In *Handbook of Texas Online*. Austin: Texas State Historical Association. Accessed May 20, 2015.
Anonymous. 1845. *Karte von Texas entworfen nach den Vermessungen welche in den Acten der General-Land-Office der Republic liegen bis zum Jahr 1839*. Braunfels [?]: n.p.
―――. 1860. *Abstract of Titles and Patented Lands Compiled from the Records of the General Land Office of the State of Texas*. Austin: John Marshall.
Armagost, James. 1986. "Three Exceptions to Vowel Devoicing in Comanche." *Anthropological Linguistics* 28: 255–66.
Arrowsmith, Aaron. 1810. *A New Map of Mexico and Adjacent Provinces Compiled from Original Documents*. London: A. Arrowsmith.
Arrowsmith, John. 1841. *Map of Texas Compiled from Surveys Recorded in the Land Office of Texas, and Other Official Surveys*. London: John Arrowsmith.
Austin, Stephen Fuller. 1822. Mapa Geográphico de la Provincia Texas. Manuscript, Dolph Briscoe Center for American History, University of Texas at Austin.
―――. 1827a. Mapa del pais de los Comanches, formado por el C. Estevan F. Austin pa. esplicar el plan de campana contra dichos Indios. Manuscript, Dolph Briscoe Center for American History, University of Texas at Austin.
―――. 1827b. Mapa del pais de los Comanches, formado por el Cuidado [*sic*] Estevan F. Austin pa. esplicar el plan de campana contra dichos Indios. Manuscript, Collection of Western Americana, Beinecke Rare Book and Manuscript Library, Yale University.
―――. 1830. *Map of Texas with Parts of the Adjoining States*. Philadelphia: H. S. Tanner.

————. 1836. *Map of Texas with Parts of the Adjoining States*. Philadelphia: H. S. Tanner.

Bädeker, J[ulius]. 1849. *Karte des Staates Texas (aufgenommen in die Union 1846.) nach der neuesten Eintheilung*. Elberfeld: J. Bädeker.

Barker, Eugene C. 1925. *The Life of Stephen F. Austin*. Nashville: Cokesbury Press. Rpt., New York: AMS Press, 1970.

Barr, Juliana. 2007. *Peace Came in the Form of a Woman*. Chapel Hill: University of North Carolina Press.

Baylor, H. W. 1929. "Recollections of the Comanche Indians." *Frontier Times* 6 (9): 373–75.

Beck, Hanno. 1956. "Heinrich Berghaus und Alexander von Humboldt." *Petermanns geographische Mitteilungen* 100: 4–16.

Becker, W. J. 1931. "The Compounding of Words in the Comanche Language." Unpublished master's thesis, University of Oklahoma, Department of English.

————. 1936. "The Comanche Indian and His Language." *Chronicles of Oklahoma* 14: 328–42.

Behr, Ottomar von. 1847. *Guter Rath für Auswanderer nach den Vereinigten Staaten von Nordamerika mit besonderer Berücksichtigung von Texas. Vorzüglich für Landleute und Handwerker nach eigener Erfahrung geschrieben*. Leipzig: Robert Friese.

Belani, H. E. R. [Karl Ludwig Häberlin]. 1841. *Die Auswanderer nach Texas. Historisch-romantisches Gemälde aus der neuesten Zeit*. 3 parts. Leipzig: C. L. Fritzsche.

Benjamin, Gilbert Giddings. 1910. *The Germans in Texas: A Study in Immigration*. Reprinted from *German American Annals*, vol. 7, 1909. Philadelphia. Rpt., Austin: Jenkins, 1974.

Berghaus, Heinrich Karl Wilhelm. 1827a. "Albert Gallatin's tabellarische Uebersicht der Indierstämme in den vereinigten Staaten von Nordamerika, ostwärts von den Felsgebirgen (Stony Mountains), nach den Sprachen und Dialekten geordnet. 1826. Mitgetheilt von dem Freiherrn Alexander von Humboldt." *Hertha* 9: 328–34.

————. 1827b. "Fortschritte in der Kultur unter den Indiern Nordamerika's nach handschriftlichen Notizen mitgetheilt von dem Hrn. geh. Staatsminister, Freiherrn Wilh. v. Humboldt." *Hertha* 9: 320–27.

————. 1837–46. *Allgemeine Länder- und Völkerkunde nebst einem Abriß der physikalischen Erdbeschreibung. Ein Lehr- und Hausbuch für alle Stände*. 6 vols. Stuttgart: Hoffmann'sche Verlags-Buchhandlung.

————. 1844. "Die Auswanderungsspeculationen. W. Grisson über die Vereinigten Staaten." *Allgemeine Zeitung* (Augsburg), December 16, no. 351: 2802–4.

————. 1845–48. *Physikalischer Atlas oder Sammlung von Karten, auf denen die hauptsächlichsten Erscheinungen der anorganischen und organischen Natur nach ihrer geographischen Verbreitung und Vertheilung bildlich dargestellt sind*. 2 vols. Gotha: Justus Perthes.

———. 1848. *Die Vereinigten Staaten von Nordamerika, geographisch-statistisch vorzugsweise nach Van der Straten-Ponthoz geschildert mit besonderer Rücksicht auf die Deutsche Auswanderung.* Gotha: Justus Perthes.

———. 1850a. "Dr. A. Wislizenus' Beiträge zur genauern Kenntnis des nördlichen Mexico." *Geographisches Jahrbuch* 1: 28–53.

———. 1850b. *Grundlinien der Ethnographie. Enthaltend in zwei Abtheilungen eine allgemeine Völkertafel oder Nachweisung aller Völker des Erdbodens, nach Sprachstämmen und Sprachfamilien ethnographisch und geographisch geordnet; und eine vergleichende, übersichtliche Beschreibung ihrer Sitten, Gebräuche und Gewohnheiten.* Stuttgart: Verlags-Bureau.

———. 1850c. "Sitten und Gebräuche der Comanches in Texas. Von Emil Kriwitz." *Zeitschrift für Erdkunde* 10: 401–9.

———. 1851. "Über die Verwandtschaft der Schoschonen, Komantschen und Apatschen. Nebst einer Karte vom Jagdgebiet der Komantschen in Texas." *Geographisches Jahrbuch* 3: 48–62.

———. 1852. *Physikalischer Atlas oder Sammlung von Karten, auf denen die hauptsächlichsten Erscheinungen der anorganischen und organischen Natur nach ihrer geographischen Verbreitung und Vertheilung bildlich dargestellt sind.* Zweite verbesserte und vermehrte Ausgabe. Acht Abtheilungen. Gotha: Justus Perthes.

———. 1860–62. *Die Völker des Erdballs nach ihrer Abstammung und Verwandtschaft und ihren Eigenthümlichkeiten in Regierungsform, Religion, Sitten und Tracht geschildert.* 2 vols. Brussels: Carl Muquardt. Orig. 1845–47.

———. 1880. *Der Sprachschatz der Sassen. Ein Wörterbuch der Plattdeutschen Sprache in den hauptsächlichsten ihrer Mundarten.* Vol. 1. Brandenburg: Adolph Müller.

———. 1883. *Der Sprachschatz der Sassen. Ein Wörterbuch der Plattdeutschen Sprache in den hauptsächlichsten ihrer Mundarten.* Vol. 2. Berlin: R. Eisenschmidt.

Berghaus, Heinrich, ed. 1863. *Briefwechsel Alexander von Humboldt's mit Heinrich Berghaus aus den Jahren 1825 bis 1858.* 3 vols. Leipzig: Hermann Costenoble.

Berlandier, Jean Louis. 1969. *The Indians of Texas in 1830.* Edited by John C. Ewers. Washington, DC: Smithsonian Institution Press.

———. 1980. *Journey to Mexico during the Years 1826 to 1834.* 2 vols. Translated and edited by Sheila M. Ohlendorf, Josette M. Bigelow, and Mary M. Standifer. Austin: Texas State Historical Association.

Berlandier, Jean Louis, and Rafael Chowell. 1828–29. [Vocabularies of Languages of South Texas and the Lower Rio Grande.] Manuscript, Additional Manuscripts No. 38720, British Library, London.

Bieder, Robert E. 1986. *Science Encounters the Indian, 1820–1880: The Early Years of American Ethnology.* Norman: University of Oklahoma Press.

Bierschwale, Margaret. 1998. *A History of Mason County, Texas, through 1964.* Mason: Mason County Historical Commission.

Biesele, Rudolph Leopold. 1927. "The Relations between the German Settlers and the Indians in Texas, 1844–1860." *Southwestern Historical Quarterly* 31(2): 116–29.

———. 1930. *The History of the German Settlements in Texas, 1831–1861*. Austin: Press of Von Boeckmann-Jones. Rpt., Austin: n.p., 1964; San Marcos, TX: German-Texan Heritage Society, 1987.

———. 2010. "Fisher-Miller Land Grant." In *Handbook of Texas Online*. Austin: Texas State Historical Association. Accessed June 4, 2015.

Biggers, Don H. 1925. *German Pioneers in Texas: A Brief History of their Hardships, Struggles, and Achievements*. Fredericksburg: Fredericksburg Publishing.

Bollaert, William. 1850. "Observations on the Indian Tribes of Texas." *Journal of the Ethnological Society of London* 2: 262–83.

Bowen, Margarita. 1981. *Empiricism and Geographical Thought*. Cambridge: Cambridge University Press.

Bracht, Viktor. 1849. *Texas im Jahre 1848, Nach mehrjährigen Beobachtungen dargestellt*. Elberfeld and Iserlohn: Julius Bädeker.

———. 1931. *Texas in 1848*. Translated by Charles Frank Schmidt. San Antonio: Naylor. Rpt., Manchaca, TX: German-Texas Heritage Society, 1991. Translation of Bracht 1849.

Bradford, Thomas Gamaliel. 1835. *A Comprehensive Atlas, Geographical, Historical, and Commercial*. New York: Freeman Hunt.

Brandenburg, Philip Donald. 1968. "A Translation of L. Constant's *Texas, das Verderben Deutscher Auswanderer in Texas unter dem Schutze des Mainzer Vereins*." Unpublished master's thesis, Southwest Texas State University [Texas State University], Department of History.

Brice, Donaly E. 1987. *The Great Comanche Raid*. Austin: Eakin Press.

Brister, Louis E., ed. and trans. 1982. "William von Rosenberg's *Kritik*: A History of the Society for the Protection of German Immigrants to Texas." Part 2. *Southwestern Historical Quarterly* 85: 299–318.

Bromme, Traugott. 1846. *Rathgeber für Auswanderungslustige*. Stuttgart: Hoffmann.

Brooks, James F. 2002. *Captives and Cousins*. Chapel Hill: University of North Carolina Press.

Brue, Adrien Hubert. 1845. *Nouvelle Carte du Mexique, du Texas, et d'une Partie des États Limitrophes*. Paris: Adrien Hubert Brue.

Brune, Gunnar. 1981. *Springs of Texas*. Vol. 1. Fort Worth: Branch-Smith.

Bunzl, Matti. 1996. "Franz Boas and the Humboldtian Tradition." In *Volksgeist as Method and Ethic: Essays on Boasian Ethnography and the German Anthropological Tradition*. History of Anthropology, vol. 8. Edited by George W. Stocking Jr., 17–78. Madison: University of Wisconsin Press.

Bureau of the Corps of Topographical Engineers. 1850. *Map of the United States and Their Territories between the Mississippi and the Pacific Ocean; and part of Mexico*. New York: Sherman and Smith.

Burr, David H. 1833. *[Map of] Texas*. New York: J. H. Colton.

———. 1846. *[Map of] the State of Texas, 1836–1845*. New York: R. S. Fisher.

Buschmann, Johann Carl Eduard. 1859. *Die Spuren der aztekishen Sprache im nördlichen Mexico und höheren amerikanischen Norden.* Abhandlungen der königlichen Akademie der Wissenschaften zu Berlin aus dem Jahre 1854. Zweiter Supplement-Band. Berlin.

Calloway, Colin G., Gerd Gemünden, and Susanne Zantop, eds. 2002. *Germans and Indians: Fantasies, Encounters, Projections.* Lincoln: University of Nebraska Press.

Camerini, Jane R. 1993. "The Physical Atlas of Heinrich Berghaus: Distribution Maps as Scientific Knowledge." In *Non-Verbal Communication in Science prior to 1900*, edited by Renato G. Mazzolini, 479–512. Florence: Olschki.

———. 2000. "Heinrich Berghaus's Map of Human Diseases." *Medical History*. Supplement 20: 186–208.

Canonge, Elliott. 1957. "Voiceless Vowels in Comanche." *International Journal of American Linguistics* 23: 63–67.

———. 1958. *Comanche Texts.* Norman, OK: Summer Institute of Linguistics.

Carlson, Gustav G., and Volney H. Jones. 1939. "Some Notes on Uses of Plants by the Comanche Indians." *Papers of the Michigan Academy of Science, Arts, and Letters* 25: 517–42.

Casagrande, Joseph B. 1954a. "Comanche Linguistic Acculturation I." *International Journal of American Linguistics* 20: 140–51.

———. 1954b. "Comanche Linguistic Acculturation II." *International Journal of American Linguistics* 20: 217–37.

———. 1955. "Comanche Linguistic Acculturation III." *International Journal of American Linguistics* 21: 8–25.

Castañeda, Carlos, and Early Martin Jr. 1930. *Three Manuscript Maps of Texas by Stephen F. Austin.* Austin: Privately printed.

Catlin, George. 1841. *Letters and Notes on the Manners, Customs, and Conditions of the North American Indians.* 2 vols. London: Toswill and Myers. Rpt., New York: Wiley and Putnam, 1844; New York: Dover, 1973.

———. 1851. *Die Indianer Nord-Amerikas und die während eines achtjährigen Aufenthalts unter den wildesten ihrer Stämme erlebten Abenteuer und Schicksale nach der fünften englischen Ausgabe deutsch herausgegeben von Dr. Heinrich Berghaus.* Brussels, Leipzig, Gent: Carl Muquardt. Orig. 1846–48. Rpt., Kassel: Hamecher, 1973; Leipzig: Paul List, 1982. Translation of Catlin 1841.

Charney, Jean Ormsbee. 1993. *A Grammar of Comanche.* Lincoln: University of Nebraska Press.

Christy, B. M., and P. D. Lowman Jr. 1998. "Global Maps of Volcanism." In Proceedings of the 20th Symposium of IHNIGEO, Naples, 1995. Edited by Nicolleta Morello, 65–90. Genoa: Brigati.

Claim of a Survivor of the Mexican War for a Pension. 1887. Form dated March 12. US National Archives and Records Administration, File Kriewitz, E., WC 13418.

Clark, William Philo. 1982. *The Indian Sign Language.* Lincoln: University of Nebraska Press. Orig. Philadelphia: L. R. Hamersly, 1885.

Clay, Comer, and Diana J. Kleiner. 2010. "Colorado River." In *Handbook of Texas Online*. Austin: Texas State Historical Association. Accessed February 16, 2014.

Comanche Language and Cultural Preservation Committee, comp. 2010. Taa Nʉmʉ Tekwapʉ?ha Tʉboopʉ (Our Comanche Dictionary). Rev. ed. Elgin, OK.

Constant, L. 1847. *Texas: Das Verderben deutscher Einwanderer in Texas unter dem Schutze des Mainzer Vereins*. Berlin: G. Reimer. English translation, see Brandenburg 1968.

Conzen, Michael P. 2000. "The Clash of Utopias: Sisterdale and the Six-Sided Struggle for the Texas Hill Country." In *Cultural Encounters with the Environment: Enduring and Evolving Geographic Themes*, edited by Alexander B. Murphy and Douglas L. Johnson. Lanham, MD: Rowman and Littlefield.

Corwin, Hugh D. 1959. *Comanche and Kiowa Captives in Oklahoma and Texas*. Lawton, OK: Hugh D. Corwin.

Coues, Elliot, ed. 1895. *The Expeditions of Zebulon Montgomery Pike*. 3 vols. New York: Francis P. Harper. Rpt. in 2 vols., New York: Dover, 1987.

Crapo, Richley H. 1976. *Big Smokey Valley Shoshoni*. Desert Research Institute Publications in the Social Sciences 10. Logan: Utah State University.

Crone, G. R. 1970. *Modern Geographers: An Outline of Progress in Geography since AD 1800*. London: Royal Geographical Society.

Crum, Beverly, and Jon Dayley. 1993. "Western Shoshoni Grammar." Occasional Papers and Monographs in Cultural Anthropology and Linguistics 1. Boise, ID: Boise State University.

Curtis, Edward S. 1930. *The North American Indian*, vol. 19. Norwood, MA: Plimpton. Rpt., New York: Johnson Reprint, 1970.

De Cordova, Jacob. 1849. *J. De Cordova's Map of the State of Texas*. New York: J. H. Colton.

DeLay, Brian. 2008. *War of a Thousand Deserts*. New Haven, CT: Yale University Press.

Delisle, Guillaume. 1718. *Carte de la Louisiane et du cours du Mississipi*. Paris: Guillaume Delisle.

Detrich, Charles H. 1894. "Comanche Vocabulary." MS 788, National Anthropological Archives, Washington, DC.

———. 1895. "Comanche-English Dictionary and Vocabulary of Phrases." MS, Western History Collections, University of Oklahoma.

Disturnell, J. 1846. *Mapa de los Estados Unidos de Méjico*. New York: J. Disturnell.

Dobie, J. Frank. 1930. *Coronado's Children*. New York: Grosset and Dunlap.

Dodge, Richard I. 1882. *Thirty-Three Years among Our Wild Indians*. Hartford, CT: A. D. Worthington.

Dolbeare, Benjamin. 1986. *A Narrative of the Captivity and Suffering of Dolly Webster among the Camanche Indians in Texas*. New Haven, CT: Yale University Library. Orig. 1843.

Domenech, Abbé Emmanuel-Henri-Dieudonné. 1872. *Journal d'un Missionnaire au Texas et au Mexique*. 2nd ed. Paris: Guame Frères et J. Duprey. Orig. 1857.

Dunt, Detlef. 2015. *Journey to Texas, 1833*. Translated by Anders Saustrup. Edited by James C. Kearney and Geir Bentzen. Austin: University of Texas Press. Orig. *Reise nach Texas nebst Nachrichten von diesem Lande*. Bremen: C. W. Wiehe, 1834.

Eckhardt, C. F. 1982. *The Lost San Saba Mines*. Austin: Texas Monthly Press.

Ehrenkreutz, Baron von. 1846. *Völlstandige Beschreibung des Staates Texas in historischer, politischer, geographischer und geselliger Hinsicht. Ein Handbuch für den Auswanderer nach diesem Staate, mit besonderer Berücksichtigung derjenigen, welche sich bei ihrer Auswanderung unter den Schutz des Mainzer oder Antwerpener-Vereins zu begeben, beabsichtigen*. Coblenz: J. F. Aug. Reiff.

Elliott, Raymond, and Mildred Padon. 1979. *Of a People and a Creek*. Cleburne, TX: Bennett Printing.

Emory, W. H. 1844. *Map of Texas and the Countries Adjacent*. Washington, DC: William J. Stone.

Engelmann, Gerhard. 1964. "Der Physikalische Atlas des Heinrich Berghaus und Alexander Keith Johnstons Physical Atlas." *Petermanns Geographische Mitteilungen* 108: 133–49.

———. 1977. *Heinrich Berghaus. Der Kartograph von Potsdam*. Acta historica Leopoldina 10. Halle: Barth.

Espenhorst, Jürgen. 2003. *Petermann's Planet: A Guide to German Handatlases and Their Siblings throughout the World, 1800–1950*. Vol. 1, *The Great Handatlases*. Edited and translated by George R. Crossman. Schwerte: Pangaea Verlag. Orig. *Andree, Stieler, Meyer & Co.: Handatlanten des deutschen Sprachraums (1800–1945) nebst Vorläufern und Abkömmlingen im In- und Ausland; bibliographisches Handbuch*. Schwerte: Pangaea Verlag, 1994.

Espinosa, Aurelio M. 1907. "Los Comanches: A Spanish Heroic Play of the Year Seventeen Hundred and Eighty." *Bulletin University of New Mexico* 45, language series 1: 1. Albuquerque.

Evans, Dennis. 1962. "Southern Plains Women's Boots, with Emphasis on the Comanche Style." *American Indian Tradition* 8 (5): 181–94.

Ewers, John C. 1957. "Hair Pipes in Plains Indian Adornment." Anthropological Papers No. 50. *Bureau of American Ethnology Bulletin* 164, 29–86. Washington, DC: US Government Printing Office.

Farmer, Walter. 1847. *Texas eine geographische Skizze bearbeitet nach Berghaus Länderkunde und den neuesten Forschungen des Prinzen Carl zu Solms Braunfels und anderer Reisenden*. n.p.

Farrand, Livingston. 1907. "Klamath." In *Handbook of American Indians North of Mexico*. Smithsonian Institution Bureau of American Ethnology Bulletin 30, Part 1. Edited by Frederick Webb Hodge, 712. Washington, DC: US Government Printing Office.

Fisher, Ed. 1994. "The River That Was: A Bibliography of Beals Creek, Texas." *Permian Historical Annual* 34: 79–96.

Flemming, Carl. 1844. *[Map of] Texas*. Glogau: C. Flemming.

Foreman, Grant. 1939. *Marcy and the Gold Seekers*. Norman: University of Oklahoma Press.

————. 1941. *A Pathfinder in the Southwest*. Norman: University of Oklahoma Press.

————. 1948. "The Texas Comanche Treaty of 1846." *Southwestern Historical Quarterly* 51: 313–32.

Foreman, Grant, ed. 1935. "The Journal of Elijah Hicks." *Chronicles of Oklahoma* 13: 68–99.

Foster, Michael K. 1996. "Language and the Culture History of North America." In *Handbook of North American Indians*, vol. 17, 64–110. Edited by William C. Sturtevant. Washington, DC: Smithsonian Institution.

Fowler, Loretta. 2001. "Arapaho." In *Handbook of North American Indians*, vol. 13, part 2, 840–62. Edited by William C. Sturtevant. Washington, DC: Smithsonian Institution.

Gallatin, Albert. 1836. *Synopsis of the Indian Tribes within the United States East of the Rocky Mountains, and in the British and Russian Possessions of North America*. Archaeologia Americana. Transactions and Collections of the American Antiquarian Society, vol. 2. Cambridge, MA: The University Press.

Gamble, John I. 1967. "Changing Patterns in Kiowa Indian Dances." In *Acculturation in the Americas*. Proceedings and Selected Papers of the 29th International Congress of Americanists. Edited by Sol Tax. New York: Cooper Square Publishers.

García Rejón, Manuel. 1865. "Vocabulario del idioma Comanche." *Boletín de la Sociedad Mexicana de Geographía y Estadística, Iª epoca*, 2: 631–59. Rpt., Mexico City: Ignacio Cumplido, 1866.

García Rejón, Manuel, comp., and Daniel J. Gelo, trans. and ed. 1995. *Comanche Vocabulary: Trilingual Edition*. Austin: University of Texas Press.

Gatschet, Albert S. 1876a. "Analytical Report on Eleven Idioms Spoken in Southern California." Appendix H 16. In *Annual Report of the Chief of Engineers to the Secretary of War for the Year 1876*, vol. 3, 550–63. Washington, DC: US Army Corps of Engineers.

————. 1876b. *Zwölf Sprachen aus dem Südwesten Nordamerikas*. Weimar: Hermann Böhlau. Rpt., Oosterhout, Netherlands: Anthropological Publications, 1970.

————. 1884. "Comanche Vocabulary and Notes." MS 748, National Anthropological Archives, Washington, DC.

————. 1893. "Comanche Vocabulary and Notes." MS 751, National Anthropological Archives, Washington, DC.

Gelo, Daniel J. 1982. "Comanche Field Notes." Unpublished manuscript in author's possession.

————. 1986. "Comanche Belief and Ritual." Unpublished doctoral dissertation, Rutgers University, Department of Anthropology.

————. 1994. "Recalling the Past in Creating the Present: Topographic References in Comanche Narrative." *Western Folklore* 53: 295–312.

————. 1997. "Review of Kavanagh's *Comanche Political History*." *Great Plains Research* 7: 145–46.

———. 2000. "'Comanche Land and Ever Has Been': A Native Geography of the Nineteenth-Century Comanchería." *Southwestern Historical Quarterly* 103: 273–308.

———. 2002. "Comanche." In *Encyclopedia of World Cultures Supplement*, 80–84. New York: Macmillan Reference USA.

———. 2011. "The Comanche Landscape: Concepts and Context." *Panhandle-Plains Historical Review* 83: 1–12.

———. 2012. *Indians of the Great Plains*. Upper Saddle River, NJ: Pearson.

———. 2013. *Ethnohistorical and Ethnographic Assessment of Comanche Activity in the Fort Hood Area*. United States Army Fort Hood, Archaeological Resource Management Series, Research Report No. 63. Fort Hood, TX.

Gelo, Daniel J., and Lawrence T. Jones III. 2009. "Photographic Evidence for Southern Plains Armor." *Visual Anthropology Review* 25: 49–65.

Gelo, Daniel J., and Wayne J. Pate. 2003. *Texas Indian Trails*. Dallas: Republic of Texas Press.

Gelo, Daniel J., and Scott Zesch, eds. 2003. "'Every Day Seemed to Be a Holiday': The Captivity of Bianca Babb." *Southwestern Historical Quarterly* 107: 35–68.

Geue, Chester William, and Ethel H. Geue. 1972. *A New Land Beckoned: German Immigration to Texas, 1844–1847*. New and enl. ed. Waco: Texian Press. Orig. 1966.

Gillespie County Historical Society. 1960. *Pioneers in God's Hills*. Vol. 1, *A History of Fredericksburg and Gillespie County: People and Events*. Austin: Eakin.

Goddard, Ives. 1996a. "Introduction." In *Handbook of North American Indians*, vol. 17, 1–16. Edited by William C. Sturtevant. Washington, DC: Smithsonian Institution.

———. 1996b. "The Description of the Native Languages of North America Before Boas." In *Handbook of North American Indians*, vol. 17, 17–42. Edited by William C. Sturtevant. Washington, DC: Smithsonian Institution.

Gracy, David B., II. 1987. *Moses Austin: His Life*. San Antonio: Trinity University Press.

Greene, A. C. 1972. *The Last Captive*. Austin: Encino Press.

Greenleaf, Jeremiah. 1845. *[Map of] Texas Compiled from the Latest and Best Authorities*. Brattleboro, VT [?]: n.p.

Grinnell, George Bird. 1920. "Who Were the Padouca?" *American Anthropologist*, n.s., 22: 248–60.

Grisson, Wilhelm. 1844. *Beiträge zur Charakteristik der Vereinigten Staaten von Nord-Amerika*. Hamburg: Perthes-Besser and Mauke.

Gwynne, S. C. 2010. *Empire of the Summer Moon*. New York: Scribner.

Hadeler, Glenn. n.d. "Kriewitz and the Comanches." In *From the Texas Heartland*. http://www.texfiles.com/hadeler/kriewitz.htm. Accessed January 27, 2014.

———. 2010. "Emil Kriewitz." In *Handbook of Texas Online*. Austin: Texas State Historical Association. Accessed January 27, 2014.

Hagan, William T. 1976. *United States–Comanche Relations*. New Haven, CT: Yale University Press.

————. 1993. *Quanah Parker, Comanche Chief*. Norman: University of Oklahoma Press.

Hale, Horatio. 1846. *United States Exploring Expedition during the Years 1838, 1839, 1840, 1841, 1842 under the Command of Charles Wilkes, USN: Ethnography and Philology*. Philadelphia: Lea and Blanchard.

Hämäläinen, Pekka. 2008. *The Comanche Empire*. New Haven, CT: Yale University Press.

Hanke, Paula Kay. 2010. "Pecan Bayou." In *Handbook of Texas Online*. Austin: Texas State Historical Association. Accessed April 12, 2014.

Häntzsch, Viktor. 1902. "Berghaus, Heinrich." In *Allgemeine Deutsche Biographie*, vol. 46, 374–79. Leipzig: Duncker und Humblot.

Harris, Marvin. 1968. *The Rise of Anthropological Theory*. New York: Thomas Y. Crowell.

Harston, J. Emmor. 1963. *Comanche Land*. San Antonio: Naylor.

Hatzfeld, Ursula. 2015. *From Dillenburg to Texas: Emigration in the District of Dillenburg from 1845 to 1846*. Translated by Henry Salzhandler. Fulton, MO: El Grito del Lobo Press. Orig. *Von Dillenburg nach Texas. Die Auswanderung im Amt Dillenburg von 1845 bis 1846*. Published by the author, 2000.

Hayter, Delmar J. 2010. "Pecos River." In *Handbook of Texas Online*. Austin: Texas State Historical Association. Accessed February 16, 2014.

Hecke, J. Valentin. 1820. *Reise durch die Vereinigten Staaten von Nord-Amerika in den Jahren 1818 und 1819: Nebst einer kurzen Übersicht der neuesten Ereignisse auf dem Kriegs-Schauplatz in Süd-Amerika und West-Indien*. Vol. 1. Berlin: H. Ph. Petri.

Henderson, E. W. 1959. "Buffalo Hump, a Comanche Diplomat." *West Texas Historical Association Year Book* 35: 112–24.

Hendrickson, Kenneth E., Jr. 2010. "Brazos River." In *Handbook of Texas Online*. Austin: Texas State Historical Association. Accessed May 23, 2014.

Herff, Ferdinand von. 1978. *The Regulated Emigration of the German Proletariat with Special Reference to Texas; Being also a Guide for German Emigrants*. Translated by Arthur L. Finck Jr. San Antonio: Trinity University Press. Orig., *Die geregelte Auswanderung des deutschen Proletariats mit besonderer Beziehung auf Texas, Zugleich ein Leitfaden für deutsche Auswanderer*. Frankfurt am Main: F. Varrentrapp, Ph. Krebs, 1850.

Herff, Ferdinand Peter. 1973. *The Doctors Herff: A Three-Generation Memoir*. 2 vols. Edited by Laura L. Barber. San Antonio: Trinity University Press.

Hodge, Frederick Webb, ed. 1907. *Handbook of American Indians North of Mexico*. Smithsonian Institution Bureau of American Ethnology Bulletin 30. 2 vols. Washington, DC: US Government Printing Office.

Hoebel, E. Adamson. 1940. "The Political Organization and Law-Ways of the Comanche Indians." Memoirs of the American Anthropological Association 54. Menasha, WI.

Hooker, William. 1836. *Map of the State of Coahuila and Texas*. Lexington, KY: J. Clark.

Humboldt, Alexander von. 1811. *Political Essay on the Kingdom of New Spain*. London: Longman, Hurst, Rees, Orme, and Brown. Orig., *Essai Politique sur le Royaume de la Nouvelle-Espagne*. Paris: F. Schoell, 1811.

———. 2014. *Political Essay on the Kingdom of New Spain*. Translated by John Black. Cambridge: Cambridge University Press.

Humfreville, J. Lee. 2002. *Twenty Years among Our Hostile Indians*. Mechanicsburg, PA: Stackpole Books. Orig., New York: Hunter, ca. 1903.

Hunt, Richard S., and Jesse F. Randel. 1839. *Map of Texas Compiled from Surveys on Record in the General Land Office of the Republic, to the Year 1839*. New York: J. H. Colton.

Jackson, Donald, ed. 1966. *The Journals of Zebulon Montgomery Pike, with Letters and Related Documents*. 2 vols. Norman: University of Oklahoma Press.

Jackson, Jack, ed., and John Wheat, trans. 2000. *Texas by Terán*. Austin: University of Texas Press.

Jeffrys, Thomas. 1775. *The West-India Atlas*; *or*, *A Compendious Description of the West-Indies*. London: Robert Sayer and John Bennett.

Jenkins, John H. 1988. *Basic Texas Books*. Rev. ed. Austin: Texas State Historical Association.

John, Elizabeth A. H. 1975. *Storms Brewed in Other Men's Worlds: The Confrontation of Indians, Spanish, and French in the Southwest*. College Station: Texas A&M University Press. Rpt., Lincoln: University of Nebraska Press, 1985.

———. 1988. "The Riddle of Mapmaker Juan Pedro Walker." In *Essays on the History of North American Discovery and Exploration*, edited by Stanley H. Palmer and Dennis Reinhartz, 102–32. College Station: Texas A&M University Press for the University of Texas at Arlington.

Johnson, E. H. 2010. "Lower Plains." In *Handbook of Texas Online*. Austin: Texas State Historical Association. Accessed February 10, 2014.

Johnston, Alexander Keith. 1848. *The Physical Atlas: A Series of Maps and Notes Illustrating the Geographical Distribution of Natural Phenomena. . . . Based on the Physikalischer Atlas of H. Berghaus*. Edinburgh: Blackwood.

Johnston, William Preston. 1964. "With Albert Sidney Johnston in West Texas: Austin to Fort Chadbourne, March, 1855." Edited by Marilyn McAdams Sibley. *West Texas Historical Association Year Book* 40: 121–45.

Jones, David E. 1972. *Sanapia: Comanche Medicine Woman*. New York: Holt, Rinehart and Winston.

———. 1980. "Face the Ghost." *Phoenix* 4: 53–57.

Jordan, Terry G. 2010. "Kapp, Ernst." In *Handbook of Texas Online*. Austin: Texas State Historical Association. Accessed December 7, 2014.

Kavanagh, Thomas W. 1996. *Comanche Political History*. Lincoln: University of Nebraska Press.

———. 2001. "Comanche." In *Handbook of North American Indians*, vol. 13, part 2, 886–906. Edited by William C. Sturtevant. Washington, DC: Smithsonian Institution.

————. 2008. *Comanche Ethnography: Field Notes of E. Adamson Hoebel, Waldo R. Wedel, Gustav G. Carlson, and Robert H. Lowie.* Lincoln: University of Nebraska Press.

Kearney, James C. 2010. *Nassau Plantation: The Evolution of a Texas German Slave Plantation.* Denton: University of North Texas Press.

Kennedy, William. 1841. *Texas: The Rise, Progress, and Prospects of the Republic of Texas.* 2 vols. London: R. Hastings. Rpt. in 1 vol., Fort Worth: Molyneaux Craftsmen, 1925; Clifton, NJ: A. M. Kelley, 1974.

————. 1845. *William Kennedy's Geographie, Naturgeschichte und Topographie von Texas.* Translated by Otto von Czarnowsky. Frankfurt am Main: Johann David Sauerländer. Translation of Kennedy 1841.

Kenner, Charles L. 1994. *The Comanchero Frontier: A History of New Mexican–Plains Indian Relations.* Norman: University of Oklahoma Press. Orig., 1969.

King, Irene Marschall. 1967. *John O. Meusebach: German Colonizer in Texas.* Austin: University of Texas Press.

Knopp, Ken. 1999. *German Immigration to America: The Fredericksburg Texas Manuscripts.* Fredericksburg, TX: Published by author.

Koch, Ronald P. 1977. *Dress Clothing of the Plains Indians.* Norman: University of Oklahoma Press.

Kozák, Jan, and Jiří Vaněk. 2002. "Berghaus' Physikalischer Atlas: Surprising Content and Superior Artistic Images." *StudiaGeo (Studia geophysica et geodaetica)* 46: 599–610.

Kriewitz, Emil. 1899. "Response to Houston Daily Post." MS, Llano County Library, Llano, Texas.

Kroeber, Alfred L. 1907. "California, Indians of." In *Handbook of American Indians North of Mexico.* Smithsonian Institution Bureau of American Ethnology Bulletin 30, Part 1. Edited by Frederick Webb Hodge, 190–91. Washington, DC: US Government Printing Office.

————. 1976. *Handbook of the Indians of California.* New York: Dover. Orig., Smithsonian Institution Bureau of American Ethnology Bulletin 78. Washington, DC: US Government Printing Office, 1925.

LaBarre, Weston. 1975. *The Peyote Cult.* 4th ed., enl. New York: Schocken.

Lich, Glen E. 2010. "Sisterdale, Texas." In *Handbook of Texas Online.* Austin: Texas State Historical Association. Accessed December 7, 2014.

Loew, Oscar. 1876. *Notes upon Ethnology of Southern California and Adjacent Regions.* Appendix H 14. In *Annual Report of the Chief of Engineers to the Secretary of War for the Year 1876*, vol. 3, 541–47. Washington, DC: US Army Corps of Engineers.

Loomis, Noel M., and Abraham P. Nasatir. 1967. *Pedro Vial and the Roads to Santa Fe.* Norman: University of Oklahoma Press.

Luther, Joseph. 2013. *Fort Martin Scott: Guardian of the Treaty.* Charleston, SC: History Press.

Maillard, Nicholas Doran P. 1842. *The History of the Republic of Texas, from the Discovery of the Country to the Present Time; and the Cause of Her Separation from the Republic of Mexico.* London: Smith, Elder, and Co., Cornhill.

Marche, Konen. 1835. *Map of Texas Shewing the Grants in Possession of the Colorado and Red River Land Company*. Brussels: Konen Marche.

Marcy, Randolph B. 1853. "Exploration of the Red River of Louisiana in the Year 1852." United States Senate Executive Document 54, 32nd Congress, 2nd Session. Washington, DC: R. Armstrong. Rpt., United States Senate Executive Document, 33nd Congress, 1st Session. Washington, DC: B. Tucker, 1854.

Marcy, Randolph B., and George B. McClellan. 1968. *Adventure on Red River*. Edited by Grant Forman. Norman: University of Oklahoma Press. Orig., 1937.

Martin, James, and Robert S. Martin. 1999. *Maps of Texas and the Southwest, 1513–1900*. Austin: Texas State Historical Association.

McAllester, David P. 1949. "Peyote Music." Viking Fund Publications in Anthropology 13. New York.

McGuire, James Patrick. 2010. "Iwonski, Carl G. von." In *Handbook of Texas Online*. Austin: Texas State Historical Association. Accessed December 7, 2014.

McLaughlin, James E. 1983. "From Aspect to Tense, or What's *-nuh* in Comanche." In 1982 Mid-America Linguistic Conference Papers. Edited by Frances J. Ingemann, 412–27. Lawrence: University of Kansas Department of Linguistics.

McLean, Malcolm D., ed. 1974–93. *Papers concerning Robertson's Colony in Texas*. 18 vols. Fort Worth: Texas Christian University Press (vols. 1–3). Arlington: University of Texas at Arlington Press (vols. 4–18).

Meadows, William C. 1999. *Kiowa, Apache, and Comanche Military Societies*. Austin: University of Texas Press.

———. 2008. *Kiowa Ethnogeography*. Austin: University of Texas Press.

Melish, John. 1816. *Map of the United States with the Continuous British and Spanish Possessions, Compiled from the Latest and Best Authorities*. Philadelphia: John Melish.

Meusebach, John O. 1894. *Answers to Interrogatories in Case No. 396, Mary Paschal et al., vs. Theodore Evans. District Court of McCullough County, Texas, November Term, 1893*. Austin: Pemberton.

Meyer, Joseph. 1846. *[Map of] Texas*. Nach den besten Quellen entw. u. gez. vom Hauptm. Radefeld. Hildburghausen: Bibliographisches Institut.

Miller, Wick R., comp. 1972. *Newe Natekwinappeh: Shoshoni Stories and Dictionary*. University of Utah Anthropological Papers 94. Edited by Jesse D. Jennings. Salt Lake City: University of Utah Press.

Mooney, James. 1896. "The Ghost-Dance Religion and the Sioux Outbreak of 1890." In 14th Annual Report of the Bureau of American Ethnology, 641–1136. Washington, DC: US Government Printing Office.

———. 1907a. "Comanche." In *Handbook of American Indians North of Mexico*. Smithsonian Institution Bureau of American Ethnology Bulletin 30, part 1. Edited by Frederick Webb Hodge, 327–29. Washington, DC: US Government Printing Office.

———. 1907b. "Delaware." In *Handbook of American Indians North of Mexico*. Smithsonian Institution Bureau of American Ethnology Bulletin 30, part 1. Edited by Frederick Webb Hodge, 385–87. Washington, DC: US Government Printing Office.

———. 1907c. "Detsanayuka." In *Handbook of American Indians North of Mexico*. Smithsonian Institution Bureau of American Ethnology Bulletin 30, part 1. Edited by Frederick Webb Hodge, 388. Washington, DC: US Government Printing Office.

Mooney, James, and Cyrus Thomas. 1907. "Illinois." In *Handbook of American Indians North of Mexico*. Smithsonian Institution Bureau of American Ethnology Bulletin 30, part 1. Edited by Frederick Webb Hodge, 597–99. Washington, DC: US Government Printing Office.

Morgenthaler, Jefferson. 2007. *The German Settlement of the Texas Hill Country*. Boerne, TX: Mockingbird Books.

———. 2009. *Promised Land: Solms, Castro, and Sam Houston's Colonization Contracts*. College Station: Texas A&M University Press.

———. 2010. "Pinta Trail." In *Handbook of Texas Online*. Austin: Texas State Historical Association. Accessed August 21, 2014.

———. 2015. *The Pinta Trail in the Texas Hill Country*. Boerne, TX: Mockingbird Books.

Mühlenpfordt, Eduard. 1846. *Der Freistaat Texas: Geographisch-statistisch-naturhistorisch und mit Rücksicht auf Auswanderer beschrieben von einem transatlantischen Reisenden*. Clausthal: Schweizerische Buchhandlung.

Neighbours, Kenneth Franklin. 1975. *Robert Simpson Neighbors and the Texas Frontier, 1836–1859*. Waco: Texian Press.

Newcomb, William W. 2001. "Wichita." In *Handbook of North American Indians*, vol. 13, part 1, 548–66. Edited by William C. Sturtevant. Washington, DC: Smithsonian Institution.

Newcomb, William W., with Mary S. Carnahan. 1978. *German Artist on the Texas Frontier: Friedrich Richard Petri*. Austin: University of Texas Press.

Noyes, Stanley. 1999. *Comanches in the New West, 1895–1908*. Austin: University of Texas Press.

Nunn, W. C. 1975. *Somervell: Story of a Texas County*. Fort Worth: Texas Christian University Press.

Oken, Lorenz. 1833–42. *Allgemeine Naturgeschichte für alle Stände*. 8 vols. Stuttgart: Carl Hoffmann.

Olmsted, Frederick Law. 1978. *A Journey through Texas; or, A Saddle-Trip on the South-Western Frontier*. Austin: University of Texas Press. Orig., New York: Dix, Edwards, 1857.

Orozco, Cynthia E. 2010. "Barnard, Juana Josefina Cavasos." In *Handbook of Texas Online*. Austin: Texas State Historical Association. Accessed May 20, 2015.

Osborn, Henry, and William A. Smalley. 1949. "Formulae of Comanche Stem and Word Formation." *International Journal of American Linguistics* 15: 93–99.

Parks, Douglas R. 2001. "Pawnee." In *Handbook of North American Indians*, vol. 13, part 1, 515–47. Edited by William C. Sturtevant. Washington, DC: Smithsonian Institution.

Patten, Roderick B., trans. and ed. 1970. "Miranda's Inspection of Los Almagres: His Journal, Report, and Petition." *Southwestern Historical Quarterly* 74: 223–54.

Paul Wilhelm, Herzog von Württemberg [Duke (Friedrich) Paul Wilhelm of

Württemberg]. 1973. *Travels in North America, 1822–1824*. Norman: University of Oklahoma Press.

Pelon, Linda. 1993. "Issues in Penatuhkah Comanche Ethnohistory." Unpublished master's thesis, University of Texas at Arlington, Department of Anthropology.

Penniger, Robert. 1896. *Fest-Ausgabe zum fünfzigjährigen Jubiläum der Deutschen Kolonie Friedrichsburg*. Fredericksburg: Robert Penniger.

———. 1971. *Fredericksburg, Texas: The First Fifty Years*. Translated by Dr. Charles L. Wisseman Sr. Fredericksburg, TX: Fredericksburg Publishing. Translation of Penniger 1896.

Penny, H. Glenn. 2008. "Traditions in the German Language." In *A New History of Anthropology*, edited by Henrika Kuklick, 79–95. Malden, MA: Blackwell Publishing.

———. 2013. *Kindred by Choice: Germans and American Indians since 1899*. Chapel Hill: University of North Carolina Press.

Perttula, Timothy K. 1992. *The Caddo Nation: Archaeological and Ethnohistoric Perspectives*. Austin: University of Texas Press.

Pike, Zebulon Montgomery. 1810. *An Account of Expeditions to the Sources of the Mississippi, and through the Western Parts of Louisiana, to the Sources of the Arkansaw, Kans, La Platte, and Pierre Jaun, Rivers; Performed by Order of the Government of the United States during the Years 1805, 1806, and 1807, and a Tour through the Interior Parts of New Spain, When Conducted through These Provinces, by Order of the Captain-General, in the Year 1807*. Philadelphia: C. and A. Conrad.

———. 1813. *Reise durch die Westlichen Gebiete von Nord-America enthaltend die Tagebücher der Reisen von St. Louis, den Missisippi [sic] hinauf bis an die Quellen dieses Flusses, durch das Innere von Louisiana und durch die nordöstlichen Provinzen von Neu-Spanien: gemacht in den Jahren 1805, 1806 u. 1807, auf Befehl der Regierung der Vereinigten Staaten*. Weimar: Im Verlag des Landes-Industrie-Comptoirs. Translation of Pike 1810.

Pimentel, Francisco. 1875. *Cuadro descriptivo y comparativo de las lenguas indígenas de México*. 2 vols. Mexico City: Isidoro Epstein. Orig., Mexico City: Andrade y Escalante, 1862–65.

Powers, William K. 1990. *War Dance: Plains Indian Musical Performance*. Tucson: University of Arizona Press.

Prewett, S. W. F. 1910. "The Adventurous Career of Charles Barnard." *Texas Magazine* 2 (8): 49–52.

Quaife, Milo Milton, ed. 1925. *The Southwestern Expedition of Zebulon M. Pike*. Chicago: R. R. Donnelley and Sons.

Ragsdale, Paul C. 2010. "von Behr, Ottomar." In *Handbook of Texas Online*. Austin: Texas State Historical Association. Accessed December 7, 2014.

Raumer, Friedrich von. 1845. *Die vereinigten Staaten von Nordamerika*. 2 vols. Leipzig: F. A. Brockhaus.

Reckziegel, Manfred. 1985. *Zur Entstehung von Berghaus' Physikalischem Atlas. Fortschritte in der geographischen Kartographie: Festband anlässlich des IV. Geographenkongresses der DDR und des 200-jährigen Bestehens der Geographisch-Kartographischen Anstalt in Gotha*, 28–37. Gotha: VEB Hermann-Haack.

Reinhardt, Louis. 1899. "The Communistic Colony of Bettina (1846–48)." *Quarterly of the Texas State Historical Association* 3 (1): 33–40. Based on interview with Rudolph Kleberg Jr. Also published as "Texas Communistic Colony" in *Houston Daily Post*, Sunday, August 13, 1899.

Rhodes, Alice J. 2010. "Camp Air, Texas." In *Handbook of Texas Online*. Austin: Texas State Historical Association. Accessed May 18, 2015.

Richardson, Rupert N. 1933. *The Comanche Barrier to South Plains Settlement*. Glendale, CA: Arthur H. Clark. Rpt., Millwood, NY: Krause Reprint, 1973; Austin: Eakin Press, 1996.

Rister, Carl C. 1940. *Border Captives*. Norman: University of Oklahoma Press.

———. 1955. *Comanche Bondage*. Glendale, CA: Arthur H. Clark.

Rivaya-Martínez, Joaquín. 2006. "Captivity and Adoption among the Comanche Indians." Unpublished PhD diss., University of California–Los Angeles, Department of Anthropology.

Roemer, Ferdinand von. 1849a. *Texas. Mit besonderer Rücksicht auf deutsche Auswanderung und die physischen Verhältnisse des Landes*. Bonn: Adolph Marcus. Rpt., Charleston, SC: British Library Historical Print Editions, 2011.

———. 1849b. *Topographisch-geognostische-Karte von Texas*. Bonn: Adolph Marcus.

———. 1983. *Texas, with Particular Reference to German Immigration and the Physical Appearance of the Country*. Translated by Oswald Mueller. San Marcos, TX: German-Texas Heritage Society. Orig., San Antonio: Standard Printing, 1935. Translation of Roemer 1849a.

Ross, Georg M. von. 1851. *Der Nordamerikanische Freistaat Texas, nach eigener Anschauung und nach den neuesten und besten Quellen für deutsche Auswanderer*. Rudolstadt: G. Froebel.

Ruiz, José Francisco. 1972. *Report on the Indian Tribes of Texas in 1828*. Translated and edited by John C. Ewers. New Haven, CT: Yale University Press.

Sachs, Aaron. 2006. *The Humboldt Current: Nineteenth-Century Exploration and the Roots of American Environmentalism*. New York: Viking.

Scherpf, G. A. 1841. *Entstehungsgeschichte und gegenwärtiger Zustand des neuen, unabhängigen, amerikansichen Staates Texas*. Augsburg: Verlag der Matth. Rieger'schen Buchhandlung.

Schiedt, Helmut. 2011. *Karl May: Oder die Macht der Phantasie*. Munich: Beck Verlag.

Schilz, Jodye Lynn Dickson. 2010. "Buffalo Hump." In *Handbook of Texas Online*. Austin: Texas State Historical Association. Accessed March 14, 2014.

Schilz, Jodye Lynn Dickson, and Thomas F. Schilz. 1989. *Buffalo Hump and the Penateka Comanches*. El Paso: Texas Western Press.

Schlecht, Friedrich. 1851. *Mein Ausflug nach Texas!* Bunzlau: Appun. Rpt., *On to Texas! The Story of a Journey to Texas in 1848*. Translated by Charles Patrick. Manor, TX: Indio Bravo 1998.

Schoolcraft, Henry Rowe, ed. 1851–57. *Historical and Statistical Information Respecting the History, Conditions, and Prospects of the Indian Tribes of the United States*. 6 vols. Philadelphia: Lippincott and Grambo.

Schulz, F. W. 2012. *Allgemeiner Wohnungs-Anzeiger für die Königliche Residenzstadt Potsdam und Umgebung auf das Jahr 1882*. Potsdam: Klaus-D. Becker.

Schultz, Johann Heinrich Siegfried. 1845. *Die deutsche Ansiedlung in Texas*. Bonn: Friedrich Encke.

Sealsfield, Charles. 1841. *Das Kajütenbuch oder Nationale Charakteristiken*. 2 vols. Zurich: Schultheß. Rpt., *The Cabin Book or National Characteristics*. Translated by Sarah Powell. Austin: Eakin, 1985.

Secoy, Frank Raymond. 1951. "The Identity of the 'Paduca': An Ethnohistorical Analysis." *American Anthropologist*, n.s., 53: 524–42.

———. 1953. *Changing Military Patterns on the Great Plains*. American Ethnological Society Monograph 21. Locust Valley, NY: J. J. Augustin.

Seele, Hermann. 1883. "Zwei Erinnerungsbilder aus der Zeit der deutschen Ansiedlung von West-Texas." In *Schütze's Jahrbuch für Texas und Emigranten-Führer für 1883*, 44–61. Austin.

———. 1884. "Die deutsche Colonie Neu Braunfels im Mai 1845. Aus Erinnerungsblättern eines alten Deutsch-Texaners." In *Schütze's Jahrbuch für Texas und Emigranten-Führer für 1884*, 93–104. Austin.

Shimkin, Demitri B. 1980. "Comanche-Shoshone Words of Acculturation, 1786–1848." *Journal of the Steward Anthropological Society* 2: 195–248.

Shook, Robert W. 1972. "German Migration in Texas 1830–1850: Causes and Consequences." *Texana* 10: 226–43.

Sibley, John. 1922. *A Report from Natchitoches in 1807*. Edited by Annie Heloise Abel. New York: Museum of the American Indian, Heye Foundation.

Simpson, Leslie Boyd, ed. 1959. *The San Sabá Papers*. San Francisco: J. Howell Books. Rpt., Dallas: Southern Methodist University Press, 2000.

Smith, Clinton. 1955. *The Boy Captives*. San Saba, TX: San Saba Printing and Office Supply.

Smith, Julia Cable. 2010. "Concho River." In *Handbook of Texas Online*. Austin: Texas State Historical Association. Accessed February 20, 2014.

Smith, Ralph A. 1959. "The Comanche Invasion of Mexico in the Fall of 1845." *West Texas Historical Association Year Book* 35: 3–28.

———. 1961. "The Comanche Bridge between Oklahoma and Mexico, 1843–1844." *Chronicles of Oklahoma* 39: 54–69.

———. 1970. "The Comanche Sun over Mexico." *West Texas Historical Year Book* 46: 25–62.

Smithwick, Noah. 1900. *The Evolution of a State or Recollections of Old Texas Days*. Austin: Gammel Book. Rpt., Austin: University of Texas Press, 1983.

Society for the Diffusion of Useful Knowledge. 1846. *[Map of] Central America II, Including Texas, California, and the Northern States of Mexico*. London: Charles Knight.

Solms-Braunfels, Carl, Prinz zu. 1846a. *Texas: Geschildert in Beziehung auf seine geographischen, socialen und übrigen Verhältnisse, mit besonderer Rücksicht auf die deutsche Colonisation. Ein Handbuch für Auswanderer nach Texas.* Frankfurt am Main: J. D. Sauerländer.

⸺. 1846b. *Karte von Texas entworfen nach den Vermessungen der General-Land-Office der Republic.* Frankfurt am Main: J. D. Sauerländer.

⸺. 1846c. *Map of the North-Western Part of Texas Received from the General Land Office in 1845.* Frankfurt am Main: J. D. Sauerländer.

⸺. 1936. *Texas, 1844–1845.* Houston: Anson Jones Press. Translation of Solms-Braunfels 1846a.

⸺. 2000. *Voyage to North America 1844–45: Prince Carl of Solms's Texas Diary of People, Places, and Events.* Translated by Wolfram M. Von-Maszewski. Denton, TX: German-Texan Heritage Society and University of North Texas Press.

Sörgel, Alwin H. 1992. *A Sojourn in Texas, 1846–47: Alwin H. Sörgel's Texas Writings.* Translated and edited by W. M. Von-Maszewski. San Marcos: German-Texan Heritage Society, Southwest Texas State University.

Sowell, A. J. 1986. *Early Settlers and Indian Fighters of Southwest Texas.* Abilene, TX: State House Press. Orig., Austin: Ben C. Jones, 1900.

Spiess, H., and F. Wrede. 1848[?]. "The German Emigration Company." *Texian Advocate* [Victoria, TX]. Solms Archive 44: 125. Sophienburg Archive, New Braunfels, TX.

St. Clair, H. H. 1902a. "Comanche." MS 877, National Anthropological Archives, Washington, DC.

⸺. 1902b. "Shoshonean Linguistic Material." MS 2048a, National Anthropological Archives, Washington, DC.

Steinert, Wilhelm. 1850. *Nordamerika vorzüglich Texas im Jahre 1849.* Berlin: K. W. Krüger. Rpt., *North America, Particularly Texas in the Year 1849: A Travel Account, a Book for Emigrants, Especially for Persons Enthusiastic about Emigration.* Translated by Gilbert J. Jordan. Dallas: Southern Methodist University Degolyer Library and William P. Clements Center, 1999.

Stempfle, G. 1841. *Karte von Texas entworfen nach den Vermessungen welche in den Acten der General-Land-Office der Republic liegen bis zum Jahr 1839 von Richard S. Hunt und Jesse F. Randel.* Augsburg: Verlag der Math. Rieger'schen Buchhandlung.

Stephens, A. Ray, and William M. Holmes. 1989. *Historical Atlas of Texas.* Norman: University of Oklahoma Press.

Strubberg, Friedrich Armand. 2012. *Friedrichsburg: Colony of the German Fürstenverein.* Translated by James C. Kearney. Austin: University of Texas Press.

Sturtevant, William C., ed. 2001. "Plains." *Handbook of North American Indians,* vol. 13, 2 parts. Washington, DC: Smithsonian Institution.

Surminski, Marc. 1992. "Dunkle Geschäfte mit deutschem Blute." *Die Zeit,* no. 47. November 20.

Tang, Chenxi. 2008. *The Geographic Imagination of Modernity: Geography, Literature, and Philosophy in German Romanticism*. Stanford, CA: Stanford University Press.

Tanner, H. S. 1846. *A Map of the United States of Mexico*. 3rd ed. Philadelphia: H. S. Tanner.

ten Kate, Herman F. C. 1885. "Notes ethnographiques sur les Comanches." *Revue d'Ethnographie* 4 (2): 120–36.

Texas National Register. 1845. [Item on Buffalo Hump]. May 15: 178.

Thomas, Alfred B. 1929. "An Eighteenth-Century Comanche Document." *American Anthropologist*, n.s., 31: 289–98.

———. 1932. *Forgotten Frontiers*. Norman: University of Oklahoma Press.

Thran, Jakob. 1848. *Meine Auswanderung nach Texas unter dem Schutze des Mainzer Vereins: Ein Warnungsbeispiel für Auswanderungslustige. Mit einem Vorwort von Dr. A[ugust] Th[eodor] Woeniger*. Berlin: E. Krause.

Thurman, Melburn D. 1988. "On the Identity of the Chariticas [Sarii Rikka]: Dog Eating and Pre-Horse Adaptation on the High Plains." *Plains Anthropologist* 22: 159–70.

Tiling, Moritz. 1913. *History of the German Element in Texas from 1820–1850*. Houston: Moritz Tiling.

Tippens, Matthew D. 2010. *Turning Germans into Texans: World War I and the Assimilation and Survival of German Culture in Texas, 1900–1930*. Austin: Kleingarten.

Todd, Tom. 2009. "Emil Kriewitz." Find a Grave Memorial. https://www.findagrave.com/cgi-bin/fg.cgi?page=gr&GRid=42266320. Accessed December 12, 2014.

Tubbs, Janie S. 2010. "Sabinal River." In *Handbook of Texas Online*. Austin: Texas State Historical Association. Accessed February 23, 2015.

Usbeck, Frank. 2015. *Fellow Tribesmen: The Image of Native Americans, National Identity, and Nazi Ideology in Germany*. New York: Berghahn Books.

Verein zum Schutze deutscher Auswanderung. 1851. *Karte des Staats Texas*. Wiesbaden: Verein zum Schutze deutscher Auswanderung.

Vermeulen, Han F. 2015. Before Boas: The Genesis of Ethnography and Ethnology in the German Enlightenment. Lincoln: University of Nebraska Press.

Viscaya Canales, Isidro, ed. 1968. *La invasion de los indíos bárbaros al noreste de México en los años de 1840 y 1841*. Monterrey: Publicaciones del Instituto Technológia y de Estudios Superiores de Monterrey.

Walker, Mack. 1964. *Germany and the Emigration, 1816–1885*. Cambridge, MA: Harvard University Press.

Wallace, Ernest. 1954. "David G. Burnet's Letters Describing the Comanche Indians with an Introduction by Ernest Wallace." *West Texas Historical Association Year Book* 30: 115–40.

Wallace, Ernest, and E. Adamson Hoebel. 1952. *The Comanches: Lords of the South Plains*. Norman: University of Oklahoma Press.

Walther, F. E. 1848. *Texas in sein wahres Licht gestellt, als geeignetster Colonisationsplatz für deutsche Auswanderer*. Dresden: Arnold.

Weddle, Robert S. 1964. *The San Sabá Mission.* Austin: University of Texas Press.

———. 2007. *After the Massacre: The Violent Legacy of the San Saba Mission.* Lubbock: Texas Tech University Press.

———. 2010a. "Los Almagres Mine." In *Handbook of Texas Online.* Austin: Texas State Historical Association. Accessed April 27, 2014.

———. 2010b. "Santa Cruz de San Saba Mission." In *Handbook of Texas Online.* Austin: Texas State Historical Association. Accessed April 27, 2014.

Wedemeyer, Adolphus F., et al. 1847. "Erklärung deutscher Kolonisten in Neubraunfels zu Gunsten des Texasvereins." *Der deutsche Auswanderer. Centralblatt der deutschen Auswanderung und Kolonisierung* 32: 503–4.

Weiss, Harold J., Jr. 2010. "Hays, John Coffee." In *Handbook of Texas Online.* Austin: Texas State Historical Association. Accessed January 28, 2015.

Whipple, A. W., Thomas Ewbank, and William W. Turner. 1855. "Report upon the Indian Tribes." *Reports of Explorations and Surveys to Ascertain the Most Practicable and Economical Route for a Railroad from the Mississippi River to the Pacific Ocean.* Washington, D.C.: War Department.

Wickham, Christopher J. 1996. "Oil and Water: The Development of the Portrayal of Native Americans by Nineteenth-Century German Painters." *Yearbook of German-American Studies* 31: 63–106.

Wied, Maximilian. 1995. *Reise in das Innere Nordamerika.* 2 vols. Augsburg: Weltbild. Orig., Koblenz: J. Hoelscher, 1839–41.

———. 2008–12. *The North American Journals of Prince Maximilian of Wied.* 3 vols. Edited by Stephen S. Witte and Marsha V. Gallagher. Norman: University of Oklahoma Press.

Wilbarger, J. W. 1985. *Indian Depredations in Texas.* Austin: Eakin Press. Orig., Austin: Hutchings Printing House, 1889.

Williams, J. W. 1979. *Old Texas Trails.* Burnet, TX: Eakin Press.

Williams, L. H. 1849. Letter to R. S. Neighbors, October 9. Letters Received from the Texas Agency, National Archives and Records Service microfilm M234, 858: 412. Washington, DC.

Willke, Hermann. 1850. *Karte von den Vermessungen im Grant und in der Gegend zwischen demselben und Neu Braunfels.* Wiesbaden[?]: Verein zum Schütze Deutscher Auswanderer nach Texas.

Wilson, James T. D. 1845. *A New and Correct Map of Texas Compiled from the Most Recent Surveys and Authorities to the Year 1845.* New Orleans: R. W. Fishbourne.

Winfrey, Dorman H., and James M. Day. 1995. *The Indian Papers of Texas and the Southwest, 1825–1916.* 5 vols. Austin: Texas State Historical Association. Orig., 1959–66.

Wislizenus, Friedrich Adolph. 1848. *Memoir of a Tour to Northern Mexico Connected with Col. Doniphan's Expedition, in 1846 and 1847; With a Scientific Appendix and Three Maps.* Washington, DC: Tippin and Strepper.

Wistrand-Robinson, Lila, and James Armagost. 1990. *Comanche Dictionary and Grammar.* Arlington: Summer Institute of Linguistics and the University of Texas at Arlington.

Wrede, Friedrich W. von. 1844. *Lebensbilder aus den Vereinigten Staaten von Nordamerika und Texas*. Cassel: Selbstverlag. Rpt., *Sketches of Life in the United States of North America and Texas*. Compiled by Emil Drescher. Translated by Chester W. Geue. Waco: Texian Press, 1970.

Wright, Muriel. 1951. *A Guide to the Indian Tribes of Oklahoma*. Norman: University of Oklahoma Press.

Wright, Muriel, and George H. Shirk. 1950. "The Journal of Lieutenant A. W. Whipple." *Chronicles of Oklahoma* 28: 235–83.

———. 1953. "Artist Möllhausen in Oklahoma—1853." *Chronicles of Oklahoma* 31: 392–441.

Wurster, Ilse. 2008. *Die Kettner Briefe. Kettner Letters: A Firsthand Account of a German Immigrant in the Texas Hill Country (1850–1875)*. Edited by Charles Kettner. Translated by Peter Benje, Carol Okewon, and Jerry Okeson. Wilmington, DE: Comanche Creek Press.

Young, J. H. 1836. *New Map of Texas with the Contiguous American and Mexican States*. Philadelphia: S. Augustus Mitchell.

Zesch, Scott. 2004. *The Captured*. New York: St. Martin's Press.

INDEX

Red Fork

(Caddoes, Tonkaways, Kikapoes)

Tuscoque

Rio Boema

(Choctaws)

Nabachho

Togaroe

Passiwono

Suriteka

d   e   r

Kitscha

Ekaoque, Pat

Manakiko

Taglkahoni

Kaesua

(Chickasaws)

Jæparishka

Quassare

(Witschitas)

Aracho

Woquequahono

Teua

Nonenoe

e   t

Tacuaraoe

Narahono

b   i

Quitarae

Pero

G

Kateumzi

Uranazwena

Tanemoc

Altes Fort

c   G

Puheua

a

Buffalo humb

Essekiata

Nokoni

J   a   g   d´

Enehokue, Conj

Pahajoko

Rio

San Saba